RESPECTFUL LGBT CONVERSATIONS

Respectful LGBT Conversations
Seeking Truth, Giving Love, and Modeling Christian Unity

HAROLD HEIE

Foreword by George Marsden

CASCADE Books • Eugene, Oregon

RESPECTFUL LGBT CONVERSATIONS
Seeking Truth, Giving Love, and Modeling Christian Unity

Copyright © 2018 Harold Heie. All rights reserved. Except for brief quotations in critical publications or reviews, no part of this book may be reproduced in any manner without prior written permission from the publisher. Write: Permissions, Wipf and Stock Publishers, 199 W. 8th Ave., Suite 3, Eugene, OR 97401.

Cascade Books
An Imprint of Wipf and Stock Publishers
199 W. 8th Ave., Suite 3
Eugene, OR 97401

www.wipfandstock.com

PAPERBACK ISBN: 978-1-5326-1790-4
HARDCOVER ISBN: 978-1-4982-4298-1
EBOOK ISBN: 978-1-4982-4297-4

Cataloguing-in-Publication data:

Heie, Harold, ed.

Respectful LGBT conversations / Seeking truth, giving love, and modeling Christian unity / Harold Heie.

Eugene, OR: Cascade Books, 2018 | Includes bibliographical references and index.

Identifiers: ISBN 978-1-5326-1790-4 (paperback) | ISBN 978-1-4982-4298-1 (hardcover) | ISBN 978-1-4982-4297-4 (ebook)

Subjects: LCSH: Homosexuality—Religious aspects—Christianity. | Sexual ethics—Biblical teaching. | Christianity and politics.

Classification: BR115.H6 R50 2018 (paperback) | BR115 (ebook)

Manufactured in the U.S.A.   05/22/18

Dedicated to Rob Barrett, Michael Gulker, and all the staff at The Colossian Forum for their deep commitment to creating safe and welcoming spaces for Christians who disagree about divisive issues to listen and talk to one another with respect and love.

Contents

Foreword by George M. Marsden | ix
Preface | xiii
Acknowledgments | xvii

1 Voices from the Gay Community | 1
2 Biblical Understandings | 21
3 Findings from the Sciences | 45
4 Constitutional Framework for Public Policy | 66
5 Same-Sex Marriage: Pluralism | 85
6 Anti-Discrimination Laws | 110
7 Voices from Younger Christians | 135
8 Churches and the LGBT Community | 161
9 Case Study Conversations about LGBT People and Issues | 205
10 Conclusion: A Possible Way Forward | 256

Recommended Readings | 287
Bibliography | 291
Authors | 295
Conversation Partners | 297

Foreword
by George Marsden

I am happy to recommend this addition to Harold Heie's important ongoing project of "respectful conversations." Serious respectful conversations are among the things that Christian communities most need. One reason for that need is in the modern era Protestant churches, especially those in the evangelical tradition, have tended to operate according to a sort of free enterprise system. Rather than institutional leadership and theological reflection coming from ecclesiastical authority from the top down, the most successful evangelical churches are built by enterprising entrepreneurial leaders from the bottom up, drawing on a populist base. Each competes with others for constituents. That, in turn, invites cultivation of polemical attitudes toward those whose beliefs or practices differ from one's own. Often differences over a single issue occur within one church family and lead to schisms and the bitterness of intra-family feuds. Such tendencies are not unique to modern popular Protestantism—there are cases in which competing popes have excommunicated each other. But in the modern Protestant case most things are settled by some degree of democracy, and so by enlisting opinion on one's own side. That means that even for lay-people the temptation to engage in polemical argument is especially strong. Such tendencies are intensified by fundamentalist heritages of many American evangelical Protestants, whose distinctive sub-traditions were shaped in part by taking firm stances against modernist theologies that challenged some of the core doctrines of traditional faith. Even more polarizing has been the openly partisan political turn that has intensified division among America Christians, especially for the past generation. Rather than Christians presenting an alternative to the world in which they are admired by how much they love one another and love even their enemies, Christians in the public sphere, at least those who get the most attention, are better known for imitating the reckless polemics of popular political discourse. Further, they are prone to add that their own positions are nonnegotiable because God is on their side.

In this wilderness of Christian incivility, Harold Heie is a welcome prophet. As his previous books on American evangelicalism have emphasized, there is a realistic alternative to the bleak landscape I have just depicted. There is a fertile evangelical center that needs to be cultivated and expanded. It is probably larger than most people realize. Partisan politics has so warped the public image of evangelicalism that one wonders if the term can survive as depicting a "gospel" of salvation in Jesus Christ that helps people find community, love, support, and reconciliation and that teaches them generosity in word and deed toward those who differ from them, even their enemies. Even within evangelical communities that are known for their partisanship, such elements do exist, but they do not make the news. Almost all church communities engage in charitable activities in their communities. And it is not often reported that regular churchgoers (not just evangelicals, but including them) are more likely to engage in volunteer work not only for church-related activities, but also even for secular causes, than are their more secular neighbors.[1] Most evangelical Christians furthermore see themselves as sisters and brothers of broadly like-minded Christians throughout the world, extending far beyond their own denominational boundaries. These days, such generosity often reaches not only to those of Eastern Orthodox communions but also to Roman Catholics. At least in their generous moments, many (perhaps most) evangelical and other Christians share the sense of commonality across communions that foster the essentials of what C. S. Lewis called "mere Christianity," or "the belief that has been common to nearly all Christians at all times."[2]

The books in this series are dedicated to the proposition that such attitudes that already exist among evangelicals need to be more intentionally cultivated. That means nurturing many of the virtues, such as love, humility, and grace, or the fruit of the spirit, "love, joy, peace, patience, kindness, goodness, faithfulness, gentleness, and self control." These biblically mandated attitudes are especially essential in discourse with those with whom one disagrees. That does not mean, of course, that those in the discussions need to come to agreement. Usually the differences will remain. Sometimes such differences may mean that fellow Christians cannot work in the same ecclesiastical or para-church organizations. Yet such divisions ought to be the last resort. And if institutional separation becomes unavoidable, then the default position should be that we regard those who differ from us as

---

1. Putnam and Campbell, *American Grace*, 445.
2. Lewis, *Mere Christianity*, viii.

still fellow Christians and fellow members of the Body of Christ who are to be treated accordingly. As Richard Lovelace says in his wonderful book *The Dynamics of Spiritual Life*, Christian groups that differ from each other need to be able to benefit from each other's genuine spiritual insights.[3] That does not mean that there are not real heresies that truly go beyond the pale regarding central teachings of the faith—there have been lots of such in the history of the church and sometime separations have been necessary. But it does mean that our first response should not be just to try to identify what is wrong with an alternative view, but rather we should also be open at least to the possibility of learning from the teaching that they are putting so much weight on. Whether we will be finally persuaded is another matter.

The current crisis regarding LGBT issues is one in which such attitudes are especially needed. If anything is clear from the conversations presented here, it is that these questions are not going to be easily or quickly resolved. One of the factors creating the current differences is a dramatic recent sea change regarding LGBT matters in mainstream Western culture. In non-Western cultures, where the majority of Christians now are found, mainstream cultures generally have not experienced that same sea change. So there is little prospect that Western and non-Western Christians are going to adjust to the new Western views at anything like the same pace. Furthermore, in the West itself, even among otherwise like-minded Christians (as these conversations show), partisans on each side believe that some fundamental Christian principles are involved.

While these and many other considerations brought forward in these conversations make an early or simple resolution unlikely, that does not mean that Christians cannot move ahead in facing these questions. That is precisely what this volume helps us do. In addition to editing the much more extensive online conversations, Harold Heie offers his own clarifications and suggestions. Most importantly in the concluding chapter, in the light of acknowledging that the issues are not likely soon to be resolved, he offers a number of suggestions for "a possible way forward." These have mostly to do with attitudes that can be cultivated on all sides with regard to taking seriously those with whom we may differ.

Many Christians today, especially those who have any sort of leadership role, are going to be deeply involved in determining policy for LGBT issues. For such people, including writers or speakers, or anyone who may be involved in councils and decision-making for Christian institutions, this volume should be high priority reading. Strict traditionalists should read it in order, at the least, to appreciate the concerns of those with whom they

---

3. Lovelace, *Dynamics of Spiritual Life*, e.g. 17, 171–236.

differ. Progressives who would like to see total acceptance right away need to read it especially in the light of the fact that Protestant institutions cannot run much ahead of their constituencies. That means that patient and respectful advocacy that takes the traditionalist side seriously is an essential component for the progressive cause. And those who, like the editor, are looking for a middle way and a way forward between the extremes will find this volume especially suited to their need. *Respectful LGBT Conversations* is a balanced primer for engaging with the major aspects of the discussions and a guide to participating in such discussions with grace.

Preface

Christians have strong disagreements about LGBT issues and have not always been gracious in expressing those disagreements. All too often, Christians have mimicked and contributed to the deplorable state of public discourse in America; discourse often characterized by demonization, name-calling, and the questioning of motives of those who disagree with you.

Given that context, my purpose for writing this book is threefold:

- To present to readers contrasting "traditional" and "nontraditional" positions regarding selected LGBT issues that are cogently argued and reveal the complexity of these issues.[1]

- To model "respectful conversations" among Christians who have strong disagreements about LGBT issues that identify areas of agreement and illuminate areas of disagreement in a manner that will provide a springboard for sustaining ongoing conversations.

- To recommend a "way forward" for Christians to continue addressing LGBT issues in a manner that is primarily guided by three foundational Christian values: The quest for a better understanding of the

---

1. In contrasting "traditional" from "non-traditional" views I am not suggesting a simple binary choice. As will be noted in chapter 9, there are at least six discernible views that Christians have taken relative to LGBT issues. However, for the purpose of providing a foundation for sustainable ongoing conversations, I believe that many of the differing views can be roughly categorized as falling within a traditional or non-traditional "family" of views. Some would call a non-traditional view a "progressive" view. I avoid the word *progressive* because it can be interpreted to suggest an improvement on a traditional view, which may, or may not, be the case.

xiii

truth, as God fully understands that truth, while giving the gift of *love* to all brothers and sisters in Christ and modeling *Christian unity*.

The bulk of this book, chapters 1–9, consists of my distillations (with some commentary on my part) of the highlights of the postings from twenty-one "conversation partners" on my web site (www.respectfulconversation.net) for nine pre-announced monthly topics around the general theme "Christian Faithfulness and Human Sexuality" that took place from July 1, 2015 through March of 2016. This electronic conversation (eCircle) attracted slightly over 34,400 page views.

For each of the first seven topics, I posed a "Leading Question" to each of two conversation partners, carefully recruited based on my expectation that one would present what can loosely be termed a "traditional" view and the other would present a "nontraditional" view. For each of the eighth and ninth topics, I had three conversation partners in light of the nature of the topics. For the fifth topic, it became apparent to me about halfway through the month-long electronic conversation that the presentations were not "fair and balanced"; both of my original conversation partners held to variations of the same nontraditional position. So, as we used to say in the aerospace industry, I made a "mid-course correction," adding a third conversation partner who was highly recommended as someone who would take a traditional position.

For those readers of the book who are not faint of heart, I highly recommend that you go to my web site and read all of the sixty-two pieces (most being 3,000–4,000 words in length) that were posted during this nine-month conversation. This recommendation is based on the unavoidable fact that when I sought to distill these many postings in this book, my own biases and preconceptions may have been given preferential treatment despite my careful attempts to be fair and balanced.

In the concluding chapter (10), I put my "oar in the water." [2] I present my views on a possible way forward for Christians regarding LGBT issues that draws heavily on what I have learned from the many postings of the conversation partners, but for which I take full responsibility due to my many embellishments and additions. The climax in my concluding chapter is a set of recommended "action steps" as a way forward that flow from a

---

2. In my past life as a Chief Academic Officer at two Christian colleges, the faculty used to say this about me because after I carefully gathered the views of the faculty on any given college issue (e.g., criteria for faculty promotion), I presented my view, after which we talked about our agreements and disagreements in the quest for a policy that would reflect the best of all of our thinking.

commitment to the priority of the Christian values of truth, love, and Christian unity (as per my third purpose for writing).

Relative to my second purpose stated above, the reader will have to judge whether or not my conversation partners modeled "respectful conversations" about their many strong disagreements. My view is that they modeled such respectful conversation to an admirable extent, stating their views with clarity and deep conviction, yet with grace-filled kindness, while also recognizing and acknowledging the deep Christian commitment of those with whom they disagreed. One of my conversation partners, Justin Lee, expresses this most eloquently in his closing reflections about his conversation with another deeply committed gay Christian, Eve Tushnet, about LGBT issues.

> I am moved by Eve's grace in disagreement and her friendship to me as we challenge one another. I am encouraged, too, by the depth of conversation we've been able to have in six simple articles. But I'm also reminded why these conversations are so important in the first place. Many hurting, lonely people's lives hang in the balance.
>
> My own position on this topic hasn't changed, but my appreciation for Eve and understanding of her view has certainly increased, and I'd say that's worth it. Respectful conversation of this sort is hugely undervalued in the church. It may not always change minds, but it is powerful and effective. Given the importance of this topic, we can't afford *not* to listen to each other.
>
> We are, after all, supposed to be known by our love.

It is especially gratifying to me that such respectful conversation has been modeled using an electronic format, given that so many electronic exchanges are what I call "hit and run": Make a blog post and expect numerous comments, most, it not all of which are cryptic comments that either applaud or, more often, vilify the author, with no genuine conversation actually taking place. We have amply demonstrated that there is a better way, a Christian way, to engage someone who disagrees with you, even online.

I share a personal observation about the content of this book that will lead to a navigation tip.

As a reader will soon find out, the issues dealt with in this book are complex (as suggested in my first purpose for writing). Those readers looking for simple answers that will fit on bumper stickers or thirty-second sound bytes will be very disappointed. You may find your head spinning as you attempt to sort through the intricacies of competing traditional and nontraditional perspectives on a given issue, both of which are cogently presented. In light of that, my modest navigation tip is that after reading this Preface, you read the concluding chapter (10) before diving into chapters 1–9. That may help you to observe some "flow" and coherence in this book (my hope being that such coherence does not only exist in my mind).

Finally, I cannot overstate my hope and prayer that the content of this book will reflect just the start of a conversation that will be a springboard for ongoing conversations about these various contentious issues. Although I identify areas of agreement between each set of conversation partners, you will soon see that major areas of disagreement remain that beg for ongoing conversation. And my concluding reflections in chapter 10 also beg for critique and further conversation. If you the reader are in a position to continue this conversation in some appropriate venue, such as a college or seminary classroom, church or denominational setting, or within another Christian organization, that will be deeply appreciated.

Acknowledgments

I first want to thank the twenty-one "conversation partners" who contributed postings to the electronic conversation (eCircle) that was the basis for this book. They modeled in an admirable way that Christians who have strong disagreements about controversial issues can engage in respectful conversations about their differences. They are the persons who made this book possible.

I especially thank one of my conversation partners, Julia Stronks, Professor of Political Science at Whitworth University, who, during the planning stage for the eCircle, helped me to formulate the sub-topics and Leading Questions for the electronic conversation.

A special word of thanks goes to Rob Barrett, the Director of Fellows and Scholarship for The Colossian Forum (TCF) and to Michael Gulker, the president of TCF, for their steadfast support of this project. It was under Michael's leadership that TCF agreed to pay most of the costs associated with managing my web site during the nine months of the eCircle. This project would not have happened if it were not for this generous financial support, for which I am extremely grateful. Rob has been a constant source of encouragement and sage advice as we create welcoming spaces for respectful dialogue in our respective spheres of influence. It is an honor for me to serve as a TCF Senior Fellow since their mission to "create hospitable space for conversations about divisive issues" comports so well with my commitment to facilitate "respectful conversations" about contentious issues.

Brian Workman and Dan Hefferan of the Five Espressos web design and development company served with distinction as my web managers leading up to and during the nine-month eCircle. I thank them for the extremely competent, efficient, and gracious manner in which they managed my website.

I thank Beth De Leeuw, who served with distinction as my Administrative Assistant in the 1980s, who was immensely helpful in formatting my entire book manuscript.

I thank Rodney Clapp, my editor at Cascade Books, as well as his associates, Brian Palmer, Matthew Wimer, and others, for the professional and efficient manner in which they brought this book to publication. I also thank John Topliff, who served as an agent for this book, for his excellent work in bringing my manuscript to the attention of publishers. It was a pleasure to work with John.

Finally, I want to express my deep appreciation to George Marsden for writing the foreword for this book. It is an honor and a source of great encouragement to have a scholar and churchman of his stature and splendid reputation express appreciation for this book and my other "respectful conversation" initiatives.

1

Voices from the Gay Community

We often resort to talking "about" or "at" persons with whom we have disagreements rather than talking "with" them. As with all of my life's work, this project emphatically rejects that approach.[1] If there is to be any hope for sorting through strong disagreements among Christians regarding LGBT issues, we first must listen to the stories and reflections of Christians who self-identify as members of the LGBT community.

Two such persons are the conversation partners for this first round of conversations, Justin Lee and Eve Tushnet, both of whom have been asked to address the following Leading Question: What are your beliefs about morally appropriate relationships between persons who experience same-sex attraction?

Justin and Eve disagree about the moral appropriateness of sexual intimacy between same-sex couples. Justin takes what has been called a "Side

---

1. The importance of talking with the persons whose lives are affected by the issues that we like to talk about in the abstract was forcefully brought home to me a few years ago when I led a seminar series on immigration issues at my home church. We started by listening to the heartbreaking stories told by our immigrant neighbors about ways in which the current broken immigration system was decimating the stability and unity of their families. Our perspectives on the "issues" that we eventually discussed were radically altered by our exposure to these stories. Editorializing for a moment, I dare to suggest that if those politicians who oppose immigration reform were willing to get to know some of their immigrant neighbors on a personal level, they would take steps to break the current political gridlock about the needed contours for such reform. But that is another story for another day (or eCircle and book).

A" position that God will bless a consummated same-sex relationship characterized by a lifelong commitment; while Eve takes a "Side B" position that sex is reserved for heterosexual marriage alone, and that there is therefore no situation in which it would be appropriate for a same-sex couple to be sexually intimate.

However, as the following narrative will reveal, they do share some common ground despite this fundamental disagreement, starting with the following point of agreement.

GAY PEOPLE TAKE PRIORITY OVER GAY ISSUES

Justin confesses that a mistake he made in his early attempts to address gay (or more broadly, LGBT) issues was that "I treated gay people as an issue instead of as people."[2]

Eve emphatically agrees with Justin that treating gay people in terms of issues rather than as people is a mistake, adding that "this is an area where both churches and individuals would do well to start with introspection and repentance."

Justin and Eve agree that a conversation about gay (or LGBT) "issues" must start with the stories and reflections of those Christians who self-identify as being gay and who are struggling with the concrete question of how best to live as faithful gay Christians. Some of these stories and reflections follow.

CHURCHES CAN BE BRUTAL

Eve reports the following about her experience in the Catholic tradition.

> I was extraordinarily lucky to come into the Church in a community where being gay was not treated as shameful or sinful. I was not sent to psychiatrists who claimed they could fix my sexuality; I was not told to fear friendship as a "near occasion of sin"; I was not ostracized, bullied, disowned, or even much gossiped about by people who claimed they were acting for my own good in the name of Jesus. Out of all the gay or same-sex attracted people I know who are seeking to lead lives faithful to the Catholic sexual ethic on homosexuality, I am the one with the least contact with "ex-gay" movements and ideologies by far.

---

2. Justin uses the word *gay* to refer to "someone with exclusively same-sex attractions," which is how this word will be used throughout this book.

Not all gay Christians have shared Eve's positive experience. One reader responds to Eve that "Of course you ponder and discern within the faith community that 'homes' you," adding the following heartbreaking testimony of his experiences of being "chopped and slashed and sliced in deep inward body-mind-feeling-heart-and-spirit places that hardly ever stop hurting" in churches (Protestant and Catholic) that were his "home."

> Honestly, between the repeat cycles of fasting and prayer, amplified by the exorcism prayer meetings, I felt like a cancer patient who is increasingly trying to bear up under the most intense but state of the art cancer treatment available. O the mighty yet arduous "cures" for being gay!
>
> Believe me when I say, it all hurt more than I can possibly report or describe. The spiritual abuse of me as a young man with a male body, my sensuality as well as my sexuality, not to minimize the brutally spiritual neglect and abuse and violence—well, gee, that has all been nearly unbearable and continues in retrospect to be nearly unbearable . . .
>
> Alas, so far, no "call to home" has ever stood even a little test of time and of heart. Lord have mercy.

In a later comment, our anonymous reader adds.

> I am very old now, well into my sixties. I tried the ex-gay and celibacy paths for at least ten years between about age thirteen and age twenty-three years. Then four or five decades on from back then.
>
> All that heartache could not, in the end, be worth it. I should have been one of those guys who hung himself in the rafters of the empty garage of the abandoned house next door, or perhaps who found a wild moment to jump from the college bell tower or high rise science buildings. Instead, I just doggedly went on and on and on.
>
> Life has just about been like a forced prisoner of war march, or perhaps in shallower extent like the Native American trails of tears.

If that story doesn't break your heart, nothing will.

"Lord have mercy" indeed.

IT'S NOT ALL ABOUT SEX

Eve makes the good suggestion that the Leading Question I posed (What are your beliefs about morally appropriate relationships between persons who experience same-sex attraction?), while "important" (because of its focus on "relationships"), is not the central question. The central question is, "How are gay and same-sex attracted people called to give and receive love?"

It appears to me that implicit in Eve's statement of the "central" question is her brief answer to the Leading Question that I posed: The most appropriate relationship between those who experience same-sex attraction is a relationship that "gives and receives love." I concur, and I would add that the giving and receiving of love is the most appropriate relationship between any two persons, whatever their sexual orientation (more about that later).

As noted by Eve, this focus on the giving and receiving of love calls into question the problematic assumption in "American Christian cultures" that sexual relationships are the only form of love between adults.

Justin shares common ground with Eve on this point, saying that "She's absolutely right in calling out our modern obsession with a particular kind of love [involving sexual relationships] and our relative neglect of other paths [for giving and receiving love]."

Before elaborating on these other paths of love, it is important to note the way in which conversations about giving and receiving love must go beyond talking about sexual relationships, as pointed out by Justin.

In brief, Justin notes that a second mistake he made earlier in his pilgrimage was to "treat a complex set of questions as if they were only *one* question . . . what does the Bible say about same-sex sex?" He now realizes there are "bigger questions" for him as a gay Christian, like "Where is my place in the church? What is my vocation? What does my future look like? If I'm single the rest of my life, what happens when I get old? Who will take care of me?" He further suggests that the church also needs to address some "bigger questions," like "How can we love the gay people in our midst—and the broader LGBT community—how can we provide them support, understanding, unconditional love, and sanctuary?"

NEGLECTED FORMS OF GIVING AND RECEIVING LOVE

Eve asserts that "Regardless of what our churches believe about gay marriage, they must rediscover the many forms of love, kinship, and care which exist outside of marriage." She then identifies four such "hidden paths of love."

Friendship: Eve suggests that "we can learn a few things from Jesus' description and practice of friendship."

First, we learn that both cross-sex and same-sex friendship can mirror the love between God and humans, since the followers and friends of Jesus included both men and women.

Second, we can see that Jesus, Love Himself, forged an intimate friendship with the "beloved disciple" John. Friendship for Jesus was not an abstract matter of obedience but a tender and personal relationship. Jesus weeps for his friend Lazarus; his friend John reclines on his breast at dinner. Friendship linked the disciples into a community which became the early church.

Eve goes on to say that "Nobody wants *every* friendship to be this kind of lifelong, promise-adorned, caregiving relationship. But both married and unmarried lay Christians would find their callings in life so much better supported if friendship-as-kinship were more recognized as a possibility.[3]

Service: Eve asserts that "In service my own neediness meets the neediness of others," citing the example of Henri Nouwen, the celibate, gay Catholic priest and "beloved spiritual author," who "found his home at L'Arche, a network of community homes for people with intellectual disabilities," adding that "In living with those who had obvious physical needs, his own spiritual and emotional longings were answered." Surely this is an example of giving and receiving love.

Celibate partnership: Eve notes that she has "friends who are living out this unusual vocation. They know that they have been called by God to 'do life together.' They live together, care for one another as kin, share a common prayer life, and grow in holiness through partnership."

While wanting to highlight the three forms of love noted above and "the challenges they pose to the view that marriage is the one adult form of love for Christians," Eve suggests that "There are many other ways of love—I know LGBT or same-sex attracted people who have taken religious vows or entered 'mixed-orientation marriages' (marriages in which one spouse is openly gay or same-sex attracted, but discerns a calling to marry an opposite-sex spouse—life is complicated, y'all). Teaching, art, godparenthood (which can be one way of honoring and deepening a friendship), adoption and fostering: All can be forms of love to which gay or same-sex attracted people are called."

Eve notes three characteristics that these various hidden forms of love have in common.

---

3. Eve recommends Wesley Hill's book *Spiritual Friendship: Finding Love in the Church as a Celibate Gay Christian* as "a terrific portrayal of the longing for friends who become brothers. Hill is alive to the complexities and challenges of forging that kind of friendship in a globalized, hyper-mobile, and market-driven society, but he also shows how our churches can help us rediscover deep and more lasting friendship."

First, "they are *caregiving relationships*," most of which "involve a long-term commitment to stability and permanence." She adds that these caregiving relationships are also "*fruitful:* They serve the next generation or the surrounding community."

Secondly, these callings also have in common the fact that they are *not imitations of marriage,* "marriage lite," or "marriage minus [X], or consolation prizes for people who can't make a Christian marriage." She notes that "My friends in a celibate partnership sometimes describe their relationship as having 'elements of marriage and elements of monasticism'" (more about that later).

Finally, "These relationships have in common the fact that *they are largely unrecognized and unsupported, not only in the broader culture but in our churches.*" Eve asks, "How often do you hear a pastor giving guidance on forging a friendship? How often do well-off or aspiring parents suggest that their children might discern a call to love and live with the poorest, not for a 'voluntourism' vacation or a part-time gig but for life?"

Eve closes this line of thought with a meddlesome set of questions: "How would our personal lives change if we considered friendship, service, and celibate life in partnership or in community to be real forms of love, as real as marriage? How would our society need to change? How would our churches need to change?"

A CLARIFICATION OF TERMS

At this point in my narrative, I need to call for a "time out," because if you take the time to read all the postings on my eCircle you will detect some consternation as to the use of certain words.

For example, Justin uses the word "romance" to describe a desirable characteristic of both heterosexual and same-sex unions. While he is clear that when he writes about the "importance of romance," he is "not talking about some mythical Hollywood rom-com fantasy," Eve and some readers have detected a lack of clarity.

For example, Eve suggests that "there is a hidden slippage" in Justin's writing "among romance, intimacy, and sex." She asks, "What work is it [the word *romance*] doing that 'love' or 'self-gift' could not do?"

A reader expresses the concern that "Generally it is said that romance is related to passing feelings and emotional experience, such as the 'honeymoon' stage of marriage when everything seems rosy," and that is "somewhat superficial . . . rather than the real substance of love." Along these same lines another reader asks, "What if emotion doesn't matter as much as intentional commitment?"

In response to such concerns, Justin clarifies that it is the importance of "human intimacy" that he is stressing: "human intimacy matters, and . . . there must be a way for gay people to experience that intimacy," adding that "whether you call it 'romance' or something else like 'spiritual friendship,' something is needed that goes beyond typical friendship as we normally think of it." Elsewhere, Justin suggests that he is talking about "a special kind of commitment—beyond what a normal friendship would offer," which may also be called by names such as "covenant partnership" or "intimate friendship." He also points us toward the importance of "self-sacrifice and fidelity" in these relationships of human intimacy.

As an example of his position, Justin points us to Genesis 29:20, which tells us that "Jacob served seven years for Rachel, and they seemed to him but a few days because of the love he had for her," adding that "When I write about the importance of romance . . . , I'm talking about the kind of driving force that would make a man agree to work for seven years—*fourteen* years by the end of the story—merely to be with the woman he loves. I'm talking about a force far more powerful than sex, something that has been part of humanity since God created Adam and noted that it wasn't good for him to be alone."

In light of the concern about the best choice of words summarized above, I will propose my own choice of words that I am hoping does justice to what both Justin and Eve have said (in agreeing on the importance of these "hidden forms of love") and the concerns expressed by some readers; daring to make a normative claim applicable to all human beings. Every human being needs to experience intimate relationships with other people characterized by enduring commitments to give and receive love that seeks to foster the well-being of the other.

IS MARRIAGE THE GOLD STANDARD?

Justice Anthony Kennedy says "yes." Eve notes this in quoting the following words from Kennedy's majority opinion in the recent *Obergefell v. Hodges* case which "made gay marriage the law of the land."

> Rising from the most basic human needs, marriage is essential to our most profound hopes and aspirations . . .
>
> Marriage responds to the universal fear that a lonely person might call out only to find no one there . . .

> *No union is more profound than marriage, for it embodies the highest ideals of love, fidelity, devotion, sacrifice, and family.* In forming a marital union, two people become something greater than once they were ... (italics mine).
>
> [Gay couples'] hope is not to be condemned to live in loneliness, excluded from one of civilization's oldest institutions.

As Eve notes, "This is a vision of marriage as caregiving and intimate love" [with which Eve and Justin would agree, as would I]. But Eve goes on to suggest that Justice Kennedy's vision is "a vision in which marriage is the *only* hope for caregiving and intimate love."

My take on Justice Kennedy's words differs from Eve's view. I don't think he is saying that marriage is the "only" hope for caregiving and intimate love. But he is clearly saying that marriage is the gold standard because it "embodies the *highest ideals* of love, devotion, sacrifice, and family" (italics mine).

Justin agrees that marriage is the gold standard, as witnessed to in the following assertions. (For those who have difficulty with his use of the word *romance*, you can substitute his clarifying words *human intimacy* or my words *intimate relationships* in my normative assertion at the end of the last section.)

> Ultimately marriage offers the healthiest and most stable from of romance.
>
> Of course, I think marriage is the best and most stable place for long-term romantic love to thrive.

Given his view that marriage is the gold standard, Justin is concerned that "many churches may be tempted to use Eve's words about 'other ways of love' as a justification for denying to gay men and lesbians a particular and important kind of love that they themselves would be unwilling to go without."

Implicit in the following comment from one reader about Justin's example of the union between Jacob and Rachel is that the possibility for "procreation" is what makes marriage the gold standard: "Jacob's romantic feelings towards Rachel were 'about' sex. Not in the sense that they were solely sexual, but in the sense that his working was for the sake of a spousal union (i.e., a unitive and potentially procreative relationship) with Rachel."

Justin's response to this comment was that "While I agree that procreation is often an outcome of marriage, I don't think it's a requirement. There are many infertile couples who are nonetheless married, and I don't think their infertility makes their marriages any less valid." In passing, I will note that I was surprised that the goal of "procreation" was not more prominent in the exchanges between Justin and Eve, especially given the prominence of that theme in Catholic perspectives on marriage.

So, it is my understanding that both Justice Kennedy and Justin propose that marriage is the gold standard for intimate human relationships. But Eve strongly disagrees, as summarized below.

Recalling Eve's contention that the "Hidden Paths of Love" are "not imitations of marriage, "marriage lite," or "marriage minus [X], or consolation prizes for people who can't make a Christian marriage," she adds that "The job of friendship or celibate life in partnership is not to be 'as much marriage as possible under the circumstances'; *these relationships have their own structure and integrity*" (italics mine).

Eve reflects on why marriage appears to be the "*only* gold standard for love—and for intimacy and commitment," and concludes that this view taken by Justin, Justice Kennedy, and many others (in our churches) "is too much shaped by contemporary American culture." Her surprising antidote is to start taking celibacy and monasticism seriously (which will now require some considerable unpacking).

CELIBACY AND MONASTICISM

Before addressing this sub-topic, here is my brief summary of the most fundamental agreements and disagreements between Justin and Eve, as reported above. Eve and Justin agree that conversations about gay "issues" among Christians should be preceded by listening to the stories of gay Christians who aspire to live faithful to their Christian commitment. They agree that issues related to same-sex relationships are not all about sex, but should rather focus on forms of giving and receiving love. They also agree that there are multiple ways for all persons, gay or straight, to give and receive love, which includes marriage, but also includes "hidden forms of love" like friendships, service to others, and celibate partnerships.

There first major disagreement is about whether marriage is the "gold standard" for giving and receiving love. Justin (like Justice Kennedy) appears to say that marriage is the gold standard (the healthiest and most stable form of human intimacy—giving and receiving love—and heterosexual Christians should not deny "gay men and lesbians a particular and important kind of love that they themselves would be unwilling to go without").

But Eve rejects the idea that marriage is the gold standard. Each of the forms of love that she enumerates has its "own structure and integrity"; no one is more valuable than another; and to suggest otherwise reflects too much accommodation to the expectations of American culture, which has taken place in many Christian churches.

At this point the option of celibacy enters the picture. For Eve, the hidden forms of giving and receiving love in celibate relationships are as valuable as the marital sexual relationship.

Justin recognizes that "celibacy has a long history in the church," and he agrees completely with Eve's assertion that "Part of the reason we don't understand the value of Christian celibacy is that we have virtually no structures for supporting it among our fellow Christians."

But Eve and Justin give differing responses to the question of whether celibacy is a special "gift" from God. Eve's experience is that "The more you talk to people who have actually vowed themselves to celibacy, the less you believe that celibacy is only meant for people who have a special 'gift' for it or who perceive a special calling to it."

However, Justin reports that his experience has "been the opposite of Eve's experience": "The more time I've spent with [gay Christians who have committed themselves to lifelong celibacy], the more I've noticed that those who have successfully made celibacy work long-term share certain traits in common—they do seem quite clearly to have a 'gift of celibacy' not present in the general population. The trends are so strong that simply knowing these people caused me to believe in the existence of such a gift, even though I didn't believe in it initially."

Justin adds that "I do believe God calls some people to celibacy, and that those who are so called are also gifted to be able to follow that call and face its challenges. But I do not believe all people have the gift of celibacy, and I think we should follow Paul's lead in not trying to force everyone onto a path they are neither called to nor equipped for" (referring to the fact that the Apostle Paul, "who was celibate himself and praised celibacy for others, remarked that 'it is better to marry than burn with passion'"[4]).

In essence, Eve is taking the position that celibacy is intended for all those who are not married and not just for those who have been granted a special "gift" for celibacy. That is not to suggest that celibacy "will come easy to us" (any more than marriage). In fact, she speaks of the unfulfilled "yearning for marriage, sex, or biological children" that gay persons have, adding that in her own case:

> Out of those three I feel the lack of sex most sharply. It's a way of making your body an icon of self-gift and union: not the only

---

4. See 1 Corinthians 7: 8–9: "To the unmarried and the widows, I say that it is well for them to remain unmarried as I am. But if they are not practicing self-control, they should marry. For it is better to marry than to be aflame with passion."

way, but one of the most powerful and urgently felt. The longing for biological children is a similar kind of intense, gut-level longing which also has such deep symbolic resonance. It's important to name this pain. By exposing the painful yearning that we feel, we can build solidarity (with other gay people, or with straight people who have suffered from the same lacks for different reasons) and honor the sacrifices we make. God doesn't want us to pretend that our surrender is costless.

Note that Eve believes that her living a life of celibacy is indeed a "sacrifice." This causes Justin to "commend [her] highly for her own willingness to sacrifice for God" (since "sacrifice is an important part of the Christian walk"), which "made me love her even more."

However, Eve's take on the nature of this "sacrifice" is worthy of note and further conversation. She presents the provocative possibility that her sacrifice is an "unchosen sacrifice" in the sense that it seems "forced by the painful collision of Church teaching and personal circumstance." She recognizes how this way of thinking runs counter to the tendency in American culture to "both overestimate and maximize how *much* we control our lives." I would like to hear Eve's response to my sense that while her "circumstances" are outside of her control, she has chosen to live a celibate life.

I close this section with a provocative question that a reader has "yet to hear any conservative evangelical or Catholic answer" and that begs for further conversation.

> What is a gay man supposed to do if he is unable to control himself, as Paul alludes to in Scripture when stating it is better to marry than to burn? Is he simply supposed to marry a woman and use her for the sake of releasing his sexual urges, even though he holds no real feelings of love and passion for her? Or is he supposed to be a super-human, for whom Paul's words don't apply, and expected to merely turn off his urges for sexual release? Is THAT what Paul told people they were supposed to do? No. He said if you cannot control yourself, it is better to marry than to burn. He gave people an "out," a concession if they couldn't control themselves. So why is there such a heavy burden placed upon gay men who experience sexual desires, but yet are not provided a legitimate way "out" so that he can release those urges and thus not burn?

An open question at this point is why a Christian would choose to live a celibate life, given the sacrifice and pain that is often experienced. To that question we now turn.

THE AUTHORITY OF THE CHURCH?

Eve's initial response to the question of whether same-sex couples should enter into a sexual relationship is simple: "I'm Catholic—that's my answer to the 'gay marriage: yes or no?' question." She elaborates by saying, "My beliefs about sex and marriage don't stem from my years of theological study (which don't exist), my ability to parse New Testament Greek (ditto), or my personal observations. They are the result of my relationship to the Church, the Bride of Christ. To ask me what *I* believe is in a certain sense the wrong question. I believe what my Church believes and teaches to be true."

Justin strongly calls into question Eve's view that "the church is 'teacher and translator'," the source she trusts to answer the complicated question [of "whether marriage should be available to same-sex Christian couples"]. As indicated below, Justin's disagreement reflects a contrast between Catholic and Protestant views of the authority of the church.

> I share Eve's love for the church, and I see it as a vital part of my Christian walk. But in some ways—perhaps in no small part because I am a Protestant—I see my relationship to the church somewhat differently.
>
> For me, the church is like my *family*. Like a family, the church provides me with needed relationships and support in my journey. Like a family, the church offers guidance and can make me aware of ways I may have gone astray. But also like a family, the church is made up of fallible human beings. I trust the church, but I do not accept everything it teaches me without question or challenge. Most of the time, I think the church gets things right. But sometimes, the church gets things wrong.
>
> I am a Protestant in part because I believe the Roman Catholic Church got some things wrong along the way—including some much bigger theological issues than the one we're discussing in this conversation. But there is no doubt we Protestants have made our share of mistakes as well. I learned about Christ and came to faith in the Southern Baptist Church, and I will be forever grateful for the Christian passion instilled in me by that denomination. Unfortunately, as much as I love the good things, Southern Baptists have also gotten some very big things very wrong, going all the way back to the beginning when the denomination was founded in part on the belief that the Bible supports slavery.
>
> ... If my spiritual ancestors had been so wrong about slavery, mightn't today's Southern Baptists be wrong about other

things—things our spiritual descendants might be embarrassed about just as we are ashamed of the mistakes of the past?

One reader echoes Justin's concern from his experiences with the Protestant Church in which he was reared.

> I worry about the implications of trusting the theology of the church.
>
> I still wrestle with the idea that the church can be our translator. What would that mean for underprivileged persons? Since Constantine for sure, the church has leaned her interpretive skills toward favoring those with privilege—the wealthy, the slavemaster, the man, the white man, the straight white man.
>
> If I looked to the church I grew up in, I would believe in a literal seven-day creation, I would believe that women cannot have a role in church leadership . . . the list goes on. But thankfully, there are those who do the leg work of intensive biblical interpretation that have enlightened my understanding of Scripture to see that when oppression and exclusion are happening in the church it is often because of bad interpretation.
>
> I for one am thankful for the opportunity to seek interpretations of the Bible outside the confines of the church family I belonged to.

Interestingly, Justin's suggests that his "disagreement" with Eve on the authority of church teaching "may actually be less about disagreement than about degree of emphasis," citing Eve's assertion that "There are things the Catholic Church could teach that would make it impossible, I think, for me to accept her as a trustworthy guide to God's will."

In response to Justin's concern, Eve says that "There's a little more to be said about my willingness to accept Catholic teaching on sexuality than just, 'Rome says it, I believe it, that settles it.' There are things I see in Scripture—and things I see in Christian practice—that help to make the Catholic understanding of sexuality credible to me." Her elaboration includes the following.

First, she says that although "Scripture uses both same-sex and opposite-sex love to model the love between God and the human soul, . . . these loves aren't used in completely parallel ways . . . . The same-sex love that mirrors the love between God and humankind is expressed most often in friendship—David and Jonathan, Jesus and John, Jesus and all the disciples—and never in marriage. When sexual love serves as a mirror it's always sexually-faithful marital love between a man and a woman."

Secondly, consistent with her experiences in the Catholic Church, where she was not shamed for her doubts and struggles about her sexuality, she has since found "other communities, small but real, where sex is reserved for heterosexual marriage and actual gay *people* are treated as beloved equals. In many of these communities the question of vocation, of how we can love, is explicitly encouraged," concluding that "If I hadn't seen that, I doubt I would have accepted the Catholic teaching."

Of course, to focus on the teachings of the church is not to diminish the centrality of the biblical record, which all church teachings aspire to mirror. The next chapter will focus on "biblical understandings" relative to LGBT people and issues. But, in the meantime, it may be helpful to consider some general reflections from Justin and Eve about biblical interpretation.

A GENERAL APPROACH TO BIBLICAL INTERPRETATION

Justin asserts that a mistake he made in his early dealings with LGBT persons and issues is that he "tried to interpret Scripture in a vacuum rather than in the context of people's lives," adding that "when hurting people's lives are involved, a compelling scriptural argument in the *abstract* is not enough."

Justin provides a number of examples from the teachings and ministry of Jesus. For example:

> In Luke 14, when Jesus heals a man on the Sabbath, the Pharisees are incensed—you're not supposed to work on the Sabbath! Jesus responds, "If your son fell into a well on the Sabbath, wouldn't you pull him out?"
>
> The Pharisees' theology begins with the abstract: *Is Sabbath work forbidden in Scripture? Yes. Is healing work? Yes. Therefore healing on the Sabbath is forbidden—and now we apply that conclusion to this man in front of us.*
>
> Jesus' approach begins with the person: *Here is a hurting person in front of me. What does he need? How can I help? Ah, but it's the Sabbath. Let me now take this man's unique situation to the Scriptures—and when we do that, we can see that the purpose of the Sabbath law is to honor God, not to cause this man to suffer.*

As a second example, Justin notes that in Mark 2, Jesus points us to "the Old Testament story of David and the Bread of the Presence. God's rule had been unequivocal: No one but priests could eat the Bread of the Presence. But David was hungry and had no other food. What should he have done?"

The Pharisees' approach would have begun with the rule ("only priests can eat this") and applied it to David ("you aren't a priest, so you can't eat this"). If he had complained of hunger, perhaps they would have reminded him that following God requires sacrifice, or encouraged him that God would provide some kind of nourishment in the future in recognition of his faithfulness.

Jesus, however, begins first with the needs of the actual human being: David was hungry. He needed food. And the only food available required breaking the rule. *So he broke the rule, and Jesus approves of this.* Not only does Jesus approve of David's actions, he suggests that the Pharisees should take this same approach to other biblical rules like the Sabbath. According to Jesus, God wants people to come first, not rules.

As a more recent example, Justin points us to Mark Noll's reminder[5] that (in Justin's words) "during the Civil War . . . the biblical arguments made for keeping slavery were much more convincing than the arguments for abolition. After all, slavery enjoys a consistent witness in Old and New Testaments and plenty of specific passages allowing it and requiring slaves to obey their masters."

But "Christian abolitionists appealed to broader biblical themes of love and freedom." Drawing on Noll again, Justin asserts that "the idea that anti-slavery *spirit of the law* could trump a pro-slavery *letter of the law* 'was not only a minority position; it was also widely perceived as a theologically dangerous position'" (which obviously is no longer the case).

Eve's take on Justin's general approach to biblical interpretation is to point us to a difference (about which she "assumes we both agree") "between what Catholics would call 'development of doctrine' (the working out of the implications of our faith over time, guided by the Holy Spirit) and culturally-influenced deviance from orthodoxy." Eve suggests that "We disagree on which things fall where" and "the question, of whether gay marriage represents a development or distortion of doctrine, is not one I will attempt to resolve." That thorny question will come to the fore in the next chapter on "biblical understandings."

ANOTHER LINGERING QUESTION

Toward the end of his final posting, Justin raises a fascinating "lingering question" related to the distinction noted above between dealing with LGBT questions in the abstract or as important in the lives of gay persons.

---

5. Noll, *The Civil War.*

As an example of the generally agreed upon view that our perspectives (on LGBT questions and all other questions) are deeply informed by our social location, Justin first notes that he detects a difference between the writings of some of his gay friends who are located in academic settings where they are expected to deal with questions using theological and philosophical categories (which can lead to "abstract" writing that gives the "impression" of lack of passion—although these friends are very passionate people) and his own writing that emerges from his "pastoral role."

In brief, Justin says that "For me, this [dealing with LGBT questions] isn't just about philosophy or theology in the abstract, or even about what might work in my own life. It's about how the church can support millions of LGBT people who want to please God."

So, this conversation comes back to the original theme: "Gay people take priority over gay issues." Justin's lingering question is: What can the church do to support, in concrete—not abstract—ways, "millions of LGBT people who want to please God?" The postings form Justin and Eve point to a number of possibilities for concrete support in churches, which I will now summarize

WHAT CHURCHES CAN DO TO SUPPORT LGBT CHRISTIANS

The horrific story already told of the brutality experienced by one gay Christian in his engagement with Christian churches should give all churches pause. As suggested by Eve, this calls for "introspection" on the part of every church, and where such self-examination reveals instances of such treatment of gay Christians, or any other failure to treat gay Christians as persons made in the image of God, "repentance" is a necessary first step.

As already noted, Justin Lee's experience with the Gay Christian Network, comprised of both Side A and Side B Christians, leads him to conclude that "millions of LGBT people want to please God." Therefore, churches need seek ways to support gay Christians who desire to be faithful to their Christian commitment.

Such support will include offering a "healing" ministry for gay Christians. Some would argue that such "healing" should come through "reparative therapies" that seek to change a person's sexual orientation. As will be discussed in chapter 3, the efficacy of such therapies is now called into question.

Rather, as Eve suggests, what is needed is "a different kind of healing ministry for gay people—where people are healed not of their same-sex attractions, but of despair, shame, resentment, corrosive anger, and self-loathing."

To be more concrete, the postings in this conversation point to some "best practices" that churches can put in place to demonstrate support and "solidarity" with gay Christians, including the following:

Listen to the Stories of Gay Christians: As suggested by both Eve and Justin, rather than jumping into contentious conversations about LGBT "issues," churches first need to "start with the stories and reflections of those Christians who identify as being gay." Justin adds that "Whatever our views on marriage . . . we need to listen to one another's stories and hearts." Getting to know on a personal level both gay and straight worshipers will help all of us to understand the ways in which each is seeking to "please God," which can eventually help us to discern our agreements and illuminate our disagreements on the many complex LGBT "issues."

Promote Neglected Forms of Giving and Receiving Love: Allowing for disagreements about same-sex marriage, churches need to focus much more on the "neglected forms of giving and receiving love" pointed to by Eve Tushnet (friendship, service, celibate partnership), which are now "largely unrecognized and unsupported . . . in our churches."

Establish Church Support Groups for "Never Married Members": As noted by one reader, "The church seems to have plenty of support groups for divorced members but nothing for never-married members," adding that "Not everyone is given the vocation of marriage or the convent." Such support should include "upholding the beauty of a life lived in celibacy, because one loves Jesus and his teachings, so that the world, which is so confused about sex, can see that Love is what matters and what is respected and honored within her walls." As suggested by Eve, such support groups can "give guidance on forging a friendship."

Help Gay Christians Address Some "Bigger Questions": As suggested by Justin, churches must help gay Christians address some "bigger questions" (beyond "what the Bible says about same-sex sex"), such as "Where is my place in the church? What is my vocation? What does my future look like? If I'm single the rest of my life, what happens when I get old? Who will take care of me?

As a preview of reflections in later chapters on the meaning of "Christian unity," one reader suggests that "Valuing the process of 'working through' division and pain without a map, patiently waiting and resisting the false hope for personal validation and specific outcomes where others change for us" may, in the long run, be the source of "true unity."

RESPECTFUL CONVERSATION EXEMPLIFIED

Hoping that what follows doesn't read too much like the minutes of a meeting of a mutual admiration society, it is important for me to point out the ways in which Justin and Eve have beautifully exemplified the type of respectful conversation among persons who disagree about divisive issues that is the purpose of this eCircle in particular, and my website in general.

First, Justin points us to the importance of recognizing complexity and exemplifying the humility that is needed to say the following words that are all too rare in discourse about contentious issues: "It's complicated," or "I don't know," or "I was wrong."

> Growing up, I used to believe that the most serious, committed Christians were the ones who could give unambiguously clear-cut answers to controversial questions. I saw nuance as a form of wishy-washiness. Black-and-white moral questions needed black-and-white answers, I thought. If someone asked a question about the morality of homosexual relationships, for instance, and someone else began their response with "Well, it's complicated," I would have been quick to jump in with, "No, it's *not* complicated. It's wrong. The Bible forbids it. God condemns it. That's all you need to know. Truth isn't relative."
>
> I still believe in Ultimate Truth.[6] I still believe God has the final word and that the Bible is morally authoritative for us as Christians. But these days, I also believe a lot of things truly *are* complicated. These days, I'd argue that the most mature, thoughtful Christians are the ones who aren't so quick to jump to conclusions. They look for the complexity. They listen before they speak. They consider the specifics of the situation, not just a general moral principle. They aren't afraid to say "It's complicated," or "I don't know," or "I was wrong."

There are also valuable lessons to be learned from reflections from both Justin and Eve on how this very conversation taught each of them to better

---

6. In the pages that follow some conversation partners refer to "Truth," some to "truth" and some to both. I believe that whichever word is used, the intent is to refer to "God's understanding" relative to the issue at hand. In my commentary in the pages that follow, I will use the word *belief* to refer to "human understanding" relative to the given issue, which can capture the truth or provide a partial glimpse of the truth, or be "all wrong" (untrue).

understand the other's differing viewpoint and to appreciate the way in which the other is aspiring to live faithful to their understanding of their Christian commitment. Starting with Justin:

> These concerns and disagreements I have with Eve are not insignificant, but I also don't want them to overshadow something else significant—that despite our disagreements, I am inspired by Eve's honesty, integrity, and commitment to her faith. Faced with a journey that I know can be challenging and perhaps discouraging at times, she has sought to pour herself into doing good for others and challenging the church to do better. That is a good, right, and holy thing, and I think it's an excellent example for us all as Christians . . . . So while Eve and I may continue to disagree on some things—and may at times be working at cross purposes—I am proud to have her as my sister in Christ and my friend, and I know I've found her writing already to bring some very important insight to this conversation.
>
> As a Christian, I believe these are important conversations to have. But, if I'm honest, these conversations can frequently be downright miserable. I've watched too many people—many of them self-professed Christians—talk to others with derision and disdain, claiming to represent truth and love while treating others in ways no one would want to be treated themselves . . . . In far too many of these conversations, the Golden Rule is nowhere to be found—on either side . . . . And that's what I appreciate most about this conversation with Eve. Over this series of essays, Eve and I have disagreed on topics of deep personal and theological significance for both of us. I know where Eve stands, and I know that she thinks I'm very wrong on some important points. Never once, though, have I felt belittled, disparaged, or dehumanized by Eve. She disagrees, but she also *understands*, and that makes all the difference . . . . A lot of people on all sides of these debates think that disparaging your opponent makes your argument sound stronger. It doesn't. It just makes people less likely to listen to you unless they agreed with you from the start. Eve, thankfully, understands that. I felt heard and respected by her in this conversation, and though we still don't agree, having this dialogue has only increased my respect and appreciation for her. I wish all conversations on these questions were so respectful!

Eve shares similar reflections:

> [Justin] is modeling the way this conversation should go.

> Justin has done so much good for people who have been harmed far more deeply by their churches than I was. This year I went to the Gay Christian Network conference for the first time. I was amazed and deeply grateful for the experience. I saw people recovering from years of shame and self-hatred, which had been reinforced by their families and churches. You hear a lot about "healing" in the context of same-sex attraction and Christianity. GCN is a different kind of healing ministry for gay people—where people are healed not of their same-sex attractions, but of despair, shame, resentment, corrosive anger, and self-loathing . . . . I hope that makes clear my deep gratitude toward Justin. He is doing so much good. But we are still not quite speaking the same language, I think—we have still not even "achieved disagreement" on what a Christian sexual ethic looks like.
>
> And with that I will check out, with many thanks to both RespectfulConversations and Justin himself. I've been challenged in some really fruitful ways, and found some common ground as well.

As already hinted at above, this good starting conversation between Side A and Side B gay Christians does not bring closure to the ongoing attempt to gain a better understanding of the nature of the truth about LGBT issues. Although some common ground has been found, significant disagreements remain. Consider Justin's concluding reflection:

> So as I wrap up my part in this conversation, I find myself deeply moved. I am moved by Eve's grace in disagreement and her friendship to me as we challenge one another. I am encouraged, too, by the depth of conversation we've been able to have in six simple articles. But I'm also reminded why these conversations are so important in the first place. Many hurting, lonely people's lives hang in the balance.
>
> My own position on this topic hasn't changed, but my appreciation for Eve and understanding of her view has certainly increased, and I'd say that's worth it. Respectful conversation of this sort is hugely undervalued in the church. It may not always change minds, but it is powerful and effective. Given the importance of this topic, we can't afford *not* to listen to each other.
>
> We are, after all, supposed to be known by our love.

I believe the mutual respect and love demonstrated by these two deeply committed gay Christians who have significant disagreements about LGBT issues will be replicated in the chapters that follow.

2

Biblical Understandings

Discussions about what the Bible teaches regarding same sex-relationships quickly focus on areas of disagreement.

To be sure, the two conversation partners for this second round of conversations, Mark Strauss and Jim Brownson, are straightforward and clear in expressing their disagreements when they respond to the following Leading Question: What is your understanding of biblical/theological teachings relevant to issues being raised by Christians who identify themselves as members of the LGBT community? These disagreements will be summarized in due time.

But it is noteworthy that Mark and Jim have identified significant areas of common ground, beliefs they agree upon. Understanding this common ground has the potential to illuminate ongoing conversations about their disagreements.

COMMON GROUND

THE AUTHORITY AND INSPIRATION OF THE BIBLE

Jim Brownson says, "I recognize and affirm Dr. Strauss's desire to take the Bible seriously, and agree that this is a core value for all who want to read Scripture as committed Christians."

In reflecting on areas of agreement, Mark Strauss says that he and Jim Brownson "agree on the authority and inspiration of Scripture. We believe that the Bible is God's Word . . . a divine message from God to humanity. It is authoritative and infallible, communicating God's will, plan, and purpose for his creation"

This agreement about the authority and inspiration of the Bible is no small accomplishment when it comes to discussing LGBT issues. I have been involved in attempts to talk about these contentious issues that hit a dead-end after hardly getting started because those on one side of the issue are viewed as having a "lower view" of Scripture than those on "my side." Fortunately, that is not the case here. Both Mark and Jim place high value on the authority of Scripture. Their disagreements reflect differing interpretations of biblical passages that they both take with utmost seriousness.

THE BIBLE IS CONTEXTUALLY GIVEN

As Mark says: "We agree that the Bible is contextually given. God has revealed himself and his will through limited human agents in diverse cultural contexts and situations. Though God's nature does not change, his purpose and intention for specific groups or individuals may differ depending on time and place." Mark then proceeds to give examples from both the Old and New Testaments.

The most obvious example of this is the old covenant laws that were given to Israel. These commands were meant to regulate and order Israel's civil and religious life in the Old Testament period and do not necessarily apply to the church. The Old Testament sacrificial system—though explicitly commanded in Scripture—was always intended to be temporary, pointing forward to its ultimate fulfillment in Christ's sacrificial death on the cross.

Even new covenant commands are contextual and potentially limited in application. Most Christians today recognize that commands related to head coverings for women, greeting one another with a kiss, and washing feet as an act of service were given in specific cultural contexts and do not necessarily apply *directly* to the church today.

Mark even notes that "biblical commands forbidding same-sex sexual relations are *potentially* within this category, applying only to certain historical contexts and situations and never intended to forbid faithful and monogamous same-sex sexual relationships." Why he believes this is not the case will soon become apparent.

EXPRESSIONS OF HUMAN SEXUALITY SHOULD BE LIMITED TO LOVING, FAITHFUL, SELF-SACRIFICIAL, MONOGAMOUS RELATIONSHIPS

As Mark says, "what I believe is a third point of agreement" is that "God's design for human sexuality is for loving, faithful, self-sacrificial, monogamous sexual relationships," adding that "Though many within the gay rights movement (as well as the heterosexual community!) claim they have the right to complete sexual freedom and multiple sexual partners, this forum is about whether God ever blesses faithful, monogamous and lifelong same-sex unions." As will soon be seen, Mark and Jim disagree in their responses to that question.

THE MORAL LOGIC OF THE BIBLE FOCUSES ON THE PURPOSES OF COMMANDMENTS

Jim and Mark utilize differing terminology in talking about this common ground.

Jim asserts that "we need to probe the 'moral logic' of the commands and prohibitions of Scripture, asking not only *what* they say, but also *why they say* what they do."

Jim adds that it is "This understanding of *why* the texts make the claims that they do gives us the wisdom to know how to apply them in complex or varied cultural contexts," suggesting that "This is not a controversial claim; in fact the church has deployed just such an approach to many issues, including the sixth commandment 'Thou shalt not kill,' particularly in its application to just-war theory, as well as more mundane commandments like the exhortation 'Greet one another with a holy kiss.' When we know *why* the Bible gives these instructions, we know how to apply them more cogently in complex or cross-cultural circumstances."

Using different language, Mark's "Hermeneutics of Cultural Analysis" embraces the "*Criterion of Purpose: The purpose, or rationale, behind a command determines its application.*" Mark provides an example that echoes Justin Lee's suggestion that "the church is like my family."

> We might say that the *purpose* of a command is more important than the command itself. For example, when Paul commands believers to greet one another with a kiss, his purpose is not to make sure that there is a lot of kissing in the church. It is to encourage believers to practice family affection. Whatever way

a particular culture expresses family affection would be an appropriate fulfillment of this command.

The following assertions from Jim and Mark point to agreement about the moral logic of the Bible.

> I . . . find Dr. Strauss's 'criterion of purpose' to be essentially in agreement with what I am saying, using the language of 'moral logic.' We agree that we need to ask why the Bible says what it does, particularly when dealing with complex, cross-cultural matters. (Jim)
>
> Another area of agreement between Dr. Brownson and myself is in his emphasis upon the *reasons* behind biblical commands. It is not just the *what* of these commands but especially their *why* that is important. This is because all commands in Scripture are culturally embedded. Determining the functional significance of cultural commands like foot washing or the holy kiss enables us to determine how God would have us to fulfill these mandates today. I am also happy to adopt the category of the "moral logic" behind the Bible's teaching. (Mark)

Consistent with this agreement, Mark concludes that "With reference to our present topic, it will be essential to determine the purpose behind biblical commands related to same-sex relationships."

This question as to the *purpose* behind biblical commands related to same-sex relationships is one of a number of key questions (more to follow) for which Jim and Mark will give differing responses. The following reflection from Jim reveals that a crucial question about "purpose" is whether the views of the Apostle Paul regarding same-sex behavior apply to "long-term, committed same-sex relationships today."

> Everyone agrees that Paul views very negatively the same-sex behavior he describes in these verses [Rom 1:24-27]. This behavior is presented as evidence of humanity's idolatry and alienation from God. The dispute arises over *why* Paul views this behavior as wrong, what sort of behavior he has in view, and whether his discussion also applies to long-term, committed same-sex relationships today.

This is the first of six questions to which we now turn.

QUESTIONS BEGGING FOR FURTHER CONVERSATION

Although the areas of agreement between Mark and Jim sketched above are significant, there are a number of questions to which they give differing responses.

IS THERE A NEW REALITY REGARDING SAME-SEX RELATIONSHIPS THAT THE CHRISTIAN CHURCH HAS NEVER HAD TO FACE BEFORE WHICH REQUIRES THAT WE GO BACK TO THE BIBLE WITH FRESH EYES AND NEW CONCERNS?

Jim answers "yes" based on his "assumption" (for which he believes there is empirical evidence) that "there are gay and lesbian Christians in committed relationships who show evidence of the fruit of the Spirit in their lives (Gal 5:22f.)."

Jim adds that "I do not intend, by making this claim, to declare that the conversation is over, and there is nothing remaining to speak of in Scripture. Rather, I make this claim to suggest that the church has a problem and a challenge in dealing with the Bible's witness regarding same-sex relationships."

A second "assumption" that Jim makes (again based on empirical evidence) is related to the "intense efforts toward 'reparative therapy' that the church has made over the last thirty years or so."

> What the church has learned over this time is that, despite the prayerful and sincere attempts of thousands of gay and lesbian Christians to pursue this goal, in the vast majority of instances, the Spirit has not brought about that sort of change to heterosexual desire in those who sought it. Now again, this does not settle the question. Resistance to change does not inherently justify the behavior that resists that change. But neither is the failure of reparative therapy irrelevant to this discussion. And I want simply to underscore, at this point, the pastoral complexity that this failure of reparative therapy creates for the church, and the accompanying need to look more carefully at texts.

In this light, Jim "poses an important question for the church: How should this tangible evidence of the Spirit's work shape the way in which we interpret the Bible on sexuality in general, and on the church's posture toward LGBT persons in particular?" Jim adds that he introduces "this frame of reference for a particular reason: unless we acknowledge the pastoral complexity of this issue, we may be tempted to read the Bible in a superficial way, and not delve to core principles and issues."

Jim further suggests that "this need to delve into deeper issues was certainly present in the early church. It was the evident fruit of the Spirit, and the reality of the Spirit's work in Gentiles that led the early church to set aside the seemingly obvious application of Old Testament laws concerning kosher eating, circumcision, and Sabbath observance for Gentile Christian converts (cf. Acts 11:15-17, Gal 3)."

Jim concludes that "it is the apparent work of the Spirit that sends us back to the Bible, to read more carefully, to delve more deeply into its witness, and to center our reading of the Bible more fully on the heart of the gospel. We do this not because experience trumps Scripture, but rather because experience often raises new questions that bring us back to the Bible with fresh eyes and fresh concerns. This was true in the early church, and it remains true today."

Mark says that he "completely agrees" with the assumption by Dr. Brownson "that there are gay and lesbian Christians in committed relationships who show evidence of the fruit of the Spirit in their lives," adding that "The fruit of the Spirit is evidence that a believer has a relationship with Jesus Christ and has God's Spirit in their life."

But, Mark qualifies this agreement with an important disagreement: "The fruit of the Spirit is *not* proof that a person is sinless or that they are not struggling with sin in certain areas," giving as an example the fact that he "had a close pastor friend who was without doubt a true believer and in whom I saw a daily demonstration of the fruit of the Spirit (love, joy, peace, patience, etc.,). Several years later I found out he was having an affair during much of this time. While exhibiting much of the fruit of a true believer, he still struggled with and succumbed to sinful desires (see Rom 7:14-25). Similarly, the believers at Corinth exhibited powerful spiritual gifts (1 Cor 1:7) and yet some continued to visit prostitutes, claiming it did not affect their spiritual life (1 Cor. 6:12-20). Paul disagreed."

In a similar vein, Mark agrees with "Dr. Brownson's assumption that so-called 'reparative therapy' is generally not successful or the simple 'answer' to a very complex situation. While God can do anything he wants in a person's life, including changing their sexual orientation, experience suggests that this is not usually how God works." Mark adds that "Similarly, God did not remove Paul's 'thorn in the flesh' when Paul asked (2 Cor 12:7-10). He instead taught Paul to rely on divine power to endure trials and temptation. None of us will be perfected (physically, emotionally, spiritually, etc.) this side of eternity."

But Mark also qualifies this agreement with another major point of disagreement: "The frequent failure of 'reparative therapy' does not prove that homosexual inclination is either natural or God's design for human sexuality. Paul's thorn in the flesh (whether disease, demon, opponents, etc.) was not part of God's good design. It was evidence of creation's fallen state."

Mark concludes that Jim has not adequately addressed the following question: "Is homosexual inclination part of God's *intentional design* for human sexuality? Or is such inclination a result of our fallen state (like other sinful sexual desires)?" Mark asserts that "the claim for God's intentional design for same-sex sexual relations seems to run counter to the paradigmatic creation account in Genesis 1–2" (more about that shortly).

Jim has the following rejoinder to Mark's critique: "Certainly people can exhibit the fruit of the Spirit while they are sinning. But if we take the New Testament seriously, it was also the fruit of the Spirit that led early Christians to say that the failure of Gentiles to abide by certain explicit requirements of Scripture (Kosher, Sabbath, and circumcision) should not be regarded as 'sin,' despite explicit texts of Scripture to the contrary (including the death penalty for Sabbath-breakers)."

But even with this rejoinder, Jim agrees with Mark's critique that he [Jim] has not adequately addressed the question: "Is homosexual inclination part of God's intentional design for human sexuality?" This is a second question that begs for further conversation.

IS HOMOSEXUAL DESIRE PART OF GOD'S INTENTIONAL DESIGN FOR HUMAN SEXUALITY?

Mark clearly answers "no": "There is no doubt in my mind that monogamous heterosexual relationships represent God's design for human sexuality. I firmly believe that homosexual desire (like my own heterosexual inclination toward lust) arises from fallen human nature and is not part of God's will for human sexuality. This seems to me the clear teaching of Scripture and also makes the most sense emotionally, socially, and psychologically. We live in a fallen world and should not be surprised to see evidence of this brokenness in ourselves and those around us." Mark elaborates, drawing on Genesis 2.

> Genesis 2 establishes monogamous heterosexual relationships as the pre-Fall standard for human sexuality. While up to this point in the Genesis narrative all of creation is identified as "good," here we learn that, "It is *not good* for the man to be alone." So from the man's own body God creates a "helper suitable for him" (Gen 2:18). Eve is brought to Adam and the narrator announces the establishment of the marriage relationship: "That is why a man leaves his father and mother and is united

to his wife, and they become one flesh" (Gen 2:24). The union is between one man (*iš*) and one woman (*iššā*).

Mark notes that "Advocates of same-sex relationships often claim that this text is not speaking about gender complementarity but about companionship, which can be equally fulfilled in a same-sex relationship."

Mark's response is that "While no doubt companionship is a key component here, in the near context both procreation and gender complementarity are also emphasized. In the first (summary) creation account in Genesis 1, God creates humanity in his own image as male (*zāķār*) and female (*nᵉqēḇāh*) and commands them to procreate: 'Be fruitful and increase in number, fill the earth and subdue it' (1:27–28). God could not have told marriage partners to procreate if he had in mind same-sex partners."

In response to Mark's position that Genesis 2 reflects God's "intentional design for human sexuality," one reader notes that "at the time of Genesis 2:24 only one man and one woman were created, therefore that was the only possibility of coupling/partnering between human beings. As we travel later on in history we will see repeatedly in the OT marriage and sexual unions between one man and multiple women. For example Abram with Sarah and Hagar; Jacob with Leah, Rachael, Bilhah, Zilpah; Judah had a wife plus his union with Tamar, which is where we get King David and eventually Jesus from; David and Solomon had multiple wives and concubines. God did not punish any of these unions and yet they were not between one man and one woman."

Jim's response to Mark's critique that he [Jim] has not adequately addressed the question: "Is homosexual inclination part of God's intentional design for human sexuality?" is based on a distinction he makes "between 'God's creative design' and what is 'sanctifiable' in God's redemptive purpose," illustrating that distinction by dealing with "disability" (being careful to point out that he is "not suggesting that being gay or lesbian is a disability").

> I think most people would agree that disability is not part of "God's creative design." God did not create human beings intending them to be blind, or unable to walk. And yet all Christians would agree that God can take our experience of blindness or our inability to walk, even if that disability is due to the Fall, and draw that disability into God's creative purpose, so that the purposes of the kingdom of God are fulfilled through it, without eliminating it.

Jim proposes that "Another example would be procreation in marriage. I would agree with Dr. Strauss that procreation is part of God's creative design for marriage. And yet the church recognizes that God's redemptive purpose can include married couples who are incapable of procreation. So it is not enough to talk about God's creative design; we also need to talk about God's redemptive purpose, including a redemptive purpose for gay and lesbian sexuality."

So, Jim claims that "what is at stake in this conversation, it seems to me, is the extent to which core aspects of God's redemptive purpose for heterosexual marriage, revealed in Scripture, can be replicated in same-sex couples. I simply don't find necessary and essential aspects of the divine purpose for marriage that cannot be fulfilled by same-sex couples. I suggested in an earlier post that the marriage vows might be a good place to start in this conversation." In his earlier post Jim said, "Think of the marriage vows that lie at the heart of a Christian marriage service. Can gay or lesbian couples make these same vows to each other using the same words, and fulfill them in a Christian way? If so, why should they be forbidden from doing so?"

More conversation is obviously needed as to whether homosexual desire is part of God's intentional design for human sexuality.

COULD CHRISTIANS HAVE BEEN WRONG FOR OVER 2,000 YEARS?

Mark raises this question:

> For three millennia the people of God have understood Scripture to teach that same-sex sexual activity is outside God's will for human sexuality. Are we really to believe that even the most godly and sensitive of believers have for millennia radically misunderstood and misapplied the Spirit's voice on this issue and are only now coming to the light? Isn't it more likely that today—as throughout history—sinful human culture is placing pressure on the people of God to compromise God's standards of righteousness?

In response to Mark's question as to whether we are "really to believe that for all that time God's people have misunderstood and misrepresented the Spirit's voice," a reader asks: "Why is that so hard to believe, when it has happened with—to list a few subjects—female clergy, interracial marriage, remarriage after divorce, slavery, geocentrism, and all the way back to Gentile circumcision? This list alone doesn't make any revisionist reading necessarily correct, but it should open our hearts."

IS HOMOSEXUAL BEHAVIOR "NATURAL"?

This thorny question that begs for further conversation, as well as the next few questions that follow, takes us into complex issues of biblical interpretation that are beyond my expertise. Therefore, I cannot do justice here to the exchanges between Mark and Jim relative to this question. I encourage interested readers to go to the original electronic postings for all the intricacies of these exchanges. What I will attempt in this limited space is to note some highlights of these exchanges; just enough to illustrate that both Mark and Jim take the biblical record and the views of the other with utmost seriousness and aspire to express their disagreements with grace and respect.

I believe it is fair to say that it is around this question that Mark and Jim have their strongest disagreements. Mark appeals to Romans 1:26-27, as follows:

> Paul here identifies homosexual behavior (females with females; males with males) as "unnatural" (*para physin*), an example of the distortion that results from humanity's rejection of God. Paul probably singles out same-sex behavior not because it is unique or a greater sin than others, but because it is *perceived* by most people (i.e. heterosexuals) as unnatural, contrary to their own sexual desires. Some advocates of same-sex relationships claim that Romans 1:26-27 only condemns "perversion" (acting contrary to one's natural sexual orientation, whether heterosexual or homosexual). But this cannot be right. Paul does not say that "certain men abandoned their natural sexual inclination" but rather that "males" (*arsenes*) abandoned "the natural use" (*tēn physikēn chrēsin*) "of the female" (*tēs thēleias*)" (v. 27). Unnatural is explicitly defined as males with males and females with females—i.e., homosexual activity....
>
> Others argue that Paul is here referring only to oppressive and exploitative behavior, like temple prostitution or pederasty, not faithful, loving homosexual relationships. While these practices were well known in the Greco-Roman world of the first century, the immediate context makes it unlikely that Paul is limiting his discussion to these. First, Paul's reference to lesbianism would make little sense in these kinds of exploitative and abusive relationships. Second, Paul's reference to mutual desire ("inflamed with lust for one another"; v. 27) rules out an oppressive or exploitative relationship. Most importantly, allusions to the creation account throughout this chapter suggest that Paul has Genesis 1-2 in mind. Paul's distinctive use of *thēlys/arsēn* (female/male) instead of *gynē/anēr* (woman/man), echoes

the language of Gen 1:27 (LXX)—"male and female he created them"—supporting the view that "natural" here refers to God's created order of human sexuality as expressed in Genesis 1–2. Same-sex sexual acts are "unnatural"—that is, contrary to God's created order.

Jim has a different reading of Romans 1:26-27, as follows:

> Lastly, we turn to the category of "nature." Paul says that "their women" exchanged the "natural use" for that which is "contrary to" or "beyond" nature (1:26), and similarly, men left behind "the natural use of woman" and had sex with men instead. But the first thing we must note is that the word "nature" (Greek *physis*) does not occur in the Septuagint, the early Greek translation of the Hebrew Bible. This is not a Jewish category, but figures prominently in Stoic philosophy, the dominant philosophical perspective among Gentiles in Paul's day. And when we look at Paul's other uses of this word, they coincide with what we also see in Stoic philosophy. "Nature" refers to a *convergence* of individual disposition (cf. the same word rendered "instinctively" in Rom 2:14), social consensus (cf. the same word used in 1 Cor 11:14-16), and the biological world (cf. Rom 11:21, 24).

Jim notes that "here is where the debate gets stuck."

> Revisionists (who argue for greater acceptance of LGBT folks) talk about the personal and social dimensions of what is "natural" and traditionalists (who argue that Scripture supports a view of same-sex behavior as inherently sinful) talk about the biological dimensions. Yet the ancient Stoic vision of "nature," like Paul's usage, encompassed a harmony between all these.

Jim elaborates on this quest for "harmony" as follows:

> I think what the Stoics longed for in their vision for nature was essentially a form of harmony and coherence between one's individual disposition, the social order, and the natural world. I think that this is what God intends as well. Our understanding of ourselves, of the social order, and of the natural world are all subject to change, but the Stoic vision of the integration of these realms is still a compelling one: how do we live, so that these various arenas of our lives exist in peaceful harmony with each other?
>
> This requires the exercise of a sanctified imagination: Can we imagine a world in which the divine pronouncement at the beginning of creation, "It is not good for the man to be alone"

(Gen 2:18) finds a range of deeply satisfying resolutions, from heterosexual marriage, to celibate communities, to gay and lesbian committed unions? Can we imagine both those with heterosexual and same-sex sexual orientation finding the deep sort of intimate communion which satisfies the longings of the heart and the body, builds stable households in society, and draws all persons more deeply into the experience of interpersonal grace which echoes and leads into the divine communion itself? Can we imagine these diverse households all contributing toward a fruitful and just society where children are conceived, sometimes adopted, and nurtured, where the hungry are fed, the poor and the sick are cared for, and where creativity and productivity is unleashed in the "natural" energy and vitality of communal life.

Mark responds to Jim's appeal to a Stoic point of view as follows.

Whether or not Stoic thought comes into play in Paul's perception of "nature" (it may), it seems hard to deny that Paul's views on homosexual behavior coincide with his Jewish background, where such behaviors were universally and unambiguously viewed as contrary to God's design for human sexuality. To claim that—despite all appearances—Paul had a higher (Stoic?) vision of convergence that would have trumped not only his Jewish worldview, but everything the Bible says about same-sex behavior, seems to me incredible.

So in the end, I have to say that I have not found the biblical or hermeneutical arguments marshaled for same-sex relationships ultimately convincing . . . .

Jim's response to Mark's response is as follows:

I agree that Jewish writers around the time of Paul use the concept of "nature" utilizing the Greek word *physis*, and that it is not unique to Paul. But I would argue that, for *both* Jewish interpreters like Philo or Josephus *as well as* for Paul, they use the word in order to communicate with a Gentile audience for whom this word is familiar and already defined. It's an apologetic move, plain and simple. They all interpret this category to be readily identifiable with divine purpose and design, finding a point of contact between what we would call "natural revelation" and the "special revelation" found in the Torah. But here's the important thing: when they use the word *nature*, their readers would not think of special revelation, but of general revelation. That's the category within which we need to envision this language.

> I agree that "Paul's views on homosexual behavior coincide with his Jewish background." But there are two further issues at stake here concerning "nature." One of them is whether Paul's understanding of the natural world is subject to change, based on further research and understanding. I think that natural revelation is not a fixed thing. Otherwise, the church would have been right to condemn Galileo's heliocentric view of the solar system, which contradicted what everyone had assumed about the natural order (but he was right!) Rather, I believe that our understanding of the "natural world" is subject to growth and enhancement. That is what I think has happened on this topic. So I think Dr. Strauss and I agree about what Paul thought. We disagree about *why* he thought it, and on whether this is a "final word" in contemporary application.

As one ponders these thoughtful exchanges between Jim and Mark as to whether homosexual behavior is "natural," it may be helpful for us to consider the following perspective from a reader (echoing the suggestions of Justin Lee and Eve Tushnet that "gay people take priority over gay issues").

> My gay friends who are Christian, some of who are in long-term relationships, married or not, find it impossible to comprehend the idea that their identity as a same-sex directed person is unnatural for them.

The above highlights of the exchanges between Mark and Jim are probably more intricate than most readers wished for. I share all of this for three reasons that are central to the purpose of this book.

First, readers need to realize that many of the issues dealt with in this chapter, and the other chapters, are too complex to be distilled into sound bytes. Those of my readers who are looking for simple black-and-white answers should stop reading about now.

Second, because of this complexity, Christians need to be generous and respectful with one another when they disagree about these issues, not thinking of those who "think otherwise" as "inferior Christians" who do not take the Bible seriously.

Finally, it is only by means of such respectful dialogue that we can learn from one another. Jim expresses this beautifully in his following concluding reflection after his exchange with Mark:

> I'm grateful for this conversation, and have learned a lot through it . . . I hope that Dr. Strauss and I will have opportunity to continue this conversation at some point face-to-face.

IS HOMOSEXUAL DESIRE ANALOGOUS TO HETEROSEXUAL INCLINATION TOWARD LUST?

Another significant point of disagreement between Jim and Mark occurs when Jim takes exception to an analogy that Mark seems to draw between homosexual desire and heterosexual inclination toward lust when Mark says the following: "I firmly believe that homosexual desire (like my own heterosexual inclination toward lust) arises from fallen human nature and is not part of God's will for human sexuality."

Jim's concern about drawing such an analogy stems from his understanding of the basis for Paul's negative view of same-sex behavior in Rom 1.

> Paul first categorizes this behavior as *lustful*. Romans 1:24 speaks of the "lusts of their hearts." Romans 1:26 speaks of "degrading passions," and Romans 1:27 speaks of how these perpetrators were "consumed with passion." Paul is not speaking here only of *misdirected* desire, but of *excessive* desire . . . . Jewish and Christian writers (including Paul) held to a particular theory about same-sex desire—that it was driven by excessive lust, by an insatiable appetite for increasingly exotic forms of stimulation.

This interpretation of what Paul is opposing in Rom 1 "raises a question" for Jim about "the applicability of this sort of logic to committed gay and lesbian unions today. Most gay and lesbian Christians do not 'leave behind' ordinary desire for those of the opposite sex as Romans 1:27 assumes; they never experienced such desire to begin with. So, while Paul appears to be speaking of those with an insatiable desire for the exotic, not content with heterosexual gratification; that analysis doesn't seem to fit the experience of gay and lesbians in committed relationships. We can all agree that any sort of sexual desire driven only by a thirst for the exotic is morally wrong. What remains questionable is whether *all* gay and lesbian relationships should be described this way, whether all such relationships are *necessarily* 'consumed with passion.'"

In a later posting, Jim elaborates further.

> I'm not at all convinced that a homosexual orientation should be viewed as analogous to a heterosexual inclination toward lust. Lust treats the other person as an object; not all gay people treat their partners this way. Lust avoids commitment; not all gay people do. Lust is essentially self-centered; not all same-sex desire is. Heterosexual lust is normal desire, but cranked up, with an absence of restraint, and a self-centered focus. I'm not convinced that all same-sex desire fits this paradigm. I would

love to hear from Dr. Strauss more about the analogy between heterosexual lust and same-sex desire. I see a lot of problems here.

Mark responds to Jim's request by saying that Paul is talking about "*both* misdirected and excessive desire."

> Dr. Brownson claims that in Roman 1:24–27, "Paul is not speaking here only of *misdirected* desire, but of *excessive* desire," and that this kind of excessive lust has little relation to mutual and loving same-sex relations. My response would be that Paul seems clearly to be talking about *both* misdirected and excessive desire. And the misdirection is explicitly defined as "female with female" and "male with male" sexual behavior. Paul's strong language related to this ("inflamed with lust," etc.) is not at all surprising considering his Jewish background. As Dr. Brownson himself points out, Jews of Paul's day viewed homosexual relations as particularly repulsive and evidence of the godlessness and corruption of the Gentile world. To claim that this Jewish repulsion related *only* to "excessive" or particularly lustful homosexual activity seems unlikely to me.

In his final posting, Mark elaborates further, proposing that both same-sex desire and heterosexual inclination toward lust are "disordered inclinations" brought about by our "fallenness."

> Dr. Brownson is also unhappy with the parallel I drew between "my own heterosexual inclination toward lust" and same-sex desire, because—he notes—lust is very different from a loving and mutual same-sex relationship. I agree that these are different. But my point was not to equate the two, but to identify both as disordered *inclinations.* My *inclination* toward lust is not in itself sinful. But it is disordered (a result of our fallenness). In the same way, the *inclination* toward same-sex relations is not sin. But it is disordered and a result of our fallenness. If we give in to these temptations (by lusting or in same-sex sexual acts), they become sin.

It is obvious that more conversation is needed.

IS HOMOSEXUAL BEHAVIOR "IMPURE" AND "SHAMEFUL?"

As challenging as it is to respond to the questions posed above, further thorny questions remain. In addition to their disagreements as to how to interpret Romans 1:24–27, Jim and Mark have significant disagreements about how to interpret other key biblical passages that appear to clearly forbid homosexual behavior (e.g., Lev 18:22; Lev 20:13; 1 Cor 6:9-10; 1 Tim 1:9-10).

Many books have been written about these disagreements (see the Recommended Readings toward the end of this book). In light of my intended purpose that this book provide a springboard for ongoing conversations, I will now merely quote some snippets from the postings by Jim and Mark pertaining to the questions as to whether homosexual behavior is "impure" and/or "shameful:"

Jim acknowledges that "Paul . . . refers to the same-sex behavior he describes in these verses [in Rom 1] as 'impurity' (Rom 1:24)," adding that "Paul frequently refers to sexual misbehavior as 'impurity' (e.g. 2 Cor 12:21, Gal 5:19)."

But Jim suggests that this language also needs to be viewed in the larger context of the New Testament's treatment of the categories of pure/impure and clean/unclean generally," elaborating as follows:

> Jesus takes a remarkably loose attitude to the Levitical standards of purity and impurity. He touches lepers, allows a menstruating woman to touch him, eats with tax collectors and sinners, and dies in a way that is, Paul reminds us, explicitly cursed by God (Gal 3:13-14, cf. Deut 21:23). But perhaps the most striking text reflecting this larger approach to purity comes from Paul himself in Romans 14:14, where Paul defines purity and impurity solely by one's internal disposition, not by external criteria . . . .
>
> What we see overall in the New Testament is a movement away from defining impurity *externally* by the law, to an approach that defines it *internally*, by whether or not behaviors are marked by selfishness and the absence of restraint. Paul clearly views the sexual behavior he describes in Romans 1 as "impurity" (as do other Jewish and Christian writers of the period) in this fuller and more nuanced way, as marked by selfishness and absence of restraint.

In that light, Jim points to "the difficulty in applying Paul's language in Romans 1 to contemporary committed gay and lesbian unions, where folks commit themselves to each other for better or worse, for richer or poorer, in sickness and in health, to love and to cherish until we are parted by death. Such commitments hardly seem to be characterized by selfishness and lack of restraint—indeed such vows entail the acceptance of substantial commitments and limitations for life!"

But Mark proposes that it is a mistake to think of the Levitical commands as relating to "merely purity issues rather than to overtly sinful behavior." Quoting Leviticus 18:22 ("Do not have sexual relations with a man as one does with a woman; that is detestable" (NIV)), Mark adds that "Leviticus 20:13 identifies the penalty for such actions as death."

Mark concludes that

> The imposition of the death penalty shows that this is far more significant than a purity issue. Purity issues are resolved through the passage of time, ritual washing or offering sacrifices, not through capital punishment. The death penalty is reserved for serious violations of God's character, his created order, and the covenant between Yahweh and his people.

A portion of Jim's response to Mark is:

> With respect to Leviticus, I agree that purity is not the only concern motivating these texts to forbid same-sex sexual activity. But I don't think that appeal to the death penalty is a helpful signal of cross-cultural relevance. The Bible calls for the death penalty for Sabbath-breakers (Ex 31:15, 35:32, Num 15:32ff), and outsiders who come too close to the tabernacle (Num 1:51), etc. One simply cannot reason automatically from the severity of the biblical penalty to its cross-cultural relevance.

Further conversation is obviously needed as to whether homosexual behavior is "impure." The same can be said as to whether such behavior is "shameful."

Jim's take on the honor-shame language of Romans 1:24–27 is as follows:

> The sexual misbehavior described here, in addition to being characterized as "lustful" and "impure," is considered "degrading" or "shameless" for a particular reason: such behavior violates established social expectations of the time regarding gender, and regarding behaviors that are seen as appropriate to males and females. For females, such dishonor arose from any sort of sexual behavior outside of marriage, as well as the failure to maintain the appropriate passive or submissive role within marriage; for males, dishonor or shame was more particularly a result of failure to "act like a man," which included (among other things) playing the passive role in sexual intercourse and being penetrated by another male.
>
> Finally, it's important to note that the categories of honor and shame are often critiqued in the New Testament (e.g. 1 Cor

1:27f; Heb 12:2). Honor and shame are not revelational categories; they are *cultural* categories that are reinterpreted in light of the gospel. I think it's fair to say that Christians in any cultural context should avoid treating people in ways that those people will experience as shameful or degrading. That's what Paul is addressing here. However, what counts for shameful and degrading varies substantially from one culture to the next, and behavioral norms need to change accordingly. And it is not at all clear that folks in our culture all experience same-sex sexual behavior as inherently degrading.

Mark's response to Jim is as follows:

> Dr. Brownson also picks up on Paul's language of shamefulness in Romans 1 (vv. 24, 26, 27) and links this passage to the important cultural values of honor/shame in the Greco-Roman world. With reference to gender, he points out that *"shame is specifically associated with failure to act in accordance with one's own gender."* For women this involved sexual behavior outside of marriage. For men, it meant failing to act as the dominant partner in sexual relations (i.e., to be penetrated, instead of the penetrator). Dr. Brownson concludes that the sexual behavior of Romans 1:24–27 is viewed as shameful and degrading not because it is homosexual *per se*, but because, "such behavior violates established social expectations of the time regarding gender, and regarding behaviors that are seen as appropriate to males and females."
>
> There is significant insight here. Shame and honor were certainly extremely important values in the Ancient Near East and the Greco-Roman world. Furthermore, although male homosexual behavior was common and widely accepted, the passive partner was often viewed with derision and shame. To be a true man meant to dominate, which meant assuming the active sexual role.
>
> While these cultural insights are valid, applying them to Romans 1 is problematic. First, they do not work well with the lesbian relationship Paul describes in 1:26. A woman's shame in the Greco-Roman world came from unfaithfulness to her family or her husband. This would be most commonly expressed in lack of submission, immodesty, promiscuity, or adultery. It would be very strange indeed to express it in terms of lesbianism, a topic seldom discussed in the Greco-Roman world. Much more likely is the explanation we have introduced previously, which is that both lesbianism and male homosexual behavior

are intended by Paul to represent obvious distortions of human sexuality as defined by the paradigmatic creation account in Genesis 1–2.

The other major problem with this shame/honor explanation of Romans 1 is that it does not apply well to what Paul says about male homosexual behavior. According to Paul, what is "degrading," "impure," and "shameful" (1:24, 26, 27) is not the passive partner in the homosexual act, but *both* partners "men . . . with other men" who were inflamed with lust "for one another." It is the acts themselves, not the particular role played, that is shameful.

This exchange of differing views as to whether homosexual behavior is shameful begs for further conversation

CONCLUDING REFLECTIONS

SIGNS OF RESPECTFUL CONVERSATION

Jim's reflections on Mark's postings reveal appreciation for two tell-tale characteristics of a respectful conversation—the quest for "balance" and "common ground," and the desire to "create space" when interpreting Scripture.

> Clearly, Dr. Strauss is seeking to take Scripture seriously. I applaud that commitment. He is seeking to find balance, and to discern common ground. I also appreciate that. I accept (with a few quibbles) the hermeneutical principles with which he begins and agree that they are a helpful starting point. Dr. Strauss clearly is trying to *create space* for cultural factors in interpreting Scripture, something that not all participants in their conversation worry about sufficiently. This is critical, I believe, to an appropriately missional reading of Scripture, as the gospel crosses cultural boundaries. [Italics mine.]

Jim also points to the importance of writing that is "accessible and clear" when engaging in written forms of respectful conversation and the importance of "hermeneutical clarity" for this particular conversation on "biblical understandings," and he applauds Mark for exhibiting these characteristics.

> I appreciate particularly Dr. Strauss's concern for hermeneutical clarity, which is a helpful perspective in this conversation. I also find his writing accessible and clear.

GRACIOUS TOLERANCE

Nevertheless, it appears that Jim and Mark may not see eye to eye as to the meaning of "gracious tolerance," another characteristic of a respectful conversation.

First, Mark clearly expresses his commitment to "gracious tolerance."

> I have to admit from the beginning that I am torn on this issue [God's design for human sexuality]. Like many other Christians, I find that my positive personal experiences with those who identify with the LGBT community are often at odds with the Bible's apparent teaching on this issue. While I respect those ... whose personal experiences have provoked them to return to Scripture with new eyes and to change their mind, I personally have found it impossible to reconcile a high view of Scripture and a consistent hermeneutic with this revisionist perspective. I bear no animosity toward any person who is gay or toward anyone who holds an inclusive perspective. I will continue to seek to love all people and live in *gracious tolerance* toward everyone, even (and especially) those who treat me with animosity or who view my beliefs as insensitive, bigoted, or offensive. [Italics mine.]

But Jim's reading of this statement from Mike (with which he "agrees") causes him to ask Mark for further elaboration.

> I would like to invite Dr. Strauss to reflect further on his own commitment to "gracious tolerance" ... (with which I agree), and his subsequent exegesis, which seems to leave little if any space for such tolerance. What is the basis on which such "gracious tolerance" should be given? How does this translate into actual church practice?

Mark responds as follows:

> Dr. Brownson also invites me to expand upon what I mean by "gracious tolerance," especially in light of my subsequent interpretation of texts (where I conclude that same-sex relationships are contrary to God's will). The implication of his invitation, if I'm understanding it correctly, is that he doesn't see how I can be "tolerant" and still believe that the Bible treats same-sex relationships as sinful. But this seems to be an inappropriate definition of tolerance. *Tolerance does not mean that I agree with or affirm someone else's beliefs or actions. It means that despite our differences, I still treat that person with love and respect.* I don't

hate them, or persecute them, or seek to harm them. Instead, I love them despite our differences. If we did not disagree, there would be no need for tolerance. For example, I have a friend who is Jewish. I love him and treat him with respect and would never intentionally harm him. But I don't agree with his beliefs. I have another friend who is an atheist. He lives a lifestyle that I consider to be immoral. Yet I show gracious tolerance to him. I love him and spend time with him and treat him with respect and dignity, and I pray for him. He knows I don't agree with his beliefs or approve of his lifestyle, but we can still share friendship, mutual love and respect. It is the same with friends who are practicing homosexuals. [Italics mine.]

Jim did not have an opportunity to respond to Mark's response. I expect he would agree that "tolerance" means that "I treat that person [who disagrees with me] with love and respect." More conversation may be called for.

WHY WE ALL NEED TO KEEP TALKING

Embedded in the conversation between Jim and Mark are some excellent reasons why they and all of us need to keep talking about our differing understandings of biblical teachings regarding LGBT issues.

First, the need for Christians to "feel deeply and empathize with those who are agonizing over these issues" calls for ongoing conversation. As Mark puts it:

> I *do* find the stories from the gay community and their supporters very compelling. And I feel deeply and empathetically with those who are agonizing over these issues. That alone is enough to keep me engaged in the conversation.

Second, many of the disagreements are on "debatable issues" (what others have called "disputable matters"—more about that toward the end of this book). As Jim puts it:

> I find that most of our disagreements are on specific and debatable issues. That, in itself, may help to explain why Dr. Strauss seeks a "gracious tolerance" with those who disagree. But it also invites a further conversation about the status of our disagreement, and the extent to which, in general, Christians should be able to recognize each other as brothers and sisters in Christ when they disagree on this question. That is an important conversation in its own right.

It is extremely important to note Jim's call for another important conversation (beyond, and, I believe, prior to this conversation about LGBT issues); a conversation about *"the extent to which . . . Christians should be able to recognize each other as brothers and sisters in Christ when they disagree"* (italics mine). It is my hope that the reader will find shades of this prior conversation at least implicit throughout this book; my own position being that Christians need to create "safe spaces" for the expression of strong disagreements about LGBT issues and many other "debatable" issues, with our "unity" being defined not by "uniformity" of belief but, rather, by our shared aspirations to be faithful followers of Jesus.

A third reason for continuing the conversation is the need to minimize "misunderstanding and ineffective communication," as pointed to by Jim.

> I am grateful for this conversation with Dr. Strauss. It helps me to see the more clearly those areas that still need work, and more particularly, those areas that are most prone to misunderstanding and ineffective communication. That, of course, is no assurance that such "misunderstanding" can be easily fixed, but it does provide a focus for further work.

A fourth reason for needing to continue the conversation is that there is the potential for each of us to "learn something" if we engage in respectful conversation with this with whom we disagree. As Jim puts it, in an elaboration of an earlier quote:

> I'm grateful for this conversation, and have learned a lot through it. I will need to think more, and perhaps say a bit more about the relationship between God's original creative design and God's redemptive purpose. These are clearly related to each other, but cannot be collapsed into a single thing. And I would love to have a wider conversation with Dr. Strauss about natural and special revelation, and how this distinction impacts Christian ethics more generally. I hope that Dr. Strauss and I will have opportunity to continue this conversation at some point face-to-face, since written conversation is always somewhat stilted and limited.

As an aside prompted by Jim's wish for future face-to-face conversation with Mark, I will note that my fondest dream is that the nine-month electronic conversation reported on in this book could be followed by face-to-face conversations involving all of my twenty-one conversation partners. That would take a lot of money, which I don't have. Maybe a reader of this book does have it. Hope springs eternal!

Mark also expresses appreciation for what he has learned by means of this exchange with Jim, noting that he expects to "keep learning."

> I have greatly appreciated this opportunity for dialogue. I have learned a great deal and expect to keep learning. I want to thank Dr. Brownson for his incisive but fair and cordial engagement.

In addition to the areas pointed to above as begging for further conversation among Christians, Mark points to a need for Christians to engage those who do not share a Christian faith commitment about these contentious issues related to human sexuality.

> Another area that needs more thought and discernment is how the church should respond in a society that is increasingly at odds with its moral standards. Some . . . have warned that the church will lose its witness if it remains at odds with the larger culture. I would say the opposite. We will lose our witness if we give in to the world's standards. The first-century church was greatly at odds with the moral values of the Greco-Roman world. Yet it survived and thrived not by changing its values, but by standing firm on God's commands while demonstrating sacrificial love, mercy, and peace toward outsiders—even when facing persecution and loss. This represents the greatest challenge for the church today, to remain true to its convictions while practicing self-sacrificial love, joy and kindness toward those who oppose us. There is no place in the church for anger, hatred, ostracism, or homophobia.

Mark does indeed point to a monumental challenge; a challenge that I believe is even greater than he portrays since, as the pages of this book reveal, there is no monolithic view within the Christian church as to "its moral standards" relative to LGBT issues. Therefore, at the same time that Christians engage one another in respectful conversations about our strong disagreements, which we should not seek to camouflage, we need to engage in respectful conversations about these contentious LGBT issues with those in our society who do not share our Christian faith commitment. Our willingness to engage in such wider conversations with love, grace, and respect for those who disagree with us may be our greatest witness.

WHAT CAN CHURCHES AND OTHER CHRISTIAN COMMUNITIES DO?

Chapter 1 included four concrete suggestions as to "What Churches can do to Support LGBT Christians." And two later chapters (8 and 9) will say a lot more about that topic. In the exchange reported on in this chapter, Mark echoes some of the suggestions made in chapter 1, echoing once again the idea that "the church is a family."

> The church also needs to be more proactive in supporting and encouraging all those who come through its doors, whether married, single, divorced or widowed, whether homosexual or heterosexual. The church is a family, and as a family it needs to work hard to provide support and accountability. This means strengthening and supporting marriages. It means encouraging healthy celibate relationships that nurture the soul with deep and caring commitment and family affection. It means acknowledging the reality of sexual temptation and providing support systems and accountability partnerships to help *all of us* maintain sexual purity.

In closing, we should all reflect on the following suggestion from one of the readers of this present conversation (which echoes once again the view that "gay people take priority over gay issues").

> Suppose we do not try to go away from the human community that is Christ's body and God's image in the world to try to suss out hidden truths without which we cannot relate to other image-bearers. Suppose we reverse the process and start with loving others in real, specific, community/congregational/pastoral relationships and then see how we read the Bible. Isn't that what Jesus did?

3

Findings from the Sciences

Christians have often struggled to forge an adequate grasp of the relationship between the knowledge claims emerging from the empirical methodologies of the natural and social sciences and their biblical/theological understandings. In theological terms, there has been tension between the understanding of Christians as to the relationship between "natural revelation" (what God has revealed through the "natural" world) and "special revelation" (what God has revealed through Scriptures and through the "Word made flesh among us," Jesus Christ).

Some of these tensions become apparent in the exchanges between two psychologists, Chris Grace and David Myers, who are deeply committed to both the Christian faith and their scientific endeavors, as they respond to the Leading Question: What is your understanding of the best findings from the academic disciplines of biology, anthropology, psychology, and sociology relative to same-sex attraction, sexual orientation, and sexual behavior for human beings?

As will be seen below, their electronic exchange reveals significant areas of agreement as well as significant disagreements that they carefully address.

COMMON GROUND

CHRISTIANS SHOULDN'T UNCRITICALLY ACCEPT CULTURAL TRENDS

As Dave points out, there has been "an astonishing transformation of public opinion" about same-sex marriage as witnessed to by changing responses to the question: "Should same-sex marriages be recognized by the law as valid, with the same rights as traditional marriages?"

> In 2015, a record 60 percent of Americans told Gallup, yes; only 37 percent said no. This flip from the 37/59 percent split a decade earlier (and from the 27/68 percent split of 1996), represents an astonishing transformation of public opinion.

Dave adds that "This momentum of gay support will likely continue as gay friends and relatives continue coming out, and as attitudes follow behavior (with same-sex marriage now the law of the land)." Later portions of this book will echo Dave's suggestion that positive attitudes toward same-sex marriage increase when the persons polled actually know friends and relatives who have "come out."

Dave also notes an "enormous generation gap" when it comes to beliefs about same-sex marriage.

> Equally striking is an enormous generation gap. Averaging across surveys, support for same-sex marriage runs about 40 percent among Americans over age 65 and nearly 80 percent among those ages 18 to 29. I am unaware of another social issue about which older and younger Americans so dramatically disagree. Today's millennials and their grandparents live in different social worlds.

But, despite this "astonishing transformation of public opinion," Dave and Chris agree that Christians should not uncritically accept cultural trends. As Dave puts it: "Our teaching of sexual ethics should not simply follow cultural trends. Rather than put our finger to the wind, we should put our nose to the Bible, aided by scholars who can help us discern its wisdom for our time."

Chris concurs, adding that in addition to turning to "biblical scholars as we reengage pertinent biblical wisdom," we must also "continue to do good science."

Dave adds that whereas we do not uncritically accept cultural trends about LGBT issues (which he refers to as "cultural traffic"), such trends should at least motivate our "stepping back to understand what science has discerned about sexual orientation and also to reengage biblical wisdom pertinent to human sexuality." This potential connection between "science" and "biblical wisdom" is a central aspect of what Christian liberal arts institutions refer to as the "integration of faith and learning," which leads us into another area of common ground shared by Chris and Dave.

THE QUEST FOR CONNECTIONS BETWEEN PSYCHOLOGY AND BIBLICAL/THEOLOGICAL UNDERSTANDING AS A WITNESS TO TRUTH

Rather than creating a false choice between accepting the findings of science regarding the natural world and adhering to biblical teachings, both Chris and Dave affirm the importance of both areas of knowledge. As Chris puts it, "I love his [Dave's] statement that 'those who aim to worship God with their minds will surely wish to attend both to natural revelation (as we explore God's 'fearfully and wonderfully made' human nature) and to biblical revelation.'"

But the goal is not just to let knowledge claims in these two spheres coexist. Rather, the goal is to "integrate" these two spheres of knowledge, which I take to mean to uncovering "integral connections" between scientific findings and biblical teachings. Dave points us toward this "integrative" goal when he asserts that his first and most important area of agreement with Chris is that "*we both respect, and seek to integrate, science and Scripture.*"

Dave asserts, and Chris agrees, that the quest for understanding in both spheres of knowledge and their integration calls for "humility" because "we are not God." Dave aptly says the following about Christians who are also behavioral scientists:

> We are fallible creatures. Knowing that some of our beliefs err (we are not God), we hold our untested beliefs tentatively and, when appropriate, use observation and experimentation to sift truth from error. Believing that God has written the book of nature, our calling is to read it as clearly and honestly as we can.

In his final posting, Chris echoes these words.

> I strive to be objective and careful when examining scientific findings, when using observation and experimentation to sift truth from error, and when integrating nature and Scripture as clearly and honestly as I can, holding untested beliefs tentatively.

Note carefully the commitment of both Chris and Dave to seek to "sift truth from error." The priority of the quest for truth is captured in Dave's view that his "calling as a Christian scholar . . . is to, as best as I can, discern and give witness to truth."

As will soon be seen, this sifting process has led Dave and Chris to differing conclusions as to the truth regarding same-sex relationships. Dave prepares us for his conclusions by saying:

> Reading the science of sexual orientation persuaded me that most evangelicals were misunderstanding sexual orientation. And reading the new biblical scholarship persuaded me that my former understanding of the Bible's supposed condemnation of loving, same-sex partnerships was a misreading of Scripture

Chris reaches a different conclusion:

> I uphold a "traditional" view to the issue of same-sex behavior. In case any may have missed the last decade of unprecedented culture shifts, to actually still believe and advocate for a traditional approach is to go counter to the prevailing winds and risk being on the wrong side of history. However, after much study and prayer and listening to experts, I am convinced that this view is on the right side of God's Word.

Details about these differing conclusions will soon follow.

But a troublesome question lurks in the background, hinted at by Chris's assertion that "Science done well—by scholars committed to objectivity and free from obvious bias and political agendas—produces the best findings, which are then published in peer-reviewed academic journals." Are the published findings in scientific journals "free from bias and political agendas"? More about that shortly. But first another area of agreement, albeit with some unanswered questions.

ALL PERSONS SHOULD BE TREATED WITH DIGNITY AND RESPECT

As Dave summarizes a significant area of agreement with Chris, "As behavioral scientists and Christians, we both begin, I sense, with the assumption that all humans have dignity but not deity."

Chris elaborates:

> This I do know: All persons—whether straight or LGBTQ—are created in the image of God and deserve dignity and respect.

> Regardless of our disagreements, each of us should seek to love our neighbor with kindness and respect. We must commit to the timeless and unchanging teachings of Scripture in a way that brings healing to the hurting or broken, and draws those with whom we journey closer to the good news of Jesus Christ.

But as Dave notes, agreement that all persons should be treated with dignity and respect leaves a number of unanswered questions as to what such dignity and respect entails; questions that will eventually need to be addressed.

> *What, specifically, does affirming "dignity and respect" imply?* Again, we agree that "All persons—whether straight or LGBTQ—are created in the image of God and deserve dignity and respect. Regardless of our disagreements, each of us should seek to love our neighbor with kindness and respect." So, does affirming dignity and showing respect include supporting the fundamental right to marry (and the more than 1000 ancillary rights, from hospital visitation to inheritance, associated with marriage in the federal register)? Does it mean equal employment opportunity at our institutions? (Should they add "sexual orientation" to their nondiscrimination policy statements?) And is it possible to affirm a gay or lesbian person's dignity while judging what is part of their identity to be a moral failure?

AREAS OF DISAGREEMENT

NATURE OR NURTURE

As background for disagreements as to the genesis of one's sexual orientation, it should be noted that, as Dave puts it, "Most are straight, some are gay." To be more exact, "European and American surveys, administered to random samples and with anonymity protected, indicate that about 3 to 4 percent of men and 2 percent of women report exclusively same-sex attractions."

Therefore, as Dave says, the "bottom line" is "whether a culture (or church or school) condemns or accepts same-sex unions, heterosexuality prevails and homosexuality persists."

But, given this data, the disputed issue pertains to the cause or causes of a person's sexual orientation. The exchanges between Dave and Chris about the genesis of a person's sexual orientation are a marvelous exemplification of the point/counterpoint nature of a respectful dialogue about disagreements.

Dave presents his view that "sexual orientation is a natural disposition," asserting that "Multiple lines of research converge in indicating that our sexual orientation is something we do not choose and, especially so for men, cannot change."

Dave adds that "Postnatal environmental influences are unknown," elaborating as follows: "Sexual orientation has no known environment influences. Contrary to what Freudians and kindred reparative therapists have assumed, same-sex attractions appear not to be the result of child abuse or molestation, or a distant father and domineering mother. If distant fathers engendered gay sons, then shouldn't boys growing up in father-absent homes (and in modern times with more absentee dads) be more often gay? (They are not.)"

As evidence that "Homosexuality, like heterosexuality, is part of the natural world," Dave notes that "Same-sex attractions are displayed by many animal species. A first clue that sexual orientation is, instead, a natural, biological phenomenon comes from the several hundred species in which same-sex sexuality has been observed—from gorillas to grizzlies, from flamingos to owls. Among sheep, some 8 percent of rams shun ewes and seek to mount other males."

Relative to the differences between "gay brains and straight brains" that neuroscientists have reported, Dave raises the following question: "Does this brain difference help explain sexual orientation? Or do people's sexual experiences leave fingerprints in their brains?" His own answer is that "Further research suggests that the brain difference is more cause than effect," thus reinforcing his view that the cause of a person's sexual orientation is biological.

Chris presents some cogent responses to Dave's view that it is "nature" and not "nurture" that causes a person's sexual orientation. For starters, while agreeing that "There are a number of findings in the scientific literature related to brain, genetic and prenatal influences that have swayed many toward a biological explanation of sexual orientation . . . other researchers and scholars do not dispute that biology plays a role, but question how big of a role it actually plays" (citing the work of Mark Yarhouse and Stan Jones).

Chris reminds us that Dave is not denying the possibility of environmental factors; rather, Dave is taking the position that "if environmental factors influence sexual orientation, we do not yet know what they are."

In addition, while agreeing with Dave that "there is evidence that sexual orientation for men may neither be chosen nor changed, for women it is not as clear," citing the work of Lisa Diamond, which leads her to conclude that "for women the question of sexual orientation is more likely a matter of conscious choice and not an irresistible urge, related to affection and bonding."

Chris also appeals to the views about "the development of sexual orientations" reported by the American Psychological Association (APA). While the APA asserts that "most people experience little or no sense of choice about their sexual orientation," Chris reports the further APA position that "'There is no consensus among scientists about the exact reasons' that someone develops an LGTBQ orientation, and 'no findings have emerged that permit scientists to conclude' that sexual orientation is determined by any one cause or factor(s)." This suggests to Chris that the APA position is that "both nature and nurture are at work."

Therefore, Chris's conclusion is as follows: "A major issue with biological influences is they cannot actually posit causality—does homosexuality or the biology/biological influences come first? Overall I am of the opinion that it is still too early and premature to render a verdict. Should future findings converge (one way or the other) perhaps more definitive verdicts will arise."

Dave responds in the following ways to Chris's response to his initial posting. First, Dave acknowledges his agreement with Chris's statement that "While there is evidence that sexual orientation for men may neither be chosen nor changed, for women it is not as clear."

But Dave adds the caveat that "Even so, most people—male or female—have a well-defined and persistent sexual orientation and that is a reality that begs for explanation. It is, methinks, also a reality that the church had best face up to."

Dave also acknowledges agreement with Chris in saying that "We both, in your words, *dispute that 'sexual orientation is determined by any one cause or factor.'*" But Dave notes the following remaining disagreement: "My understanding is that an interplay of genetic, prenatal hormonal, and brain differences conspire to influence our sexual orientation. You are less persuaded, but—reflecting your science-respecting humility—you are open to new evidence: 'Should future findings converge (one way or the other) perhaps more definitive verdicts will arise.'"

So, Dave summarizes his disagreement with Chris about the "nature and nurture" question as follows:

> *Is biology the chicken or the egg?* You [Chris] wonder: "Does homosexuality or the biology/biological influences come first? . . . . [and your overall opinion is] that it is still too early and premature to render a verdict."
>
> We differ, because I *am* comfortable rendering a verdict: The accumulating evidence persuades me today more than ever that sexual orientation is a natural disposition. The observations of same-sex attraction in sheep, the new genetic evidence from the

> "gay brothers" study, the accumulating evidence of gay-straight brain and trait differences, the influence of prenatal physiology, and much more adds up to a compelling case that *biology matters*.... And that explains why the American Psychological Association has asserted, as you noted, "most people experience little or no sense of choice about their sexual orientation."

Dave also asks Chris the following question: "If, as you seem inclined to believe, nurture (environment) rather than nature shapes sexual orientation, what specifically are the environmental influences? A distant father? An overbearing mother? (Those Freudian ideas, embraced by reparative therapists, seem pretty well discounted.)"

But, it is extremely important to note Dave's assertion that his disagreement with Chris about the "nature or nurture" distinction seems not to be "fundamental to our faith."

> Ergo, you and I are living and working on the same planet, Chris—both of us rooted in a science-affirming faith tradition that seeks to be open to the Spirit's continuing work, through new biblical and natural revelations. Moreover, our differences seem not fundamental to our faith. When together affirming the Apostle's Creed we say nothing about sexual orientation.

Dave also goes so far as to wonder whether the "nature or nurture" distinction "fundamentally matters."

> Given the reality of sexual orientation—its strength and persistence for most people—does the nature versus nurture explanation of sexual orientation fundamentally matter?

Ongoing conversation about the "nature or nurture" issue is obviously needed. In addition, Dave suggests the need for further conversation about the following questions:

- Why do many Christians resist a biological explanation of sexual orientation?
- If bias influences psychological science (as you and I agree), might it not also influence biblical and theological interpretation?
- Why not offer an inclusive Christian pro-monogamy norm?

The second and third questions will be addressed below. Chris responds as follows to the first question:

> There can be many answers to this question. It may be that many Christians seek to avoid a naturalistic fallacy (the erroneous

notion that "biological" or "natural" implies moral goodness or acceptance). Perhaps many believe that the innate effects are not sufficient or compelling enough to morally justify any resultant behavior, as many commentators have frequently implied. Perhaps they feel that with this issue it is still too early to draw any causative statements, given the correlational nature of these studies, the relative newness of the research, and the small sample sizes used in most studies.

ARE THE BIASES OF SCHOLARS REFLECTED IN THEIR RESEARCH?

Chris raises this probing question relative to the research results that have been reported by the APA concerning "children with gay and lesbian parents": "In 2005 APA declared that there was 'not a single study' showing that children of gay or lesbian parents were disadvantaged compared to children from mother-father homes. They identified seventy-seven scholarly studies that met our criteria for addressing the well-being of children with gay or lesbian parents. Of those studies, seventy-three concluded that children of gay or lesbian parents fare no worse than other children."

The APA reached the following conclusion: "This research forms an overwhelming scholarly consensus, based on over three decades of peer-reviewed research, that having a gay or lesbian parent does not harm children."

But Chris wonders about the other four studies. He notes that these studies "have been criticized by many scholars as unreliable assessments of the well-being of LGB-headed households" since they "took their samples from children who endured family break-ups, a cohort known to face added risks."

Chris finds this alarming: "Not a single study showing the opposite effect? . . . This type of consensus raises an antenna for me. It feels too neat, too tidy, and a little too fresh . . . . When I read that 77 scholarly studies converge, and the only four that don't are dismissed as full of errors, the word that comes to mind for me is '*Really?*' This seems unusually tidy for our social sciences."

Chris asks: "What if there are some articles published in leading, peer-reviewed journals that challenge the APA claims above, finding that children do best in married mother-father homes? What if numerous well-respected scholars do not find the evidence as overwhelming and consensus-forming as APA would have us believe?" He then cites some research in peer-reviewed journals that call into question that supposed consensus, and raises the possibility that there may be "other explanations for such an overwhelming scholarly consensus and convergence." His pointed question is: "Could bias be playing a role in dismissing alternative perspectives?" Chris then responds to his own question by noting that:

> Respected social psychologists from the University of Pennsylvania, Rutgers, NYU, Stockholm University, the College of New Jersey, and Arizona State (none who identify as conservative or Republican) have gathered strong research evidence suggesting that social psychology is not a welcoming environment for traditionalists or conservatives. They published their findings in *Behavioral and Brain Science* stating "the collective efforts of researchers in politically charged areas *may fail to converge upon the truth* [emphasis from Chris] when there are few or no non-liberal researchers to raise questions and frame hypotheses in alternative ways.". . . They note that while this is not a threat to the validity of most studies, it "causes problems for the scientific process primarily in areas related to the political concerns of the left—areas such as race, gender, stereotyping, etc." They ask: "Might a shared moral-historical narrative in a politically homogeneous field undermine the self-correction processes on which good science depends?"

In his desire "just to be clear," Chris says that "I do not believe that most of the studies in the area of same-sex attraction, sexual orientation, and sexual behavior are flawed or erroneous. . . . However, any research, even scientific research, is subject to bias. Far too often researchers are able to find what they are looking for, thus reflecting their initial biases. This becomes even more problematic when popular culture is also strongly (if not vehemently) biased in a particular area."

Chris's penultimate conclusion is that:

> We should care about any evidence of bias influencing how we conduct or evaluate research. And if we deny even the possibility of such a bias, without reference to empirical investigation, then we will have failed as responsible scientists committed to the pursuit of truth. And ironically so, given that another of the most important lessons from social psychology teaches that we are in no position to evaluate the objectivity of our own decision-making.

Chris raises another "troubling possibility" that "Scholarly research papers may be reviewed differently depending on whether they are considered to support liberal vs. conservative positions," citing a research paper "now in press" that supports this contention.

Chris's final conclusion calls for a "proper tentativeness."

> At such a time [as this], and perhaps there has been no greater time than now, we must demonstrate a proper tentativeness. Just this week new questions are being raised about replication problems in psychology (see *Science*, August 2015). The scientific account is still in its early stages. Though there is a dramatic and unprecedented shift of popular opinion on topics related to same-sex attraction, orientation, parenting, behavior, etc., scientists must continue carefully and thoughtfully to pursue good, unbiased scholarship, if only because respected researchers still disagree.

Dave's initial response to Chris's concern about "gay parenting studies" is that "I would, for two reasons, put my money on children's tending to flourish when co-nurtured by two parents who are enduringly committed to them and to each other (regardless of parental sexual orientation)."

First, "there is considerable evidence to support this, and it's not just from the APA. The American Academy of Pediatrics (2013) reports that what matters is competent, secure, nurturing parents, regardless of their gender and sexual orientation. The American Sociological Association . . . in a lengthy Supreme Court brief, concurs: Decades of research confirm that parental stability and resources matter. 'Whether a child is raised by same-sex or opposite-sex parents has no bearing on a child's wellbeing.'"

Second, "this finding fits the larger conclusion, amply and surprisingly documented by behavior genetics research, that parental nurture—or, more generally, the 'shared environment effect'—has surprisingly little influence on the development of children's traits. Even adopted children tend to share personalities and aptitudes more akin to their biological than adoptive parents (while benefitting greatly from adoption in other ways). In 'the largest twin study of same-sex sexual behavior' the contribution of shared environment (including parental influence) to men's having same-sex sexual partners was *zero*."

Having said that, however, Dave agrees with Chris's concerns about the possibility that a scholar's biases can be reflected in his/her research.

> *We both understand that psychologists' assumptions and values can penetrate their teaching, writing, researching, and practicing psychology* (a point also made by psychology's feminist critics). As you note, "any research, even scientific research, is subject to bias."

But Dave suggests that the same concern can apply to scholars in biblical studies and theology, leading him to pose the following question for further discussion.

> *If bias influences psychological science (as you and I agree), might it also influence biblical and theological interpretation?* Believing that a) there is a God, and b) it's not us, isn't our religious thinking also subject to test, challenge, and revision? Shouldn't it, like science, be ever-reforming? As gay evangelical Ralph Blair notes in his new synopsis of the modern history of Christian thinking about sexual orientation, . . . publications that today are vigorously objecting to same-sex marriage and touting sexual reorientation ministries were, in the past, using the Bible to justify racial segregation and opposing interracial marriage. (Thankfully, this is not the entire Christian history, as the church also helped lead the abolition of the slave trade and the civil rights movement.)

Clearly more conversation is needed as to how to minimize the potential for distortion due to biases in all areas of scholarly research.

CAN SEXUAL ORIENTATION BE CHANGED?

The importance of this question is highlighted by Dave's observation that

> We have all heard claims of people who, thanks to therapy or an ex-gay ministry, are said to have done a sexual U-turn, from actively gay to happily straight and married. And we have all heard stories of gay people who, hearing such stories, have sought change—only to end up depressed, suicidal, or in broken marriages.

Dave's response to this question is that "sexual orientation is enduring." He notes the fact that "Leading mental health associations—psychiatry, psychology, social work, pediatrics—have cautioned against sexual reorientation therapy. 'Efforts to change sexual orientation are unlikely to be successful and involve some risk of harm,' declared the American Psychological Association's governing body in a 125-to-4 vote."

Dave also notes that there is "a growing list of ex-gay ministry leaders who have recanted their testimonies [regarding a change in sexual orientation]—the so-called "ex-ex-gays," citing a number of examples, most notably that of Alan Chambers, the long-time leader of Exodus who effected the closing down of the Exodus ministry in 2013, declaring the following at that time.

> I am sorry for the pain and hurt that many of you have experienced. I am sorry some of you spent years working through the shame and guilt when your attractions didn't change. I am sorry we promoted sexual orientation change efforts and reparative theories about sexual orientation that stigmatized parents . . . . More than anything, I am sorry that so many have interpreted this *religious* rejection by Christians as God's rejection. I am profoundly sorry that many have walked away from their faith and that some have chosen to end their lives.

Chris begins his response to Dave by saying that "In the areas of sexual orientation and sexual orientation change efforts I am interested in scientifically valid findings that both support and run counter to the (now) widely held APA position."

Chris is careful to note that he is "not dismissing the importance of anecdotal evidence of ex-gay ministry leaders recanting past beliefs," but "there are many good articles in respected journals that elaborate different and valid perspectives." He cites a number of such research results.

The most notable counter-example Chris notes is the work on "Sexual Identity Therapy" (SIT) spearheaded by Mark Yarhouse. Chris notes that this research focuses on "sexual identity issues, which is not the same as sexual orientation or attractions. Sexual identity is about how we label ourselves—straight, gay, lesbian, bisexual—and may include our attractions, behaviors, values and beliefs. Someone with same-sex attraction may identify as gay and Christian, but could also identify as being a believer in Christ who has same-sex attraction, and not identify as gay."

Chris notes that when focusing on such "identity" issues: "For one person the feelings of same-sex attraction may be weighed more heavily. For another person, religious beliefs might play a larger role. For yet another, it all comes down to the actions they have taken. How you identify yourself is a decision based on any number of factors working in numerous and complicated ways." His most telling observation is that "for those who seek to identify first as being 'in Christ,' they may choose not to make same-sex attraction the defining element of their identity."

Chris reports that the SIT research conducted by Yarhouse and Stan Jones[1] is "a longitudinal study [that] meets empirical standards for valid research and uses large sample sizes," and "Such research was completed with persons seeking to change their sexual orientation by exploring therapy

1. Jones and Yarhouse, *Ex-Gays?*

that included religious perspectives." Chris elaborates as follows: "Sexual Identity Therapy (SIT) . . . does provide a place for clients to examine ways to live and form an identity in light of their beliefs and values . . . . The psychologists who pioneer this approach help clients find congruence 'so that their behavior and sexual identity line up with their beliefs and values.'"

Chris also says that "These researchers note that change is rarely complete or categorical, but it can occur along a continuum, and it does not appear to be intrinsically harmful," reporting Yarhouse's summary as follows:

1. Although some people do experience a change in sexual orientation, most experience modest gains, and many share that they continue to have same-sex attractions at times.

2. It does not appear to be intrinsically harmful to try to change sexual orientation, especially if a person has realistic expectations.

3. Where people may struggle the most is with unrealistic expectations or messages that they are not trying hard enough or do not have enough faith.

Chris's conclusion regarding the results of SIT research is that:

> Contending that all same-sex attraction is immutable is a distortion of reality. Attempting to characterize all sexual reorientation therapy as "unethical" violates patient choice and gives an outside party a veto over patients' goals for their own treatment. A political agenda shouldn't prevent gays and lesbians who desire to change from making their own decisions.

Relative to Chris's concern about Dave relying heavily on the anecdotal testimonies of leaders of ex-gay ministries that reparative therapies have not been effective, Dave's response is: "You and I surely would agree that 'the plural of anecdote is not evidence.' But in this case, the number of ex-gay ministry leaders who have recanted—saying that neither they nor anyone they knew actually had changed (despite their one-time testimonies to the contrary)—is striking."

As to Chris's take on the SIT work of Yarhouse and Jones, Dave asserts that "their data . . . actually showed very few people from all the Exodus ministries willing to be surveyed, and very few of these reporting a 180 degree sexual reorientation." Dave also quotes the following concern that Ralph Blair's has about SIT: "Instead of seeking to change homosexual orientation, SIT reframes the person's identity to bring it into 'congruence' with the belief that homosexuality is sinful. 'Congruence,' he [Yarhouse] says, 'is achieved when a person is able to identify themselves and live in a way that reflects that identity and is consistent with their principles and values.' So successful 'congruence' is identifying with what one's supposed to believe, not with what one actually feels."

So, disagreements about the effectiveness, or not, of reparative therapies persist. More study and conversation is needed.

CAN CHRISTIANS SUPPORT SAME-SEX COVENANT PARTNERSHIPS?

Dave raises the possibility of biblical support for same-sex covenant partnerships, as follows: "Among the Bible's 31,103 verses, only seven explicitly mention same-sex behaviors (and none of those discuss same-sex covenant partnerships). That leaves scholars to interpret Scripture's moral wisdom, based also on what else it has to say about marriage and human relationships."

Dave begins his elaboration by saying that "we have massive evidence indicating that:

- humans do live fuller and happier (and healthier) lives if married,
- children fare better in households with married parents (even after controlling for income and race), and
- communities with high marriage rates experience less crime, educational dropout, and poverty."

Dave concludes that "These findings fit well with what we have learned about the human 'need to belong.' We are social animals. We—all of us, whether gay or straight—flourish when deeply connected with others in close, enduring, mutually supportive relationships. We were not made to be alone," which fits with his understanding of an overarching biblical theme.

In that light, Dave poses the following question:

> Why not stand up for healthy relationships that satisfy the human need to belong within covenant partnerships? Rather than advocating a sexual double standard for straight people (marry or be celibate) and gay people (sorry, you must be celibate), why not proclaim a single Christian sexual ethic? Why not yoke sex with faithfulness? Why not seal love with commitment? Why not foster a conservative, marriage-supporting positive argument: that the world would be a happier and healthier place if, *for all people,* sex, love, and marriage routinely went together?

In other words, Dave is asking: "Why not offer an inclusive pro-monogamy norm?"

To those who are concerned that Dave's proposal of "an inclusive pro-monogamy norm" that would embrace both opposite-sex and same-sex marriage changes the Christian understanding of "marriage," Dave asserts that "over time" Christians who have taken a "Reformed and ever-reforming" approach to their faith that allows them to take a "fresh look at Scripture" have "changed their minds about marriage."

> For those who embrace a "Reformed and ever-reforming" faith tradition—one that esteems a spirit of humility and is open to the continuing work of the Spirit—this fresh look at Scripture is how it should be. And so it has been across time, as people of faith have changed their minds about marriage—from practicing arranged marriages to favoring romantic choice; from assuming polygamy to mandating monogamy; from viewing marriage as inferior to celibacy to seeing it as an equal calling; from assuming male headship to preferring mutuality; from shunning interracial marriage to welcoming it; from disciplining divorced people to welcoming them into our faith communities. In each case, our religious ancestors found proof texts to support their cultural assumptions, and later biblical scholarship led us to a read and respect Scripture in a fresh way.

Chris responds to Dave's question about the moral legitimacy, or not, of "an inclusive pro-monogamy norm" by asserting that there is no biblical support for same-sex covenant partnerships. He does so by responding to two questions that he poses:

1. Are there any passages or verses in the Bible that approve, affirm or bless same-sex behavior?

    The answer is a clear and convincing "No." There is not a single known passage that approves or blesses same-sex behavior. This is beyond contestation, and it is not controversial.

2. Do the biblical texts that deal specifically with same-sex behavior condemn it unconditionally and call it a sin to be repented of, forsaken and forgiven?

    The short answer: Scripture calls us to refrain from all non-marital heterosexual or homosexual sexual behavior, whether loving and monogamous or not.

As for the idea of a "pro-monogamy norm" that is "inclusive," Chris says "One can just as easily ask, Why offer a pro-monogamy norm at all?" adding that "once Scripture is changed to fit the view that Genesis and other passages allow for same-sex behavior, then the sexual ethic of monogamy doesn't make sense for gay or straight." Chris concludes by asking: "Once we go with a biological effects argument in supporting homosexuality, is not the next step to accept polyamorous affairs within all marriages?"

Along similar lines, Chris concludes by addressing another question posed by Dave: "Rather than tie 'onto people's backs loads that are heavy and hard to carry,' as Jesus said of the Pharisees, why not offer a positive affirmation of monogamy?" Chris's response is to first pose a parallel question: "Are traditionalists placing undue burdens on same-sex attracted and oriented people when we claim that same-sex behavior is immoral, and the only option available for them is chastity, not marriage? Is this demanding too much?"

Chris's response to his own parallel question is:

> The truth is the New Testament and Jesus consistently call believers to behave in ways that can only be defined as "burdensome" (e.g., "give a blessing for an insult," 1 Pet. 3:9; "Take up your cross daily and follow Me," Luke 9:23; and "Do good to those who hate you," Matt 5:44) *unless we understand that true life and joy and happiness is found in obedience to God's ways.* All of these commands are hard if not impossible—apart from the power of the Holy Spirit (Phil 2:13).

Chris then says that "Perhaps the best thing I can do to answer this question is to point people to authors like Wesley Hill and Eve Tushnet, both same-sex attracted, who make compelling cases for a traditional view of marriage and dispel the assumption of impossible burdens."

Chris then "implores" us "to read Eve's posts [on her Patheos blog] and especially *Washed and Waiting*[2] and *Spiritual Friendship*[3] by Wesley Hill. Chris adds: "Wesley is a gay Christian who advocates for celibacy because as a theologian he finds the case for marriage between one man and one woman the clear and compelling sexual ethic taught in Scripture." Chris then concludes as follows: "And the burden is clearly hard for Wesley and Eve and many other celibate Christians. After meeting and speaking with Wesley just one time I found myself both encouraged and humbled, and now pray for him on a regular basis. There are no easy answers. But at least read their story and then decide if these charges of Pharisaical burdens are fair or unfair."

---

2. Hill, *Washed and Waiting*.
3. Hill, *Spiritual Friendship*.

WHAT IS THE RELATIONSHIP BETWEEN THE QUEST FOR TRUTH, EXTENDING LOVE AND KINDNESS, AND SEEKING CHRISTIAN UNITY?

Chris points us toward this important question when he says the following:

> Clearly some in the church have not modeled *love and kindness* while holding to the *Truth*. And while we may disagree about the morality of same-sex behavior and hold views contrary to popular opinion, we must give no cause to being viewed, fairly or unfairly, as hateful or unkind (italics mine).
>
> The church is at a crossroads, and our future actions must carefully and prayerfully reflect God's hope for us—to be *united with Christ*, like-minded, that our love may abound still more and more in real knowledge and all discernment (italics mine).
>
> We have a long way to go . . .

There is much to unpack here as to the relationship between the quest for truth, extending love and kindness, and seeking Christian unity. For starters, both Dave and Chris affirm the importance of the quest for truth. It is clear from Dave's quoting with approval David Hume's comment that "Truth springs from argument among friends," that he [Dave Myers] views his conversation with Chris as a quest for the truth.

Chris similarly affirms his commitment to the quest for truth.

> A friend recently wrote "an argument among friends lies at the heart of our enterprise as Christian scholars. We each aim to give witness to the truth . . ."
>
> As scientists and Christians we are eyewitnesses to God's Truth. What an awesome endeavor!
>
> We are eyewitnesses to his truth when we study nature as found in the observable created world . . .
>
> Yes, even in an argument with a friend.
>
> We are also eyewitnesses to his Truth as revealed in Scripture, which he supernaturally authored . . .

Both Dave and Chris agree that each should "speak the truth in love," although they embrace differing beliefs about what that truth is regarding LGBT issues. As Dave puts it:

> *What does it mean for us, as you admonish, to "speak the truth in love?"* Yes, let's aspire to speak the truth in love. And we can further agree that "Love does not mean that all things are acceptable. Love does not preclude upholding a standard. The

> New Testament does not define love as acceptance of a behavior that transgresses God's moral law."
>
> Your admonition, Chris, helpfully takes us to the heart of the issue. Might "the truth" include the reality of sexual orientation and the human need to belong?

Thankfully, throughout their conversation Chris and Dave have both modeled admirably their shared commitment to speak the truth in love, as witnessed to by the following reflections on their exchanges.

> Thank you, Chris, for your gentle and empathic spirit. And thank you for so aptly summarizing the gist of my first essay. You listen well. I now understand why you are so gifted at helping people create healthy relationships! (Dave)
>
> Thank you, Chris Grace, for your courage and kindness in engaging mutually respectful conversation (Dave).
>
> It has been a joy and privilege to participate in this blog and converse with talented authors and scholars, if only by reading their insightful posts. I have sensed that we are fellow sojourners, each seeking encouragement from *being united with Christ*, comfort from his love, being like-minded, praying that our love may abound still more and more in real knowledge and all discernment. The previous post by David Myers, my conversation partner, reveals that this is his heart as well. (Chris—italics mine)

Chris provides an extremely important example of an approach to modeling love and kindness while holding to one's understanding of the truth that focuses on "getting to know" the other person.

> I take heart in one working relationship that I have recently started that gives me hope. A faculty colleague from another institution was initially wary of my connection to a conservative Christian university and the impending judgmental attitudes she expected of me. She and her wife had recently adopted a young toddler, and she beamed as she showed me pictures. Her fears and concerns were soon alleviated as we worked and laughed together throughout the week. I was relieved and grateful that she did not disparage my sincere convictions that a biblical marriage is one that is between one man and one woman. She did not challenge me, nor seek to change my views, and neither of us experienced the other as hateful, bigoted, intolerant, or mean.

The question remains as to how commitment to the quest for truth and the expression of love and kindness toward those who disagree about that truth is related to the seemingly elusive goal of "Christian unity." Chris makes the following "pledge."

> I pledge to treat all Christians as new creations in Christ, remembering that our true identity is not based on sexuality or self-expression but on *our union with Christ* (italics mine).

Dave's observation about his disagreements with Chris is that "our differences seem not fundamental to our faith. When together affirming the Apostle's Creed we say nothing about sexual orientation."

In offering thanks to this eCircle project "for offering a public platform for this conversation," Dave views this as a conversation "among people who concur on basic matters of faith, but differ on its implications in today's world."

So, both Chris and Dave hold out hope that Christians will commit to the quest for "unity" in the midst of disagreements about LGBT issues. Surely that will be easier said than done.

CAN THE NEGATIVE "PUBLIC IMAGE" OF CHRISTIANITY BE CHANGED?

I close this chapter by addressing a concern that both Dave and Chris share, an overwhelmingly negative "public image" of Christianity that has driven many, especially the young, away from the Christian church. As Dave puts it most strongly:

> The ascendancy of the extreme fundamentalists/evangelicals, and their grip on the GOP, has meant that the ugliest, meanest, most anti-science, most intolerant side of Christianity—anti-abortion, homophobic, racist, sexually repressed and woman-hating, and hating anyone different from them—has become the public face of Christianity. In states where they have enacted their hard-right agenda, the polls show a huge backlash from Millennials and young people who are much more tolerant of gays, other races, and much more pro-science and feminist in orientation. These young people have not switched to more liberal Christian denominations, but left religion altogether.

Dave notes with approval the advice of columnist David Brooks: "Put aside a culture war that has alienated large parts of three generations from any consideration of religion or belief. Put aside an effort that has been a communications disaster, reducing a rich, complex and beautiful faith into a public obsession with sex. Put aside a culture war that, at least over the near term, you are destined to lose."[4]

Chris shares Dave's concern.

> I am encouraged that David seeks to present a more winsome and biblically authentic spirit that attracts the next generation. He laments the "counter-evangelism effect" that an anti-gay stance has on the irreligious "nones," the lost and the un-churched. How sad for Christianity to be described as "anti-homosexual" above any other descriptor by those aged sixteen to twenty-nine. Even worse is how we are described by anti-religious academics—ugly and mean and hateful—and these are just the start.

The big question, then, as asked by Dave, is: "Might a more winsome—and also biblically authentic—spirit attract rather than repel the next generation?"

Both Dave and Chris point us toward the beginning of a response to this closing question when they encourage Christians to "speak the truth in love" (Eph 4:15). I conclude this chapter with my own reflections.[5]

The major challenge is that the very idea that there may be some truth about any given issue (like an LGBT issue) is increasingly unfashionable in contemporary culture.

As a result, those of us who believe that there is some truth about LGBT issues, as only God fully understands it, and who are, therefore, committed to the quest to better understand that truth, are surely swimming upstream. Our only hope for navigating these troubled waters is for us to extend the gifts of love and kindness as we talk, first with other Christians, and then with others, about disagreements concerning LGBT issues. If those who do not profess commitment to the Christian faith can witness such respectful conversation among Christians, then the present negative "public image" of Christianity could change for the better. This present conversation is intended to model such respectful conversation.

---

4. Brooks, "The Next Culture War."
5. For elaboration, see Heie, "Truth and Civility."

4

Constitutional Framework for Public Policy

As revealed in chapter 2, Christians disagree as to the most adequate interpretations of biblical teachings related to LGBT issues. But, even if Christians agreed on their biblical understandings, it is another question as to how, if at all, their Christian perspectives should inform the shaping of policy in a pluralistic public square shared by citizens who embrace other worldviews, religious or secular.

One of our conversation partners for this fourth round of conversation, Micah Watson, points us to this important question as to how Christian perspectives should inform, or not, the shaping of policy in a pluralistic public square after first laying his "own cards out on the table" relative to his biblical understanding of "marriage."

> Just to lay my own cards on the table, I think Professor [Mark] Strauss is right to identify orthodox Christian sexual ethics with chastity in singleness and marriage as a lifelong and exclusive union between one man and one woman [see chapter 2]. Yet biblical understandings do not necessarily yield straightforward conclusions as to what a Christian should advocate in a pluralistic public square with regard to public policy.

As evidence that biblical understandings do not necessarily lead to straightforward public policy conclusions, Micah notes that "We have no shortage of disagreement about how Christians should think about public policy, let alone how the Constitution should inform this thinking."

Therefore, in this chapter Micah and Kathy Lee address the following Leading Question: How should the US Constitution inform Christian thinking about public policy issues in America? Since the conversation in this chapter deals with public policy issues in general (not only LGBT issues), the next chapter reports on the follow-up round of conversation about the stance Christians should take relative to public policy for or against same-sex marriage, given the pluralistic nature of American society.

WHAT ARE THE FUNCTIONS OF THE US CONSTITUTION?

In his first posting, Micah suggests that all constitutions, including the US Constitution, serve three functions.

> Constitutions do a number of things, but for our conversation I want to highlight three functions. First, constitutions express the vision of what a political community aspires to, and reveals an underlying view of human nature . . .
>
> Second, constitutions allocate power by authorizing various political entities at varying levels to exercise that power. Of course, constitutions also limit power . . .
>
> Finally, and somewhat paradoxically, constitutions are comprised of laws that create the mechanisms whereby we create more laws.

Kathy expresses "appreciation" for "Micah's overview of the functions of a constitution," calling it "invaluable" and requesting permission to use it in lower-level courses. Her summary is that "a constitution expresses aspirations of a people, allocates and limits powers, and provides structure through which a polity can make more laws."

OTHER AREAS OF AGREEMENT

THE US CONSTITUTION AND LAWS SHOULD PROMOTE HUMAN FLOURISHING

As already noted above, both Micah and Kathy view the role of a constitution as expressing what a political community "aspires to," which can be thought of as facilitating "human flourishing." As Kathy puts it, "Micah and I agree that government should be about creating conditions where humans can flourish," adding that their shared view "stems from our faith commitments."

Micah makes the important point, already alluded to above, that a distinction must be made between agreement as to the "end" of human flourishing and the "means" by which public policies can best foster those ends, about which there may be significant disagreement (although the following quote deals specifically with public policies relative to "sexuality," I believe this distinction is crucial for all public policy issues).

> We can think of the biblical discussion as a way of articulating certain grounding truths about human nature and its purposes with regard to sexuality. We might think of this as a discussion about human *ends*, the fulfillment of which contributes to God's vision of human flourishing (whether in marriage or in singleness). The policy discussion, on the other hand, is mainly about *means*: how best to promote and protect that vision in the many tangible ways that laws and policies touch on and regulate marriage, sex, and family life. What a constitutional discussion does is fill in the gap between the normative ends or purposes and the public policy means. For policy, law, and life together do not occur in a vacuum. They occur in a political community, and the operating blueprint of any political community is its constitution.

HUMAN FLOURISHING REQUIRES THE DOING OF JUSTICE

Kathy views the Constitution as "a 'living' document. It is, like the Bible, a text that requires interpretation; it is not self-interpreting." And she proposes that it "'lives' in the actual circumstances of people's lives," which allows for individuals and various groups of people to "come to the court seeking a remedy for a perceived injustice."

> I do not think of the Constitution as a free-standing document; it is grounded in the details of people's lives as fleshed out in Supreme Court decisions. So when I think about the Constitution influencing how Christians thinks about public policy, I begin with the fact that the document "lives" in the circumstances of people's lives. Individuals and organizations, as well as other groups of people, come to the Court seeking a remedy for a perceived injustice.

Kathy notes that her belief that the Constitution is a vehicle for doing justice is informed by her view, as a Christian embedded in the "Reformed tradition," that "government is an institution that can be used to achieve justice."

Kathy adds that those who seek redress from perceived injustices are "often the real people ... [who] have been stigmatized by society because of custom, tradition, religion, and law," asserting that some of the stigmatized have been oppressed because of their class, gender, or race.

Kathy concludes that "Those who have not experienced oppression based on certain identities need to hear the stories of those who have" and we must always be "examining whether through interpretation of this 'living' document [the Constitution] justice is diminished or advanced."

Micah concurs with Kathy's concern with "how the law affects actual people" and her concern for the "least of these" who cry out for justice.

> It seems to me that Kathy is rightly motivated by a concern for how law affects actual people, and her exemplars are those who cry out for justice for the least of these.

LIMITATIONS OF THE CONSTITUTION DUE TO HUMAN FINITUDE AND SIN

Kathy points out that the US Constitution was written by human beings who were not "neutral"; they inevitably brought their own perspectives to what they wrote.

> ... the Constitution, along with statutes and common law traditions, was written and interpreted from certain perspectives, and is therefore a flawed document.... This is not to suggest that we cannot approach better interpretations, more just interpretations; it is only to acknowledge that the framers were not neutral observers and neither are contemporary judges.... It is indeed Christian, in my view, to suggest that law and adjudication can never be completely neutral.
>
> So in thinking about the Constitution, one needs to acknowledge that it is stand-point dependent. That is, to ignore the race, class, and gender of the framers is a serious error if we want to understand the reasons for their writing what they did.

In that light, Kathy asserts that "when we talk about the Constitution we must talk about people, [including] those who wrote it, those who interpret it, and then those who seek redress through it."

As to those who seek redress by means of the Constitution, Kathy asserts that Christians need to focus on those who have been stigmatized in society, often because of "class, gender and race."

> I would suggest that the incarnation compels the Christian to place "the least of these" at the center of analysis, those who have been stigmatized. In their respective interrogations of liberal legalism, critical legal studies, feminist jurisprudence, and critical race theory focus on categories omitted on purpose from traditional analysis, namely class, gender and race.

As an example, Kathy suggests that the US Constitution is not "colorblind." Rather, it reflects "racism."

> Because race is a significant category of analysis, critical race theorists challenge the race-neutral idea of a colorblind Constitution, a tenet of liberal legalism. To seek a colorblind Constitution would be to ignore how racism is entrenched in institutions. Law professor Charles Lawrence argues that the notion of a colorblind Constitution is attractive and would be in fact a worthy goal in a world where individuals were valued as individuals. But the United States is not such a world.

In that light, Kathy asserts that the US Constitution needs to be read with a "hermeneutic of suspicion."

> Knowledge is embodied, which is both glorious and problematic at the same time. The framers were rooted in eighteenth-century America, with its time-bound customs and traditions and understandings. I honor the Constitution but must, as a Christian, read it with a hermeneutic of suspicion.

Kathy then asserts that "the fall should prompt a 'deep criticism of the law,'" especially on the part of those who are members of "socially constructed" groups which have been "stigmatized in our society."

> The fall and the incarnation create a "double consciousness" in the Christian who wishes to understand law, and in particular the Constitution and Court decisions. The fall should prompt a "deep criticism" of law. Law can be, after all, an instrument of death. It put the Word to death. But it should not be rejected as completely irrational or completely indeterminate. It simply means that the law, including the Constitution, is one of the institutions upon which we rely for so much, is more deeply flawed than we may care to imagine. Also, if one is a gay Christian, a Christian of color, a Christian who is challenged

> because of a mental illness or physical disability, or any socially constructed identity which has been stigmatized in our society and has been a basis of social and legal discrimination, then law, the Constitution and Court decisions are going to be even more skeptically scrutinized and should be. And if one is Native American, one's relationship to the US Constitution is even more complicated because tribes have an extraconstitutional relationship to the US. And there is and ought to be a strong hermeneutic of suspicion.

Kathy concludes that "The rule of law, including the US Constitution and Court decisions, can be the ideology of the oppressor."

Micah finds much to agree with in the views that Kathy expresses above, while also noting some disagreements that call for further conversation. First, he agrees that the Constitution is not a "near-fallible authority for the meaning of justice . . . that we as citizens must accept without question."

> . . . we each proceeded to cast strong doubts on an understanding of the Supreme Court as the most important and near-infallible authority for the meaning of justice and the American political tradition. Neither of us believe that Supreme Court jurisprudence, despite the robes and the Greek columns, delivers for us unalloyed wisdom from on high that we as good citizens must accept without question.

Micah also believes that "Kathy is rightly motivated by a concern for how law affects actual people, and her exemplars are those who cry out for justice for the least of these. Moreover, we do well to remember the pervasiveness of sin and its seeping into every human institution no matter how lofty or respected," concluding that "the Constitution as a human political document gives us both evil and good."

Therefore, Micah found "Kathy's call for a 'double consciousness' [of both the fall and the incarnation] regarding the Constitution to be persuasive, and her account of how Christian faith informs a hermeneutic of suspicion moving," albeit acknowledging the possibility that "I may not be suspicious enough for her liking."

Micah also agrees with Kathy that "no one of us enjoys a view from nowhere, completely objective and untouched by our identities or perspectives . . . . We are, all of us, affected by the fall. We are affected by our place in society, our family background, our gender, age, faith commitments, history, and the list goes on . . . critical perspectives [critical legal theory, feminist legal theory, and critical race theory] from the academy can disabuse any of us who still thinks that we can attain a version of Cartesian certainty about the law or any other subject."

But here the seeds of a disagreement emerge, as embedded in the following statement from Micah.

> I have no problem accepting that every author has interests and may be, consciously or not, exercising and pursuing her power in writing. This is true whether the authors are framers of a Constitution, Supreme Court justices interpreting that Constitution, critical legal theorists, or Kathy and myself. The observation about the ubiquitous presence of power dynamics strikes me as fine as far as it goes. But such dynamics have to be able to co-exist with *genuine insights into justice and truth*, or the critical legal theorists have a self-referential puzzle to tease out, namely how their own power interests do not vitiate their claims to accurately describe how legal discourse operates for everyone else (italics mine).

Here, then is Micah's expression of "disagreement," or at least "puzzlement."

> My area of disagreement, or perhaps puzzlement, then, with Kathy's affinity with these critical theories lies in how these approaches would inform judicial and political decisions about the *common good*. If we were to have another Constitutional Convention, of course we would want it to be much more representative than the one held in Philadelphia in 1787. I couldn't agree more that a new Constitutional Convention would be terribly *unjust* if it was as restricted as the previous one, and did not include those whose voices have historically not been empowered (italics mine).
>
> What I'm not sure about is what we think would emerge from these groups, *as groups*. That is, I'm not sure what it means to say there's a meaningful "women's" perspective on politics.

In my own words, here is the first question I believe Micah is asking Kathy: How is the position she is taking relative to the "limitations of the Constitution due to human finitude and sin" related to their shared belief that the US Constitution should "promote human flourishing" and the substance of the "justice" that human flourishing requires? More specifically, who gets to decide on the substance of human flourishing and justice? Is it duly elected legislative bodies or is it non-elected members of the judicial system? As will soon be seen, Kathy and Micah have a major disagreement when they respond to that question.

In the meantime, a second question embedded in the above exchange is: If one grants that all "identity groups" should have a voice in conversations about the Constitution and the laws that "pass constitutional muster," who speaks on behalf of these groups? It is to this question that we now turn.

WHO SPEAKS ON BEHALF OF WOMEN AND OTHER IDENTITY GROUPS?

As already noted, Micah says that he is "not sure what it means to say that there is a meaningful 'women's perspective on politics.'" He elaborates as follows, suggesting that the same issue can be raised relative to other "identity groups" such as African Americans.

> I think we should listen to women's voices, and women should be included in the "we" that is doing the listening. But it is obvious that women are divided about many political issues. Whatever women bring to a particular issue *as women* seems to be as susceptible to the same disagreements about justice and the common good that divide men. Thus while I firmly agree that the exclusion of women from voting and office-holding in the past was unjust, and women's voices must be heard now, I don't know what it would mean for a judge to consider women's voices as such. One would need to fall back on discerning whether the *reasons* offered for this or that position *truly advanced justice* (italics mine), and only secondarily on the gendered nature of the persons offering those reasons falling on opposite sides of an issue.
>
> ... If what counts is a common history of belonging to an oppressed group, then one is faced with either distinguishing between the incommensurable political views of President Obama and Justice Thomas, or determining that one of those two African-American men cannot genuinely speak from the African-American experience.
>
> ... I'm not sure what specific political wisdom or positions one can expect from listening to various people groups defined by what Kathy refers to as socially constructed identities.
>
> What I'm getting at here is the distinction between calling for the inclusion of all sorts of different voices in our politics, and thinking about who can legitimately *speak on behalf* of those different voices. I could not agree more that we should hear from everyone, and particularly those who have not been

the "winners" in our society. I am doubtful, however, that members of the judiciary have the ability or the warrant to do so.

The Supreme Court was not designed to represent the people of the country, and given the difficulties I've mentioned, it's hard to see how it could . . .

If judges are not equipped by their training or office to speak on behalf of the various constituencies in the country, who is? As I suggested before, the answer is public servants who must compete in order to win the votes of citizens so they can serve in the legislature. This is not to say that legislatures always get things right. Far from it. But there is no human institution free of that liability. And unlike judges, the very purpose of a representative is to represent her constituents, who can throw her out if they judge that she has not taken their concerns seriously enough.

I agree with Kathy that we cannot trust judges to arrive at completely unbiased and objectively fair conclusions in their deliberations about constitutional questions and controversial policy matters. I don't pretend that legislators always get it right, nor that our Constitution is a flawless document. It is, however, the system that we have, and a system has included within it a "promissory note" that has expanded opportunities for a flourishing life to more and more people. That system puts the power to make decisions about the issues that define us into the hands of those most immediately responsible to the people.

As can be seen from this extended quote, although both Micah and Kathy agree that legislators can make mistakes, they have a major disagreement about who has the authority to correct those mistakes, a topic to which we shall soon turn. But first, we consider Kathy's response to Micah's concern about who should speak for various "identity groups."

Kathy says that "Micah is absolutely correct to point out the diversity of women's voices, that no one group can speak for all women."

But Kathy adds that "to suggest that because no one woman can speak for all women or no black citizen can speak for all black citizens, that no group is monolithic in its views *does not mean common experiences cannot form a common narrative* (italics mine)."

Kathy's view that "common experiences" shared by members of an "identity group" can "form a common narrative" leads her to propose that the composition of the Supreme Court should have greater diversity, including more women.

Ironically, the fact that women do not speak with one voice suggests that more efforts should be made to have the federal judiciary have more women on it.

Kathy gives the example of the appointment of Sandra Day O'Connor to the Supreme Court by President Ronald Reagan.

> Micah and I differ regarding our views on representation and the judiciary. Micah writes, "The Supreme Court was not designed to represent the people of the country." And he rightly points out the elitism of the educational backgrounds and social backgrounds of justices, although I would suggest that Justice Sotomayor differs from the other justices in terms of wealth. I am not at all asserting that a justice represents a constituency in the same way elected representatives do. What I am suggesting is that it matters that candidate Ronald Reagan promised that he would appoint a woman to the Court and that President Reagan fulfilled that promised when he appointed Sandra Day O'Connor to the Court. She would have been the first to say she was not representing women qua women, but did it not matter that she was appointed? Representation can mean and signal many things, and one of the things it can signal is now a woman could aspire to have a seat at the conference table and sit on the bench of the most august court in this country. Did it matter that someone who had gone through pregnancy and borne children now was present at discussions about abortion cases? I would suggest yes. And studies of O'Connor's decision-making suggest that her experiences as a woman affected her outlook. Justice O'Connor herself noted the importance of a diversity of backgrounds on the Court when she paid tribute in 1991 to Justice Thurgood Marshall, the first black justice, upon his retirement.

Kathy concludes with the suggestion that "the legitimacy of the Court is enhanced when the court looks more like the population," adding that "there is something to be said for symbolic representation when a group in our society can look at the Court and say there is someone who is like me, like me in an identity that has historically been stigmatized and marginalized."

MAJOR AREA OF DISAGREEMENT: WHO HAS THE AUTHORITY TO OVERTURN LEGISLATIVE DECISIONS?

To recapitulate some points of agreement, both Kathy and Micah believe that the US Constitution and laws should promote human flourishing, which requires the doing of justice; and the US Constitution is a fallible "human document" that reflects the particularities of the social locations of the framers, and the "pervasiveness of sin" could influence both its content and its interpretation.

But a major disagreement now comes to the forefront: Who decides when a legislative action is contrary to the content of the US Constitution and how should that be decided?

Micah clearly asserts that "We the People" should make such decisions through our elected political representatives (using both "ordinary" and "extraordinary" political means—more about that distinction later). Decisions to overturn a legislative action should not be made by "unelected" persons like Supreme Court justices.

> . . . the Constitution presupposes that American citizens are competent to make their own decisions about the common good and how to achieve it. The government, then, is a creature of the people, rather than the other way around. We call our representatives and other government officials public *servants* for a reason. The corollary to this point about the importance of the people is that we should be very wary when non-representative actors overturn duly enacted decisions of the people, whether made directly by popular referenda or through the votes of their representatives in Congress or the state legislatures.

Micah adds that "There is nothing in our Constitution, our political history, or in any study of human nature I am aware of that shows that legally trained judges are any more capable of getting a moral question right than the rest of us."

Kathy disagrees with Micah, arguing that the authority to overturn legislative decisions lies with the Supreme Court. Her disagreement is based on distinguishing between the content of the Tenth and Fourteenth Amendments to the US Constitution, with an overarching purpose of the Fourteenth Amendment being to "protect minority rights from being violated by legislative majorities." In her own words:

> While the Tenth Amendment reserved to the states those powers not delegated to the federal government, the Fourteenth Amendment, when passed, was specifically aimed at the actions

of states. It seems to me that in order to understand how the Constitution might inform a Christian's views on political issues that the Fourteenth Amendment should be part of the conversation, a place where the Court has pegged its role to protect minority rights from being violated by legislative majorities.

To illustrate her position, Kathy appeals to the *Loving v. Virginia* case, which came to the Supreme Court in 1967, which she describes as follows:

> I cannot help but think of Mildred and Richard Loving whose case regarding interracial marriage reached the US Supreme Court in 1967. The Lovings were an interracial, married couple (she was of African-American and Native American descent; he was white). While in bed, in the early morning, they were arrested in Virginia for violating the state law prohibiting interracial marriage. They were convicted, sentenced to prison for one year; however, the court stated that if they left Virginia for twenty-five years they would not have to go to jail. At the trial, the judge noted that Virginia's anti-miscegenation law rested on the fact that God had placed "the races . . . on separate continents," a fact that reflected that God "did not intend for the races to mix." With the help of the ACLU, the Lovings sued the state of Virginia, claiming the law violated the Fourteenth Amendment. In its decision, the US Supreme Court noted that the state court had pointed out that the regulation of marriage should be left to the states under the Tenth Amendment. But the Supreme Court ruled that states did not have complete power over the regulation of marriage and that state anti-miscegenation laws violated the equal protection clause of the Fourteenth Amendment. This despite the fact that the state police power gives states power over marriage law. At the time, polls indicated that 70 percent of the American population was opposed to interracial marriage. *Should the Court have told the Lovings, "You need to wait until the American people come around"?* (italics mine)
>
> When the Fourteenth Amendment was passed in 1868 the contours of federalism changed forever; now the Tenth Amendment would have to be looked at in conjunction with the Fourteenth. States were to treat freed slaves equally and state laws that appeared to infringe the rights of freed slaves were now subject to review by federal courts. What is important is that the language of the Fourteenth Amendment is general; it speaks of citizens and their rights to due process and equal protection under the law.

Kathy also appeals to the overturning of "Segregation Laws" by the Supreme Court on the basis of the Fourteenth Amendment.

> If legislative majorities in the South were in fact protecting the rights of freed slaves then the Fourteenth would not have been necessary; they were not. The political process did not protect social outcasts; now federal courts could be places where oppressed and marginalized voices could be heard. I agree with Micah that federal judges do not have a corner on discerning what a society should look like. That said, I am not as optimistic as he is about elective bodies. There is indeed something called the "tyranny of the majority." Segregation laws demonstrated that fact.

Finally, Kathy appeals to the *Reed v. Reed* case in 1971 that expanded the "rights" of women.

> The Fourteenth Amendment has been a tremendously important source for my rights as a woman to be secure against the action of states. Should women have waited for state legislatures to come around to a more progressive view regarding the role of women in society? In 1971, in *Reed v. Reed*, the Supreme Court, for the first time, used the equal protection clause of the Fourteenth Amendment to strike down an Idaho law that automatically named men to be appointed executors of wills. That law was based on traditional views of women's roles, expressed through a male-majority state legislature. It was a duly enacted law, but was it fair? *Should the women of Idaho have just waited for views to change? How long?* (Italics mine.)

Kathy concludes with the following assertion: "Yes, federal judges are unelected, but a constitutional democracy is not simply about resolving disputes through voting in legislatures. There are fundamental rights which should be protected from being limited by legislative majorities," adding that "In a post-Citizens United political regime, those with more money have more access to the political process. For these reasons, I am not as optimistic about the political process protecting rights of marginalized groups" and "while it is always wise to think about the role of courts and judges in a constitutional democracy, it is just as important to think about the limits of the political process to protect the rights of those who historically have not been the 'winners' in that arena."

Micah prefaces his response to Kathy with an empathetic understanding of the position she is taking.

> Kathy understandably presses me on my preference for legislatures when it comes to representing the people's vision of the common good. The people, after all, can authorize their representatives to pass unjust legislation. Isn't it the case that our Constitutional system, and the Fourteenth Amendment in particular, empowers the courts to police the excesses and injustices of our legislatures?

Micah's response starts with the observation that "Many people, conservative and progressive, seem to think that the judges should look at the policy or law in question and determine, based on their own sense of what justice requires, whether the law is constitutional or should be struck down." Micah then says that he doesn't "think of it this way." Rather, here is his way of thinking about who has the authority to overturn legislative decisions.

> When courts intervene they (should) act on behalf of the *extraordinary* politics that have already been enacted and which supersede the *ordinary* politics that have resulted in an unconstitutional and possibly unjust situation. The Court should be acting on what the people have already established as constitutional. (Italics mine.)

But what is Micah referring to when he appeals to "the extraordinary politics that have already been enacted?" His answer flows from his response to the following prior question: "What rules do we agree upon for the resolving of those things we disagree about?"

> *The default and constitutional method for resolving our incompatible visions for promoting the common good is voting, and that is done by representatives who are accountable for their votes.* Whatever our cause, when we lose in the legislative arena we can at least take solace in having had a fair shot, or even a long shot. We can regroup, reorganize, and perhaps rethink our position and our tactics. We can back another candidate, or another legislative route to our policy goals. We've not only had our say, we can try again. We agreed to the process in the beginning and though disappointed, we can accept the outcome because the risk of losing is the price we pay to live together in relative peace in a pluralistic political community. (Italics mine.)

Therefore, my understanding of what Micah means by embarking on "extraordinary" politics to address a perceived injustice is to go through the process of seeking to change the laws, or, if need be, amend the US Constitution itself, in a manner that addresses the injustice, noting that either strategy requires voting of the citizenry.

This "way of thinking" can be illustrated by Micah's reflections on the *Loving v. Virginia* and *Reed v. Reed* cases that Kathy has addressed.

> Should the Court have told the Lovings to wait until the American people came around in *Loving v. Virginia*? Should the Court have told women in Idaho to wait in *Reed v. Reed*?
>
> No. The Court did not need to tell people to wait around for some future moment but instead declared what We the People had *already* spoken in the Fourteenth Amendment, and that a straightforward application of the democratically enacted principles in that super-legislation trumps the ordinary legislation that had denied Americans their rights. The Court did not rely on the individual and personal views of its nine members in either of those cases but did what judges are trained to do: interpret the people's law and apply it to these particular circumstances. . . . In short, *the Court struck down the decisions of the people of Idaho and Virginia on behalf of the People of the United States by appealing to the Fourteenth Amendment, which in turn was ratified by the legislatures of the states* (italics mine).

As I see it, the main point in Micah's response is the sentence italicized in the above quotation. But this raises the question, at least in my own mind (and hinted at in a few of my previous italicized portions of quotes): If a person or group believes that a legislative action is treating them unjustly, do they have no recourse *until such a time* when some type of "extraordinary" politics takes place that calls into question perceived long-standing injustices, such as the passing of an Amendment to the US Constitution? Alas, we ran out of time in this conversation before we ran out of questions. More conversation is called for.

REFLECTIONS ON OBERGEFELL V. HODGES

As background for the next round of conversation regarding public policy pertaining to same-sex marriage (chapter 5), it is important to summarize the positions that Kathy and Micah take regarding the recent Supreme Court decision in *Oberfgefell v. Hodges* that appealed to the Fourteenth Amendment to require states to license and recognize same-sex marriages. As expected from the exchanges reported above regarding a constitutional framework for all public policy decisions, Kathy and Micah view this Supreme Court decision in different ways.

Kathy "rejoiced" in the Supreme Court decision, although she thinks that decision could have been based on "stronger grounds" (guessing that this possibility will be addressed in the next round of conversation reported in chapter 5).

> ... it will not come as a surprise that I rejoiced in the Court's decision. In fact, I was in Washington, DC, outside the Supreme Court, when the decision was announced and celebrated with the hundreds of people there. I do not agree with the traditionalist view of marriage and think that there is room within the Christian church for both gay, lesbian, and straight married couples. Although I celebrated the *Obergefell* outcome, I do think that the majority's opinion could have had a different analysis that would have placed the decision on stronger grounds, but that question is for the next participants in this conversation to discuss.

Micah has a different view of this Supreme Court decision, as follows.

> I do believe the *Obergefell* decision of this last summer is an egregious example of Supreme Court judges substituting their own moral judgments about the common good for the duly enacted laws passed by the people of Tennessee, Michigan, Kentucky, and Ohio, and every other political community committed to traditional marriage.

Micah adds that "the burden of my argument in this essay [his first posting] is that Christians (and everyone else) should have a problem with Obergefell and other cases like it, because of what it does to the prospects of *our shared civic community*" (italics mine).

In his first posting, Micah elaborates somewhat on how he sees the Obergefell decision having a negative effect on "our shared civic community," as follows:

> We should expect our public servants to respect the decisions made by ourselves and our representatives. We should hold our courts to the highest standards when they are asked to review current law by strict requirements of constitutional law. Whatever our political principles, we should object when the rules by which we have agreed to resolve our disagreements are changed mid-stream by those unauthorized for the task. *We should respect those on the other side of our political arguments by competing in the legislature and in the court of public opinion, not short-circuiting the democratic process* (italics mine).

Micah further elaborates on the portion of the above quote that I have highlighted. I will now turn to that elaboration in the next section, with some embellishment on my part.

A PROPOSAL FOR MORE CONVERSATION ABOUT CONTENTIOUS PUBLIC POLICY ISSUES LIKE SAME-SEX MARRIAGE

Before presenting my embellishment, I will quote a portion of Micah's further elaboration on his suggestion that "We should respect those on the other side of our political arguments by competing in the legislature and in the court of public opinion, not short-circuiting the democratic process."

> There is no plausible way to understand the Court as speaking on behalf of We the People [in the *Obergefell* decision]. There is no doubt that the Court spoke on behalf of some of the people, but in doing so it shifted in its role from interpreting Constitutional law to creating it. It is more accurate to describe the Court as speaking for "we the people as we the court would like them to be."
>
> ... The American people were debating this issue and that healthy debate should have been allowed to continue ... unless ... .the stakes for justice are so high that achieving the desired result is worth breaking the social contract—the Constitution—that not only expresses our aspirations but guides how we settle our differences. To return to my first essay, the Constitution assumes that we the people will differ on fundamental issues about justice and the common good. It is better to agree on how to adjudicate those differences [by means of "extraordinary" politics] than to stomp out those differences from above. But if an issue is so paramount to our convictions that we cannot compromise in good faith, then we may be tempted to forgo our common bonds and either force the issue or break apart. The latter, of course, is what happened in 1861.

As an *entre* to my embellishment, note that Micah continues by noting that his "primary concern" is "the prospect of citizens who support traditional positions on marriage and sexuality being deemed the equivalent of racists who supported segregation or sexists who opposed women's suffrage," adding that "this is already happening."

In sharp contrast to this "demonizing" [my word, not Micah's] of those who oppose same sex-marriage on religious grounds. Micah poses the following "closing questions for my more progressive brothers and sisters."

> Do you see your more traditional Christian neighbors as the contemporary equivalent of George Wallace? Do you think our position is necessarily motivated by irrational animus? Or do you agree with President Obama that we can approach this issue in good faith? Will you defend the rights of Christian churches, colleges, and businesses to operate according to the dictates of their consciences, even if you would decide differently? Can Christians in good faith seek to promote their vision of what marriage is in the public square? Can we still share this public space? Can progressives and conservatives still meaningfully speak of *our* Constitution?

By now, the reader can surely see my embellishment coming. (What follows are my reflections, not to be attributed to either Micah or Kathy.)

It is obvious by now that Kathy and Micah have engaged in respectful conversation about their significant disagreements, not "demonizing" one another. Rather, they have expressed deep appreciation for one another, as follows.

> One of my former teachers used to say that we have to *rise* to the level of argument. That is, we have to so clarify our terms and our meanings such that our claims and counter-claims can actually engage each other. I think we've achieved some degree of that, and I want to again express my appreciation for this project and to Kathy Lee for pressing me to think harder about justice and our constitutional order. While there is no doubt we will not have exhausted our exploration of this issue, I think we've clarified some things and done so with more light than heat (Micah).
>
> I have appreciated Micah's reminders about the role of courts and also the dangers in assuming that groups based on certain identities ever speak with one voice and for his pointing out the ways in which we agree. So, thank you, Micah, for engaging in this conversation (Kathy).

So, my "bold embellishment," which is surely utopian, is that whatever strong disagreements Christians and all others may have relative to their understandings of a "constitutional framework for public policy issues" and all the other issues related to human sexuality that are addressed in this book, they will proceed in "good faith" to respectfully talk about their disagreements for the purpose of uncovering common ground and illuminating remaining disagreements enough to "keep the conversation going" in a shared public square.

If I may be so bold, I will suggest that this book models the realization of this utopian dream among my conversation partners. It is my hope and prayer that this "redemptive witness" on the part of twenty-one Christians that "it can be done" will inspire many other Christians, and those holding to other worldview commitments, religious or secular, to continue the conversations about human sexuality that are started in this book, and to extend this respectful approach to engaging those with whom we disagree to public conversations about the many contentious public policy issues that we face in our nation.

5

Same-Sex Marriage
Pluralism

As my good friends can tell you, I am fond of asserting that "one cannot predict beforehand the results of a respectful conversation." A noteworthy example of the truth of that assertion emerged in the conversation reported in this chapter. The results of this conversation surprised me.

For starters, it became apparent that I needed to make a midcourse correction to my prior pattern of asking two conversation partners to post essays dealing with a Leading Question, which for this present topic was: Given the pluralistic nature of American society, what stance should Christians take relative to public policy for or against same-sex marriage?

My two original conversation partners were Mikael Pelz and Julia Stronks, chosen with the expectation they would give differing responses to the Leading Question, loosely called "traditional" and "nontraditional." After their initial postings, it became apparent that, although they had some disagreements, they basically agreed on a nontraditional response informed by a common commitment to "principled pluralism" (more about that later).

So, in my attempt to ensure that the remainder of this conversation would exemplify a fair and balanced presentation of contrasting views, I asked Adam MacLeod if he would join the conversation, midstream, based on a recommendation from an astute reader that Adam would present a strong traditional view. On extremely short notice, Adam graciously agreed to join Mikael and Julia as a third conversation partner. But the surprises were just beginning.

I believe it is fair to say that in my first four monthly conversations, the two conversation partners for each topic presented contrasting traditional and nontraditional responses to their respective Leading Questions, from which it was possible to discern significant areas of agreement and to identify and illuminate areas of disagreement in a way that opened the door for ongoing conversations about their disagreements.

However, for this conversation, areas of agreement were scant and areas of disagreement were so stark as to appear intractable, now or forever. How is it possible to proceed in light of this apparent dead-end? Julia sees hope for fruitful ongoing conversations if we reject the notion that the purpose of this conversation is to "win the argument." Is it possible that a "higher purpose" than "winning the argument" can be well served by means of respectful conversations between those who disagree strongly about any given contentious issue? We will consider this provocative possibility at the end of this chapter. Before that, I will summarize highlights of the exchanges between Mikael, Julia, and Adam.

A PRINCIPLED PLURALIST POSITION

Both Mikael and Julia approach the issue of same-sex marriage from a "principled pluralist" perspective. As Mikael observes, "I was struck by how similar Julia's view on same-sex marriage was to my own view. We both seem to be solid principled pluralists. And our different articulations of pluralism are complementary."

FOUNDATIONAL PRINCIPLES OF PLURALISM

Julia notes that the pluralist perspective "involves two kinds of pluralism: institutional and confessional pluralism," which she summarizes as follows:

> *Institutional pluralism* draws from a Reformed theological concept of sphere sovereignty to demonstrate that in public life there are many different ways in which we engage the world. We are family members; we worship; we can be entrepreneurs. And, it is important to remember that the institutions that support these activities have different responsibilities. A church is not a family; a family is not a business; a government is not a church. Our responsibility is to think through the different callings of these different institutions. God's creation can flourish only when there is room in society for people to function in all the different capacities that God has called them to.

> *Confessional pluralism* means that while we live in a broken world we recognize that people have to have room to live according to the worldview they feel called to. For Christians thinking about citizenship the important question is what sorts of responsibilities do governments have toward people of other worldviews and faith traditions?

Julia suggests that "The biblical foundation for this kind of pluralism is centered in three different places," elaborating as follows:

> First, the Old Testament is filled with directives from the prophets that demonstrate civil authorities have a responsibility to the poor, the sick, and those without power. The books of *Micah* and *Amos* are replete with commands to those in authority to *do justice* and to *let justice roll down like a river* . . .
>
> Second, Christ's life demonstrates that the kingdom of God is not to be brought about by the sword. Christ used stories, persuasion and encouragement to demonstrate what our lives should be in this world. Political pluralism is a tool that protects other institutions as they engage in other kinds of persuasive work. The church has room to be what the church is called to be. Families and businesses have room to flourish in the way that they are called. There is room to share the love of Christ and to act in accordance with the way Christ calls us to live, but there is *not* room to coerce others to do the same.
>
> Third, in the parable of the Wheat and Tares (Matt 13) Christ shows us that it is not our job to separate the wheat from the weeds. In this parable the farmer's workers asked if they should pull out the weeds from the fields. The farmer said no. So, the sun and the rain fell equally on the wheat and the weeds until the harvest. Political pluralism allows public, legal justice to fall equally on everyone in society, even if we consider that some of the people are weeds.

IMPLICATIONS FOR SAME-SEX MARRIAGE

The Leading Question asks "what stance should Christians should take relative to public policy regarding same sex-marriage?" Because the focus of the question is on "public policy," Julia presents the "counterintuitive" assertion that "you can't start a conversation about same-sex marriage policy by focusing on marriage. You have to start by looking at the foundations of public policy: what is the government supposed to do?"

Julia then observes that some Christians respond to this question as to the role that God intends for government based on a perspective that has been called "theonomy," with a clear implication regarding public policy for same-sex marriage.

> Some Christians believe that God intends their Christian worldview to be the law of the land. They point to the Old Testament laws of Israel and argue that if something is a sin it ought to also be illegal. Government and church are not differentiated. God's desire for one is the same as God's desire for the other.
>
> These Christians would argue that same-sex marriage ought not to be legally recognized. Homosexual relationships are wrong; therefore, government should not recognize these marriages.

Julia presents a differing response to the question of the role that God intends for government in general, and the implications for public policy regarding same-sex marriage in particular, based on the "principled pluralist" perspective that she views as an alternative to "theonomy."

> So, as we apply this pluralism to our view of government we have to consider the responsibility of all these different institutions [of society]. *And*, we have to think about what it means to do justice to people of worldviews other than our own. Christians want government to recognize our right to shape institutions like schools, churches and non-profits according to our own worldview, but we also have to challenge ourselves to determine whether we are supportive of the worldview expression of other groups in society. Is it more biblical to encourage freedom of worldview no matter what the foundation of that worldview might be (pluralism), or is it more biblical to support only institutions that reflect Christian presuppositions (theonomy)? Is the public square intended by God to be for everyone (pluralism) or mainly for Christians (theonomy)?
>
> I fall into this pluralism approach to government and I strongly support the legal recognition of same-sex marriage. I believe that all Christians no matter what their beliefs about homosexuality ought to support same-sex marriage as a matter of *justice*. The focus has to be on thinking about what it means to do justice to all people who are functioning in loving, committed relationships raising children, caring for each other and fulfilling all of the responsibilities that exist in marital unions. If the government chooses to benefit heterosexual marriages

in particular ways then homosexual relationships functioning similarly should be benefited in exactly the same way.

God created us with the ability to engage in political community and this engagement carries not just rights but obligations. People in this pluralism perspective argue that Christian politics means that we must not look for privilege for our own perspective, whatever that might be. Rather we must seek to live with others in a fallen but redeemed world, sharing public goods and advocating for the well-being of all people. This requires that we listen to them about what their well-being entails. And, I'd say that Christians should be *enthusiastic* in their eagerness to achieve justice for LGBT people that have long been loving each other, caring for each other, and raising children in ways that have benefited society over hundreds of years.

Note carefully, for later reference, Julia's suggestion that "justice" for "married" same-sex couples requires that they be treated the same way as married heterosexual couples if they also "are functioning in loving, committed relationships raising children, caring for each other and fulfilling all of the responsibilities that exist in marital unions."

While presenting a similar description of the contours of "principled pluralism," Mikael adds the observation that the term "pluralism has undergone a radical transformation in Christian circles over the past three decades." He elaborates as follows:

> In my view, the first treatment of this term among Christians was largely reactionary. The fading dominance of the Christian worldview in American society beginning in the 1970s caused anxiety among some quarters of Christianity. These sentiments fueled the rise of the New Christian Right and the ushered in the culture wars in the politics of the 1980s and 1990s.
>
> However, I believe a more constructive connotation of pluralism has emerged over the last decade, one that seeks to respect individual differences within society and attempts to meet people where they are spiritually, intellectually, and relationally. For instance, in their recent book, *Amazing Grace* (2010),[1] David Campbell and Robert Putnam find that those who regularly attend church increasingly support civil liberties for opponents of religion and for homosexuals. These broad shifts have depoliticized Christianity and cultivated more political diversity within the Christian community.

---

1. Putnam and Campbell, *Amazing Grace*.

Mikael reaches the same conclusion as Julia regarding public policy for same-sex marriage.

> ... in order for gays and lesbians to fully participate in public life as equal citizens, same-sex marriage should be upheld as a fundamental legal or civil right.
>
> ... For gays and lesbians to be full members of civil society, they should be entitled to the same rights and privileges as any other member of society. This, of course, means they should have the right to marry same-sex partners, but also not be subject to any forms of discrimination in areas of public life including voting, housing, education, and employment. This position is based on a pluralistic understanding of public policy that seeks to serve the common good, which must be informed by all members of society in order to be legitimate. I would also add that this position does not hinge on one's personal view of homosexuality, but on the precepts of a civil society.

Once again, for later reference, it is important to note that Mikael's position on the legitimacy of same-sex marriage "does not hinge on one's personal view of homosexuality, but on the precepts of a civil society." Julia echoes Mikael on this point:

> I argue that no matter what Christians think about homosexuality, we should all support the legal recognition of same-sex marriage as a matter of biblical civic justice.

CHRISTIANS ENGAGING OTHERS IN A PLURALISTIC SOCIETY

Mikael notes that those persons committed to principled pluralism must "enter into a larger collective community and interact with people with different realities or belief systems than our own," adding a personal example: "As a white male, I have a very limited point of reference for the everyday experiences of other racial and gender groups in society. However, citizenship requires that I consider these experiences in evaluating the overall effectiveness or value of public policy."

Mikael notes that this responsibility requires "that citizens must be committed to engaging in meaningful political conversations with different groups in society," adding that "This model of citizenship is increasingly difficult in an era of political and cultural polarization, but is nonetheless critical to defining the common good."

The question then arises as to the "role of religion" in these public conversations. In particular, Mikael asks "what does a pluralistic society that promotes individual freedom require of Christians as thoughtful and responsible citizens" who are called to be "salt and light in society (Matt 5:13–16)." His own response is:

> First of all, Christians can and should actively participate in political debates in order to promote a public agenda that advances justice, peace and reconciliation for all people. Within the public realm, this is how Christians can love our neighbors (Mark 12:30–31). Christians have the opportunity to be spokespersons for a common good that seeks to uplift every member of society, respects the God-given dignity of every human being, and builds meaningful communities based on mutual respect. These activities are connected to a cosmic view of redemption in which Jesus Christ seeks to reclaim all facets of creation.

Mikael also argues that such involvement in public discourse will require the exercise of "tolerance."

> A core value of liberal democracies is tolerance. Initially instituted to address religious diversity and the conflict it can inevitably breed, tolerance for other citizens is a necessary backdrop for a just political order that allows free people to play a role in public deliberation and decision . . . . Promoting the virtue of tolerance does not mean that God is absent from society in general or individual lives. It does mean that Christians give space for God to exercise his sovereignty.

Mikael also asserts that the commitment to public discourse about contentious public policy issues must also be practiced within the "Christian community" when it discusses same-sex marriage.

> In order for this discussion [of same-sex marriage from a biblical and theological perspective] to be fair, thorough, and determinative, Christians who oppose same-sex marriage have to be allowed to speak their conscience. Openness and charity are needed as Christians come together to affirm the commitments of being a follower of Jesus Christ and to honestly explore how these commitments relate to same-sex relationships. Many of these discussions have already taken place; however, they must not stop because of the recent US Supreme Court case recognizing same-sex marriage. We must continue to listen to each other and move forward on this issue together.

Mikael also proposes that whether conversations about same-sex marriage involve just other Christians or the broader public, Christians need to demonstrate both compassion and humility.

> As Christians begin to consider how to respond to the recognition of same-sex marriage, compassion and humility should guide our public policy approach. Christians have the opportunity to demonstrate compassion by ensuring that gays and lesbians can exercise fundamental legal rights that enable them to function in society and to flourish.... Moreover, non-state structures can play a vital role in cultivating compassion for everyone touched by this issue.
>
> Christians should also approach this issue with a healthy dose of humility.... We can only enter in such a discussion if we are open to God's revelation, and practice humility in our own understanding of his Word and his general will. Christians can enter into this dialogue with full confidence of who God is and his continuous process of reconciliation for all things.

EXEMPTIONS TO PUBLIC LAW?

You will recall that Mikael has already asserted that "in order for gays and lesbians to fully participate in public life as equal citizens, same-sex marriage should be upheld as a fundamental legal or civil right," which he has called his first "basic public policy position on same-sex marriage." But his commitment to principled pluralism also leads him to commit to a second public policy position that allows for the possibility of "exemptions" to "public laws" on the basis of religious convictions, such as the public law established by the Supreme Court decision in the case of *Obergefell v. Hodges*.

> ... religious institutions that oppose same-sex marriage should not be compelled to support this public law [that same-sex-marriages are legal]. Thus, public policy should grant exemptions from participating in same-sex marriage ceremonies to institutions that are inherently religious. This position is consistent with the concept of principled pluralism, which reflects the diversity and differentiation of God's creation. This exemption also provides space for the church to pursue a healthy and honest discussion on this issue.

Mikael explains how this second commitment flows from principled pluralism.

Principled pluralism has two important implications for the public policy debate regarding same-sex marriage. First, according to this concept, organizations that are not tied to the state play a vital role in social life. Theologically, principled pluralism views God mediating his power on earth through various offices or representatives. Thus, it suggests that religious and other types of organizations can rightly and with authority speak to the conditions of same-sex couples, family issues relating to same-sex couples, and the cultural impact of same-sex relationships. As such, these structures offer a unique space for Christians to discuss the moral, ethical, and theological dimensions of homosexuality.

Second, the concept of principled pluralism sees the world as a diverse and differentiated creation designed by God. As a result, no one structure should dominate the others as each serves a specific purpose. This notion suggests that non-state structures should have the ability to exercise some independence from the prescribed public policy, as long as these activities do not deprive citizens of basic legal protections. For religious structures, this independence has been pursued in religious free-exercise arguments pertaining to the First Amendment of the Constitution. These arguments have been used to exempt individuals and organizations from complying with certain portions of the law that contradict a sincere religious conviction.

Of course, arguing that religious convictions may be the basis for exemptions from public law raises the extremely thorny question as to when such an exemption is warranted. With respect to the *Obergefell* decision relative to same-sex marriage, Julia expresses "appreciation" for the court's work, but has the following concern about "the opinion itself": "The Court's decision did little to guide us in balancing the rights of the gay community with the interests of conservative religious people. This balance is at the root of a lot of conflict in the areas of employment and consumer protection. It's also at the root of a lot of upcoming litigation." The next chapter on "Anti-Discrimination Laws" will address this issue in detail. In the meantime, both Mikael and Julia share some reflections on when religious exemptions to public law may be warranted.

First, Mikael argues that:

> Religious organizations should be given a narrow religious exemption on the issue of same-sex marriage. Specifically, church clergy and religious institutions should be able to exercise their religious freedom found in the First Amendment and not be

> compelled to perform or take part in same-sex marriage ceremonies.... such exemptions do not deprive gays and lesbians from exercising the legal act of marriage through the state or other types of religious institutions that approve of same-sex marriage.

However, Mikael makes it clear that this "narrow religious exemption" would not include exemptions in a recent case that has garnered much news coverage.

> However, I want to be clear on when this religious exemption would not apply. First, it would not allow an individual acting on behalf of the state to refrain from the administration of same-sex marriage because of a personal religious belief to the contrary. Under this policy, Kim Davis, the Kentucky county clerk who refused to issue marriage licenses because of her objection to same-sex marriage, would not be able to exercise this religious exemption. Granting such an exemption in this case would cause too much harm to the legal rights of gays and lesbians. If this exemption were allowed, it would likely lead to a cascading effect across the country where more and more public officials would assert their own belief system rather than follow the law. The end result would be less and less freedom for gay and lesbian citizens.

Similarly, Mikael argues that "this religious exemption would also not permit individuals in a private business setting to deny a variety of wedding services to gays and lesbians," his rationale being that "this exemption is not good public policy because it could easily be abused by individuals and businesses who may not have a sincere religious objection to same-sex marriage. It is much more apparent for religious organizations to demonstrate this objection because of their explicit religious mission, which would also encapsulate individuals with similar personal views. Moreover, the discriminatory nature of granting this type of religious exemption in largely the public sphere of commerce seems unnecessary and completely avoidable."

Julia has a different view on the question of whether "exemptions should extend to for-profit businesses," albeit with some uncertainty.

> For myself, I think the main distinction is not whether organizations are owned by religious people but whether the owners have made an effort to craft the entire organization along the lines required by their faith. If a baker will make a cake for anyone, then the baker may not say, "I won't craft a cake for a same-sex couple." But, if a baker has a whole faith-based approach to his

or her craft, and faith not only permeates the baking of all goods but also is a part of the baker's entire approach to consumer relations—then I feel a little differently. Can a democracy handle a for-profit business that serves only people who align with a specific understanding of a faith tradition? Or, would we say that all business engaged in consumer transactions must serve and hire without regard to sexual identity?

Julia concludes that she "will be eager to learn from" the conversation partners for the next topic of anti-discrimination laws."

AN ALTERNATIVE POSITION: A DEFINTION OF MARRIAGE THAT PRESERVES THE "NATURAL RIGHTS" OF CHILDREN THAT ARE PRIOR TO LAWS

A stark alternative to the "principled pluralist" position on an same-sex marriage taken by Julia Stronks and Mikael Pelz, as outlined above, is presented be Adam Macleod. To suggest that Adam and Julia/Mikael ended up "talking past one another" is gross understatement. After Mikael's response to Adam's initial posting, Adam responded to Mikael's response as follows:

> Mikael has so thoroughly mischaracterized my essay that I do not think my time would be well spent to bridge the gap between what I wrote and his critique of what he attributed to me. Instead, I'll briefly restate the argument I did make [more about that later] and then offer some observations about Michael's proffered definition of marriage.

In response to this response from Adam, Mikael acknowledges that he and Adam didn't find much common ground. Mikael then apologizes to Adam, but expresses hope that the conversation can continue.

> I thank Adam for his follow-ups to my essay. I don't see much common ground between our positions. My essay sought to examine the broader public policy implications of Adam's legal arguments. And I honestly sought to understand Adam's perspective in drawing these wider implications.
>
> However, a discussion is not very fruitful if one party believes he or she is being misrepresented. I apologize to Adam for mischaracterizing his position or implying too much from his essay. A 3,000-word essay is limiting, especially for a topic this expansive. Discussions between two very different perspectives often require a lot of grace to find common ground, and I ask for

Adam's grace in this instance. I do sincerely hope the conversation can continue.

Despite this apparent impasse, I hope that what follows will illuminate some of the disagreements.

QUESTIONING THE LEADING QUESTION

Once again, the question that I initially posed to all three "conversation partners" was: Given the pluralistic nature of American society, what stance should Christians take relative to public policy for or against same-sex marriage? When providing Adam with instructions for his posting, I abbreviated this initial question to: "Is allowing same-sex marriage good public policy?"

Adam found both questions to be "loaded." His commentary on my initial Leading Question was as follows:

> That seems to me something like asking whether, given American pluralism, Christians should oppose a policy that approves moving bodies staying at rest. The law of inertia will not change whatever public policies say.

It is extremely important for the reader to understand Adam's concern. Laws of physics, like the law of inertia, are not dependent on what people think about them. They are "laws," after all. Similarly, I understand Adam to be arguing that when it comes to human sexuality, there are certain "laws" that apply (he later calls them "natural laws") that are not dependent on the diversity of beliefs that people have about human sexuality or the public policies that government decides upon.

Adam then calls into question any public policies about human sexuality (or anything else) that are in violation of "natural laws" about human sexuality (or anything else): "a positive law contrary to the natural law is unjust," a "conviction" that stretches "from Augustine to Martin Luther King, Jr. and beyond."

So, contrary to Julia's assertion that a conversation about "same-sex marriage policy" should start with the question of what government is supposed to do, Adam asserts that the conversation should start by asking "What is marriage?"; the implication being that if we can understand the "natural laws" about the meaning of marriage, that will determine what our public policies ought to be.

Therefore, we now turn to the question "What is marriage?" starting with Adam's answer.

WHAT IS MARRIAGE?

Adam's response to this foundational question flows from his understanding of "features of human nature and natural law," as follows:

> ... the fundamental right of marriage is necessarily and essentially grounded in the natural duties that mother and father owe to their children and the corresponding rights of children to have legal connections to, and support from, their own mother and father. Those jural relations [between mother-father and children], being grounded in nature and established since before ancient memory, are pre-political and pre-legal—fundamental rights and duties.
>
> *The legal norms of marriage have always included the moral norms of natural law not because American evangelical Protestant Christians said so but because they are natural rights and duties arising from a biological reality*: Sex between a man and woman has consequences, namely offspring. Marriage is pre-political and fundamental, existing in all known civilizations as a man-woman institution to link fathers and mothers to their children by binding them to each other for life. (Italics mine.)

It is important to note at this point, from the italicized sentence above, that Adam is not embracing the "theonomy" position that Julia referred to, since he is not arguing that the *only reason* that government should legislate in favor of the "traditional" view of marriage is because that is what a Christian worldview demands. Rather, Adam is presenting a broader argument that the traditional view of marriage reflects "natural law" that can, and should, be embraced by all human beings, regardless of their worldview commitments.

Note carefully Adam's assertion that the "fundamental right of marriage" and the "corresponding rights of children to have legal connections to, and support from, their own mother and father" are "pre-political and pre-legal fundamental rights." Therefore, these fundamental rights are not established by law; they exist prior to enacted laws. Adam elaborates as follows:

> This complex of jural relations is vested in a discrete group of people—the family, composed of father-mother-children—to which governments gives recognition but did not create and are not free to rearrange. The integrity of the family is a source of obligation that does not owe its existence to positive law, and

that fact constrains the freedom of lawmakers to alter positive laws governing the family.[2]

In this light, Adam expresses his concern that "Perhaps the most troubling aspect of this most unusual moment in American history is the extent to which courts [are] inventing 'same-sex marriage' [in a manner that does not comport with the pre-legal understanding of the "fundamental right of marriage"]."

It is important to note the negative consequences that Adam perceives if his time-honored position on the meaning of marriage is abandoned.

In brief, Adam laments the negative effects on the well-being of children who have been denied the right to support from their mothers and fathers, citing the "chaos" that results when "heterosexual intercourse, procreation, and child care" are disconnected, as is becoming commonplace "in many of America's cities today."

> We are witnessing . . . social chaos in many of America's cities today, including my adopted hometown of Montgomery, Alabama. Here, more than two-thirds of children are born out of wedlock and are therefore at elevated risk of all the well-known negative outcomes—poverty, lack of education, unemployment, incarceration, sexual abuse, drug abuse, depression, and much else. Same-sex couples did not create that mess. But to create equality between marriage and "same-sex marriage" would require us to break the remaining normative bonds of the only institution capable of fixing the problem.

The problem with legally disconnecting marriage from parentage, from Adam's perspective, is that it could weaken the sense of obligation that parents should have for caring and supporting their biological children. Adam puts it this way:

> I think it is reasonable to think (I did not have space to demonstrate this, but I have elsewhere, as have many others) that laws affect choices and actions, and that eliminating those laws that connect marriage to parentage is likely to disconnect parentage from marriage in the choices and actions of people who have children.

In that light, Adam asserts that "all Americans, but especially Christians—have a responsibility to rebuild our broken marriage culture and defend the laws that protect children, rather than encouraging the elimination of natural marriage's remaining vestiges."

2. Macleod, "Rights, Privileges," 6.

Adam does see some potential light at the end of the tunnel. He projects the possibility that "the fundamental norms of the common law—the natural duties and rights of the mother-father-child triad—will reassert themselves by necessity as states come to grips with the devastating consequences of fatherlessness in our post-marriage culture."[3]

A challenge that Adam presents to Julia or Mikael is to "identify the essential characteristics of marriage and distinguish them from peripheral and non-essential traits." Mikael's response to this challenge is:

> Marriage is a commitment between two people, in which they share in each other's lives and rely upon each other for emotional, financial, and spiritual support. Married couples also fulfill each other's sexual needs. For Christians, marriage is also an opportunity to intimately understand Christ's self-sacrifice in the context of a physical human relationship. These relationships necessitate a certain level of legal protections so that couples can pursue this type of commitment. Marriage does not always include children, though children can benefit from a healthy marriage.

There appears to be overlap between Mikael's definition of marriage as "a commitment between two people in which they share in each other's lives and rely upon each other for emotional, financial, and spiritual support" and Adam's enumeration of four "norms" of marriage—"monogamy (two people), fidelity (to each other only), non-consanguinity (not close blood relations), permanence (for life)."

But the fatal flaw in Mikael's definition, according to Adam, is that Mikael's "redefinition of marriage logically entails the elimination of those four norms" because "the foundational norm that renders those norms rational—conjugality (man-woman union)" is missing. In Adam's own words:

> [Stronks and Pelz embrace an unstated assumption that] marriage will retain its norms—monogamy (two people), fidelity (to each other only), non-consanguinity (not close blood relations), permanence (for life)—without the foundational norm that renders those norms rational—conjugality (man-woman union)—after some of the best contemporary thinkers on both sides of the question have argued (persuasively, it seems to me) that the redefinition of marriage logically entails the elimination of those norms.

---

3. Ibid., 36–37.

A perusal of the writings of some of the "contemporary thinkers" who Adam cites in the above quote (links to which Adam provides in his posting) reveals that a common concern is that "those who embrace same-sex civil marriage leave no firm ground—none—for not recognizing every relationship describable in polite English, including polyamorous sexual unions, and that enshrining their view would further erode the norms of marriage."[4]

Adam's expression of this concern is as follows:

> Michael states that marriage is a commitment in which the participants "share in each other's lives and rely upon each other for emotional, financial, and spiritual support." But he also states, "Married couples also fulfill each other's sexual needs." Yet if marriage is not inherently a sexually-complementary union of man and woman who together form a one-flesh unity when united in coitus, why must it involve sex? His definition discriminates against couples who share each other's lives and rely upon each other for support without sex—bachelor brothers or spinster sisters, an adult caring for an elderly parent, long-time roommates, etc. Is there any reason for this discrimination?
>
> And why only two people? Michael's definition discriminates against throuples, quartets, polyamorous households, and other groups. But such groups also "share in each other's lives and rely upon each other for emotional, financial, and spiritual support." Some of those groups even share sex, satisfying Michael's other element. If marriage is not a real, one-flesh union of one man and one woman then the number two seems arbitrary.

Alas, the month of conversation ended before Mikael or Julia could respond to this concern. But this was only one of a number of "loose ends."

QUESTIONS BEGGING FOR FURTHER CONVERSATION

An unavoidable and unfortunate consequence of my midcourse correction is that the month ran out before Julia, Mikael, and Adam could respond to a number of questions or issues raised.

Most significantly, responses were not forthcoming to the two radically different perspectives presented regarding possible public policies relative to same-sex marriage. On the one hand, Julia and Mikael presented a strong case for a "principled pluralist" perspective that focused on their view that public policies regarding "marriage" should emerge from the need to foster

---

4. George et al., *What is Marriage?*

"public justice." Due to lack of time, Adam was not able to give an in-depth response to the contours of the "principled pluralist" position.

On the other hand, Adam presented a strong case for a "natural law" perspective that the "natural rights and obligations between parents and children" should define "marriage" and determine public policy regarding marriage. Mikael and Julia did not have time to give an in-depth response to this "natural law" approach to the issue of same-sex marriage.

It is my hope that sometime in the future, Julia, Mikael, and Adam, and their respective allies, will be able to continue a conversation about these fundamentally differing perspectives.

In addition to that possible future conversation, a number of other questions were raised during the electronic exchange that beg for further conversation.

IS THERE AN "IDEAL" FAMILY STRUCTURE?

In his response to Adam's position, Mikael expresses two concerns.

> My concerns regarding Adam's arguments are two-fold: 1) He confounds the goals of marriage with the goals of raising children. They are related but they are not the same and should be treated separately, and 2) he upholds an ideal of family that is unnecessarily exclusive and does not create opportunities for other members of society to love and care for children when this ideal is inevitably unmet.

Adam responds to Mikael's two concerns by asserting that "Michael has so thoroughly mischaracterized my essay that I do not think my time would be well spent to bridge the gap between what I wrote and his critique of what he attributed to me." But he does briefly address Mikael's two concerns.

First, Adam asserts that "I did not argue for any ideal type" or "ideal family structure." Rather:

> I described the law. I distinguished between the new privilege of "same-sex marriage," whatever that is, and the fundamental law of marriage, which has always been grounded in the pre-political, common-law jural relations of mother-father-child and remains grounded in those fundamental jural relations in all fifty states . . . . And I summarized an argument that I have made elsewhere, demonstrating that states cannot make man-man "marriage" and woman-woman "marriage" equal to real marriage without eliminating those jural relations. Producing "marriage equality" would therefore necessarily destroy the

right of each child to have legal connection to her mother and father....

Adam also responds that he did not "conflate marriage and raising children," explaining that:

> The fundamental liberty (not a claim-right to official recognition, as Michael seems to assume) of the natural family is grounded in the jural relations of the biological family in the sense that those jural relations provide its justification. But the liberty itself protects a natural marriage whether or not that marriage results in children. The law does not inquire into fertility when assessing the validity of a natural marriage; it is content to note that a natural marriage—man-woman union—is the only kind of social relation capable of producing children naturally.

Time did not allow for Mikael and Adam to sort out this apparent impasse. Much more conversation is needed. And I believe that ongoing conversation needs to take into account the following sub-issues.

WHAT IS BEST FOR CHILDREN?

At last, we come to an important element of common ground. Adam, Julia, and Mikael all agree on the importance of fostering the well-being of children. As Mikael puts it:

> His [Adam's] primary concern for the well-being of children is evident in his essay, and is something all three contributors to this ... discussion undoubtedly share. We all want children to grow in loving and nurturing families, though we may disagree on how to achieve this.

Adam agrees:

> I am sure that they [Julia and Mikael] share my concern for the rights and well-being of children. I take it that we disagree about the nature of those rights and the best *means* to promote children's well-being.

What, then, is the best means for promoting the well-being of children? Adam's view on how to foster the flourishing of children is that "children are most likely to flourish when raised by their own mother and father." He refers to "a strengthening consensus among social scientists and public figures on the right and left that children flourish when raised by a married mother and father, that they do best when raised by their own biological mother and father, and that natural marriage is sui generis in this regard."

On the other hand, as we saw in chapter 3, not all social scientists agree that there is a scientific consensus that children do best when raised by a married mother and father. So, more conversation about that issue is called for. That conversation should include discussion of the following reflections from Mikael.

First, Mikael suggests that even if having children raised by their biological mothers and fathers is "best" (the "ideal") for raising children, that is not always possible in our broken world.

> While this ideal [for all couples to conceive and raise a child together] is often the case, countless individuals, couples, and children face a different reality that Adam does not acknowledge. As a result, Adam's conceptualization excludes many other instances of a loving and supportive family . . .
>
> To simply base families on God's original design of procreation precludes all of the wonderful and unexpected things God can reveal through other non-natal relationships and the broader community. The Bible is full of accounts of unorthodox or unconventional families that God used to bring his people closer to him. Narrowly defining family as natural parental rights denies us the full richness and possibilities of God's creation. Using this definition also makes it easy to forget the role of extended family members, churches, and various forms of community in building strong families.

Mikael concludes by saying that he is "not prepared to defend" a particular position on the question of whether "these unconventional family arrangements [should] extend to same-sex couples," which he suggests will require a "separate discussion." Hopefully, ongoing discussions prompted by this chapter will address that thorny question.

HOW ABOUT CIVIL UNIONS WITHOUT MARRIAGE FOR SAME-SEX COUPLES?

As Julia notes, some who hold to a "principled pluralism" perspective (other than her or Mikael) have proposed granting same-sex couples the "civil rights of marriage without actually calling it 'marriage.'"

> There is some disagreement among Christians in this pluralism perspective.[5] Some would say we can grant all the public, civil rights of marriage without actually calling it "marriage." To them marriage is a distinctively male/female institution. But, others say this is not full justice and elevates biology over the relationship aspect of marriage. They would say true justice occurs only when the legal term of marriage is offered to all.

Other than what Julia said above, our three conversation partners did not discuss the perceived pros and cons of this option. Nor was there any discussion of a similar option that I have heard expressed verbally from time to time: Government should get out of the "marriage business" completely by only granting civil unions to all interested couples (opposite-sex or same-sex), with "marriages" being reserved for religious settings—any couple wishing to share marriage vows would simply find a church that is willing to perform such a marriage ceremony.

To be sure, these are controversial options, and further conversation is called for.

WHAT DOES "LOVE" REQUIRE?

Julia reports that over the twenty years or so that she has struggled with LGBT issues, including the question of whether same-sex couples should be allowed in the church (a question that will be dealt with in-depth in chapter 8), she found wisdom in the following advice from a mentor.

> This man said, "I do not know which approach is the right one. But, I do know that if I err, I choose to err on the side of loving and accepting those who follow Jesus no matter what their sexual identity. When I stand before God I would rather defend myself having made a mistake by accepting gay Christians as full brothers and sisters at the table of God than defend myself having made a mistake by rejecting them.

Mikael responds to this report from Julia as follows:

---

5. As Julia points out, "The US organization that most closely represents this [principled pluralist] perspective on government is the Center for Public Justice" (CPJ). However, Julia adds that she does not speak for CPJ "in any way" and her "perspective on the issue of homosexuality and same-sex marriage is different from theirs." The position of CPJ on marriage is that "marriage . . . should be recognized as a life-long covenant between a man and a woman . . ." (http://www.cpjustice.ork/index.php/public/page/comtent/homosexuality). In the interest of self-disclosure, I served for a number of years as a trustee of CPJ.

> Julia said that she received helpful advice from someone who conveyed that if he erred, he would choose to err on the side of loving and accepting those who follow Jesus regardless of their sexual identity. While we should always love, many Christians disagree on what love requires us to do on this issue. I imagine those who are opposed to same-sex marriage would say that they are also erring on the side of love by not sanctioning what they would consider as harmful homosexual relationships. Putting pluralistic arguments aside for a moment, this is perhaps the crux of the matter that defines our view of "the good" in public policy. I wonder *if both sides of this issue can agree on a basic understanding of what love requires*, apart from how they view homosexuality, much like Rawl's veil of ignorance. If this is possible, it could be a starting point for finding common ground on this issue among the church and lead the way in public policy. (Italics mine.)

This fascinating suggestion begs for further conversation. Chapter 8 will report on such a subsequent conversation.

WHERE DO WE GO FROM HERE?

For starters, it is my hope that the many unresolved disagreements and loose ends reported in this chapter will be the subject of ongoing respectful conversations in many venues, including further conversations involving Julia, Mikael, and Adam.

It is also my hope that as such future conversations take place, participants will be open to the risky possibility that genuinely listening to the views of those who disagree with them and talking about their disagreements can cause them to refine or change their perspectives. Julia and Mikael share their experiences with this dynamic process.

> For the past twenty-five years of my professional career I've written books on First Amendment jurisprudence and articles on same-sex marriage. And, one of the things that surprises me and keeps me interested is that my perspective on both of these topics has changed over time (Julia).
>
> I was not initially open to same-sex marriage. After hearing from several prominent Christians struggling with this issue as well as befriending Christians who are gay, I began to open up

> to other perspectives. I also have relied upon many important Christian thinkers in defining a biblical view of justice. This process of listening and thinking encouraged me to reexamine how the Bible and the Christian walk speak to same-sex marriage. That said, I still feel like I am living in the gray on this particular issue, and I constantly fight the urge to prematurely resolve this matter in my own mind (Mikael).

Note especially the influence on Mikael of his having developed friendships with "Christians who are gay." Based on my own experience, I firmly believe that we open ourselves to the possibility of a profound change in our perspectives when we get to know those who disagree with us on a personal level.[6]

And, of course, it is my hope and prayer that all future conversations about the contentious issue of same-sex marriage be characterized by respect, the kind of respect that was demonstrated by the conversation partners in this conversation in the midst of their strong disagreements, as witnessed to by the following testimonials.

> I thank Adam for sharing his perspective. It is now clear we have a robust debate on this question! And while I disagree with many of the arguments Adam outlines in his essay, I appreciate his vigorous defense of traditional marriage and his willingness to engage arguments to the contrary (Mikael).
>
> Mikael also avoids ad hominem and sticks with reasoned discourse, which is a rare feat these days among proponents of his position, and I thank him for it. The tone of Michael's essay is (mostly) charitable, and it appears that he made a genuine, good faith effort to understand my argument (Adam)
>
> The Respectful Conversations project is a unique opportunity to show the world that we can achieve disagreement in good faith, and the previous entries in this series admirably avoid unpleasantness. (Adam).
>
> Pelz correctly acknowledges that many of us act in good-faith obedience to conscience and not out of enmity. That is a promising starting place for a respectful conversation (Adam).

I conclude this chapter with a more provocative proposal from Julia as to "where we can go from here."

> One way (but not the only way) of looking at the conversations that have been reported on in this book up to this point (and in much of what

---

6. For a report on my experience of the truth of this maxim in an area of discourse unrelated to LGBT issues, see Heie, "Politics in the Trenches."

follows) is that the "conversation partners" would like to "win the argument," at least in the sense that they hope that readers will find their arguments persuasive because they have presented their perspectives in a compelling manner with clarity and conviction. But Julia raises the fascinating question as to whether the purpose of these conversations is to "win the argument." To begin to engage that question, she compared her experience as a lawyer with her experience as a political science professor.

> Long ago when I practiced law I spent a lot of time in the courtroom. This was a good place for me because I am by nature argumentative and competitive. I like to win. It was also a bad place for me because by nature I am argumentative and competitive. Winning is too important to me. Being a litigator brought out aspects of my personality that on my best days I work to suppress.
>
> When I left the practice of law to become a college professor I thought I was leaving competition behind me; I was wrong. While lawyers might manipulate facts and the law to win, academics often use jargon to dismiss others. I struggle with this every day because I can be really good at it. I struggle with it in my writing and I struggle with it in the classroom. When I teach, I can be tempted to see the classroom like I saw the courtroom—a place to instruct and to win. If you see things differently than I do, you are wrong. Let me tell you all the ways in which you are wrong.
>
> But, teaching is different than litigating. Though I often instruct, my main job is different. When I am at my best I spend my time helping students to understand what they believe about the world, who they are in the world, and how they are to engage a world that is fallen but has been redeemed. This takes a gentleness that does not come to me by nature. It takes willingness to stand in the shoes of another and it takes humility and delight in learning from those who differ from me. My students are gay, straight, conservative, liberal, undocumented, African American, Caucasian, Asian, Native American, Christian, atheist, wealthy, poor, middle-class, male, female, transgender, and so much more. I have taught for over twenty years and I still learn more from students than I give them. This staggers me.

Julia then observes that for the current conversation about same-sex marriage, no one "won the argument," primarily because the three conversation partners "see the world differently."

> Mikael, Adam and I are all Christians, all trained similarly in the field of politics and law. But, we see the world differently. We interpret history differently, and we value early theorists and church leaders differently.

For Julia, this raises the all-important questions: "*Is the primary issue who is right? Or, is the primary issue how we will live together despite our differences?*" In particular, Julia raises these questions relative to the role of government.

> Is the role of government to elevate the right way of doing things? Or, is the role of government to accommodate and organize, so far as possible, different ways of being in the world?

Julia then gives a dire warning: "*If the job of government is to get it right, and have us all live according to the right, then I see no hope in this world for peace and respect.*" She notes that if "we [Julia, Mikael, and Adam; all of whom share a commitment to the Christian faith] can't agree, who can?"

> Here we have three white, upper-middle class highly educated Christian academics, similar in our orientations, teaching at similar schools—who nonetheless disagree about something so foundational to human life. If we can't agree, who can? If government is going to be about one of our perspectives winning, then government will never be more than majority and minority perspectives trying to gain ground.

So, Julia concludes that "*Christian citizens need to focus more on accommodating differences than on winning the argument,*" adding that:

> The real challenge is in figuring out what the accommodation should look like. Under what circumstances might accommodation of different perspectives be a matter of justice? And, under what circumstances might accommodation of different perspectives lead to harm?

For Julia, such attempts at "accommodation" must focus on doing "justice" to all citizens, including "those who view the world as Adam does."

> Public opinion and law are beginning to reflect what I think of as a just way of treating LGBT citizens. For me this is cause for rejoicing. But people who think like I do must challenge ourselves to also think about those who differ from us. What does it mean to do justice to those who view the world as Adam does? *What room should they have in society to organize their families, places of worship or places of business according to their deepest beliefs?* (italics mine).

The question italicized above will be the focus of the next chapter devoted to "anti-discrimination Laws." Julia concludes by suggesting that answering that question is "a really hard task," adding that "Sometimes it is easier to just try and win the argument."

6

Anti-Discrimination Laws

It is not uncommon for LGBT persons to experience discrimination because of their sexual orientation or gender identity. As a result, both states and the federal government have passed some anti-discrimination laws to protect LGBT persons. Further legislation is being considered, which has led to considerable debate and dispute as to the optimum terms for such legislation.

A particular point of dispute centers on a perceived tension between protecting the rights of LGBT persons and protecting the "religious freedom" rights claimed by faith-based organizations that believe that sexual relationships between same-sex couples are contrary to their faith commitments. Faith-based organizations holding to such beliefs argue that that should be granted certain exemptions to anti-discrimination laws that protect LGBT persons. Are such exemptions ever warranted, and, if so, how should they be crafted?

That is the issue that is discussed by the conversation partners for this sixth round of conversation, Chelsea Langston Bombino and Kathryn Brightbill, as they address the following Leading Question: Both states and the federal government have anti-discrimination laws relating to employment, housing, and consumer protection for members of the LGBT community. Should faith-based institutions, both nonprofit and for-profit, be eligible for exemption from these laws?

OBERGEFELL V. HODGES DOES NOT ANSWER THIS LEADING QUESTION

As Chelsea observes, the Supreme Court decision *Obergefell v. Hodges* "requires states to accept same-sex marriage but does not tell governments what they must require of private persons and organizations with respect to same-sex marriage."

One consequence is that "a gay couple can get married but then both people get fired or they can't find housing in those many states and localities without laws protecting the LGBT community from discrimination." Furthermore, "The federal government itself does not have any comprehensive SOGI [Sexual Orientation and Gender Identity] protections."

As a result, there is now "a heightened push to create new laws, including at the federal level, that would make SOGI a new protected class."

As will soon be seen, Chelsea affirms the need for such anti-discrimination laws. But she expresses the concern that "unless well written, such laws, while protecting LGBT people in their identity, will harm faith-based organizations that have a different religious paradigm regarding human sexuality and desire to live in conformity to it without denying the legal rights of others."

If the *Obergefell v. Hodges* Supreme Court decision does not provide an inroad into addressing our Leading Question, where can we start? We begin with a perceived ideal for a pluralistic society.

EQUAL OPPORTUNITY TO PARTICIPATE IN SOCIETY

Kathryn points us toward an ideal for a democratic, pluralistic society: "On the most basic level, for a democratic, pluralistic society to function, all members of that society must be given the equal opportunity to participate in society."

Kathryn then reminds us of two examples of the devastating effects in American history when this ideal has not been embraced.

> When one segment of the population is barred from full participation the effects are far reaching. We see that with slavery and Jim Crow—African Americans are still paying the price, economically, physically, and socially for the generations in which they were denied access to full participation through slavery and segregation. Similarly, prior to the passage of the Americans with Disabilities Act, those living with disabilities were prevented from full participation in society because public

spaces were inaccessible. Whether through the active discrimination of Jim Crow or the passive discrimination that ignored the needs of those with disabilities, people were prevented from using their talents and denied access to goods and services, and they and society suffered as a result.

Kathryn also notes that discussion of this ideal is deeply existential for those, like her, who identify as being LGBT, echoing again the earlier suggestion from Justin Lee and Eve Tushnet that "gay people should take priority over gay issues."

> I would like to begin by noting that it is an altogether singular experience to be called upon to argue for one's right to do what most of society takes for granted—to participate in society without having to think about whether you will face discrimination based on who you are. For my esteemed colleague in this conversation, this is an academic discussion. For those who are LGBT, the direction this country ultimately takes on this question will have far-ranging consequences for their lives and ability to contribute as productive members of society.

Kathryn adds that "what we are actually discussing is whether LGBT people can legally be denied access to large swaths of public life," citing once again the experience of African American families under Jim Crow and pointing to her concern about "religious exemptions" to anti-discrimination laws (much more about that later).

> It was so bad [under Jim Crow] that travel guides had to be published so that African American families could travel safely and find places where they could sleep and eat. In some communities, other African American families had to open their homes because otherwise African American travelers had no place to stay. Jim Crow wasn't just lunch counters or bus seats, it was a system that prevented African Americans from participation in all the areas of public life that white Americans take for granted . . .
>
> Whether supporters of religious exemptions intend to create an outcome for LGBT people not unlike the one African Americans experienced under Jim Crow, the reality is that this is the door they are opening. A society that allows faith-based discrimination is a society that cuts LGBT people off from full participation in society.

Kathryn has presented a compelling case for enabling LGBT persons an equal opportunity to participate in society. But if the ideal is to provide "all persons" an equal opportunity to participate in society, the thorny question remains as to the appropriate nature of such participation in society for those non-LGBT persons and their organizations that, based on their religious convictions, wish to provide social services that contribute to society but oppose expressions of sexual intimacy for same-sex couples. We will eventually address that difficult issue. But, we will next seek to identify a foundation for the assertion that all persons should have equal opportunity to participate in society.

HUMAN DIGNITY AS THE BASIS FOR PROVIDING EQUAL OPPORTUNITY FOR PARTICIPATION IN SOCIETY FOR ALL PERSONS

What is the "key to human dignity"? Chelsea notes the proposal from an elder of the Church of the Latter Day Saints (LDS), Dallin H. Oaks, that "religious faith . . . is the key to human dignity."

Chelsea observes that "many disagree" (with Oaks) by "identifying factors, such as race or sexual orientation, as the axis on which human dignity hinges." Therefore, Chelsea concludes, "our society has at least two different concepts of human dignity. One response has been to place 'freedom from discrimination . . . above the constitutional guarantee of free exercise of religion'—marginalizing religion."

Based on her conviction that "Both sexual orientation and religious faith, and the conduct that follows from each, are fundamental to human identity," Chelsea takes a both/and rather than an either/or stance: "Better . . . to [safeguard] both concepts of dignity by protecting religion as well as LGBT rights."

Of course, this both/and approach raises the critical question, to be addressed later, as to how to balance commitment to protect both religion as well as LGBT rights. But, however that balance is struck, it is an appeal to human dignity that is the basis for the ideal of enabling all persons to participate equally in society.

Before embarking on the challenging task of attempting to strike a balance in protecting both religion and LGBT rights, it is important to point out that both Chelsea and Kathryn agree on the need for creating such a balance.

THE NEED FOR BALANCE BETWEEN PROTECTING RELIGION AND LGBT RIGHTS

Both Chelsea and Kathryn affirm the need to protect both gay rights and religious liberty. First, Chelsea quotes with approval the following position taken by Douglas Laycock, a "religious freedom scholar at the University of Virginia."

> The proper response to the mostly avoidable conflict between gay rights and religious liberty is to protect the liberty of both sides. Both sexual minorities and religious minorities make essentially parallel claims on the larger society. Both sexual orientation and religious faith, and the conduct that follows from each, are fundamental to human identity . . . . Both same-sex couples and religious dissenters also seek to live out their identities in ways that are public in the sense of being socially apparent and socially acknowledged.

Kathryn also eloquently takes a both/and position that calls for "balancing."

> I want to begin by underscoring the importance of religious freedom as a fundamental right that we all enjoy. I've lived and worked in a country that doesn't have the same religious freedoms that American Christians have and I can absolutely say from experience that the ability to practice one's faith should not be at the whims of a government. The question at hand is not one of whether people of faith should have religious freedom, but rather what should happen when one person's religious beliefs impinge on another's ability to exist and function in a free society.
>
> The free exercise of religion is not an absolute freedom and never has been one. Religious freedom does not extend so far as to allow a person to harm another in the name of free exercise of religion. Because we live in a nation of laws, we are constantly balancing religious freedom with the rights of others not to have their lives and well-being harmed by the religious practices of another.

Interestingly, both Kathryn and Chelsea appeal to the position of the Dutch statesman Abraham Kuyper relative to "sphere sovereignty" (an aspect of the "principled pluralist" position outlined in chapter 5) in support for their call for balance in protecting both religious liberty and gay rights, but they differ in their concerns about where imbalance can occur.

First, based on sphere sovereignty, Kathryn argues for the need for government to protect gay rights from intrusion by faith-based persons or organizations committed to "religious freedom," as follows.

> ... let us now move on to the reasons why, regardless of beliefs about the morality of same-sex relationships, Christians should support non-discrimination laws. I will be writing from a Kuyperian sphere sovereignty framework [that is] . . . well-suited to a discussion of how Christians should relate to a pluralistic society.
>
> Under a sphere sovereignty framework there are different spheres or domains that are ordained by God, and society functions best when one sphere doesn't try to overreach into the domain of another sphere. For example, the family unit is a sphere, as is the church, as is the civil government. The civil government should not overreach and meddle in the church's sphere of ecclesiastical governance, and the church should not try to overreach into the civil government and try to implement religious law in the civil sphere. Doing so would then result in the civil government imposing laws on the spheres of other churches and faiths that would infringe on those groups' ability to function in their own spheres.
>
> Moving to the discussion at hand, the church sphere, civil government sphere, and the public sphere are all in play in a discussion of non-discrimination laws. The public sphere is that area where all of us operate, and while as people of faith we all bring our religious beliefs (or lack thereof) into the public sphere, the public sphere is not the church. We have a model for what happens when a church or religious sphere operates outside of its bounds within the public sphere—we get something akin to Sharia law in Iran or Saudi Arabia, where religious police are able to enforce ecclesiastical law not just on their own congregants, but on the population as a whole. And while I am not suggesting that religious exemptions are equivalent to Sharia law, they are a form of churches and religious groups enforcing their ecclesiastical law on the community as a whole. Religious exemptions to civil laws allow the religious sphere to overreach into the public sphere and to impose religious law on those who are not members of that faith community. Rather than protecting religious freedom, such exemptions take away the ability of everyone to freely operate within the public sphere.

Chelsea also appeals to Kuyper's sphere sovereignty position, but in the opposite direction, arguing for the need to protect faith-based persons and organizations from unwarranted intrusion from a government committed to protecting gay rights.

> In response to Kathryn's application of sphere sovereignty, ... I would suggest that, when it comes to overreach, the civic government is actually extending into the religious sphere when it tries to set requirements for how explicitly religious organizations, whether they are houses of worship or social services organizations, make employment decisions.

I believe that Abraham Kuyyer would say that overreach is possible in both directions. This suggests the need for a both/and approach that protects both gay rights and religious freedom, raising once again the need for creating an appropriate balance between these two "protections."

The areas where such balance is needed are numerous, including housing, credit opportunity, public accommodations, and hiring practices. Therefore, consideration must be given to an appropriate scope for anti-discrimination laws, a topic to which we now turn.

AGREEMENTS AND DISAGREEMENTS REGARDING THE DESIRABLE SCOPE FOR ANTI-DISCRIMINATION LAWS

After some initial misunderstanding, Chelsea and Kathryn express agreement on certain elements of an appropriate scope for anti-discrimination laws. For starters, they both agree on the need for anti-discrimination laws that focus on "housing and credit opportunities." As Chelsea says, "People and organizations of faith should then support SOGI laws focused on housing and credit opportunity without much reservation."

Kathryn concurs:

> I am glad to see that [Chelsea] does not support discrimination in housing and credit. Shelter, along with food and water, is among the most basic of needs, and the inability to find housing essentially precludes individuals from participation in society. Similarly, in our credit-based economy, cutting off groups from access to credit makes participation difficult. A commitment to the basic dignity of all humans requires that we do not prevent some from accessing the tools necessary to support themselves and to find safe housing.

But a misunderstanding then arises. Kathryn understands Chelsea to be advocating for exemptions for "religious shelters," which Kathryn finds extremely problematic: "The exemptions [Chelsea] suggests for religious shelters would, in many communities, leave homeless LGBT people and LGBT survivors of domestic violence without a roof over their heads."

Chelsea responds as follows:

> I never suggested that we should exempt shelters, religious or otherwise, from serving LGBT people.... [I] completely agreed with [Kathryn] that there should be public accommodations laws that protect LGBT people from discrimination, and that faith-based orgs should not be exempt from serving the LGBT community.

Chelsea further elaborates on her position as follows, noting that whereas "there are instances where members of the LGBT community have been denied admittance to a shelter because of their sexual orientation," that is not "the standard practice, nor would it be accepted or tolerated by the larger faith-based community."

> I completely support SOGI laws that would not wholesale exempt religious shelters from serving everyone eligible regardless of their sexual orientation and gender identity. At the same time, in my work with hundreds of faith-based social service organizations, I have never come across a shelter, food bank, or jobs program that denied services to an individual because of their sexual orientation or gender identity. That is not to say that these instances of SOGI discrimination by faith-based social services providers (those providing housing, food, workforce training, or other such services) do not happen. I am sure there are instances where members of the LGBT community have been denied admittance to a shelter because of their sexual orientation. But I point this out simply to say that my organization has worked closely with a large segment of the faith-based nonprofit social services sector, and SOGI discrimination in these sorts of services simply is not the standard practice, nor would it be accepted or tolerated by the larger faith-based community.

As an example of this assertion, Chelsea quotes the Rev. Michael Brown, Executive Director of the Kalamazoo Rescue Mission:

> Because we recognize that Muslims observe different eating habits, we have attempted to accommodate this and to ensure that an alternative is available when pork is served as the main course. There are [also] persons from our community residing at the Gospel Mission who are gay or transgender and many

who are not Christian. They are all welcomed to the services of the Mission.

Chelsea summarizes her position as follows, pointing to what she sees as "significant *housing, credit opportunity, secular employment, and/or public accommodations* areas of consensus" between her and Kathryn.

> I want to acknowledge our agreements, as I believe we have significant areas of consensus. I agree that SOGI laws should be passed on a local, state and federal level that protect LGBT individuals from discrimination in the areas of housing and consumer protection, and that such laws generally do not require exemptions for religious institutions. I agree that a landlord should not be able to turn away a same-sex couple for "religious reasons." I agree a transgender woman should not be denied access to credit. Such acts of baseless discrimination do happen, disproportionately, to members of the LGBT community. These are not hypothetical wrongs, but real instances of invidious discrimination that have unfairly impacted LGBT individuals. SOGI laws are especially necessary in light of *Obergefell*. It is wrong that a same-sex couple now has the legal right to marry, yet their doing so could still result in discrimination or disparate treatment in *housing, credit opportunity, secular employment, and/or public accommodations* (italics mine).

Note Chelsea's punch line that the scope of anti-discrimination laws should include the areas of "housing, credit opportunity, secular employment, and/or public accommodations." Elsewhere, Chelsea expands the category of "secular employment" to "secular and governmental employment," arguing that there should be no exemptions to anti-discrimination laws relative to employment in those sectors of society. At the same time, Chelsea acknowledges that "This level of protection [for LGBT employment in the secular and governmental sectors], sadly, is still absent in over half of the states. Right now, in approximately thirty-eight states in this country, LGBT employees have no legal recourse if their employer were to fire them tomorrow for their sexual orientation or gender identity."

Since Kathryn argues against SOGI discrimination in hiring practices for any sectors of society, she would certainly agree with Chelsea that such discrimination should not take place in the "secular and governmental sectors." But it is with respect to hiring practices for faith-based organizations that strong disagreement with Chelsea emerges. This disagreement pertains to a distinction between the services that should be provided by faith-based organizations (about which Chelsea and Kathryn have significant agreements) and, as Chelsea says, "how they [faith-based organizations] staff and how they provide services."

To emphasize that the fundamental disagreement is not about the social services being provided, Kathryn points to the important role that faith-based organizations play in providing such services.

> In this country we rely on faith-based non-profits to provide a lot of social services. In some communities, Catholic hospitals are the only ones available, the Salvation Army and other faith-based groups do much of the work of providing services to the homeless, and faith-based non-profits provide adoption services, to name a few examples. This is a good thing, and as a public policy matter we should be encouraging faith-based community development and relief work. The government cannot provide a total safety net, and dedicated individuals working in their communities often have a better sense of what their community needs than a bureaucrat hundreds of miles away.

Holding off until later the question of "how" faith-based organizations provide social services and the controversial related issue of whether faith-based organizations providing such social services should receive taxpayer support, the main area of disagreement between Chelsea and Kathryn that we will now address is whether there is a need for anti-discrimination laws relative to "staffing" (i.e., hiring practices) of organizations that provide social services.

EMPLOYMENT REQUIREMENTS FOR FAITH-BASED ORGANIZATIONS

The issue of employment requirements for faith-based organizations is complex and contentious. To put this issue in historical perspective, Chelsea reminds us of the anti-discrimination stipulations in Title 7 of the Civil Rights Act of 1964, the 1972 amendment to this Act and subsequent court rulings.

> While the Civil Rights Act of 1964 prohibited employment discrimination based on race, color, national origin, sex, and religion, it upheld religious freedom by allowing organizations whose "purpose and character are primarily religious" an exemption to consider religion in staffing decisions. The 1972 amendment to the Civil Rights Act expanded the exemption to cover every position in a religious organization, and not only positions with religious duties.

In 1987, the US Supreme Court unanimously affirmed the religious staffing exemption for all positions in a case concerning a Mormon-run gymnasium's practice of hiring only Mormons in janitorial positions (*Corporation of the Presiding Bishop v. Amos*).

Because of the religious staffing exemption, faith-based organizations generally have the freedom to hire employees who fully embody their religious mission, and thus are best equipped to share it. Generally, courts interpret this so-called religious staffing or religious hiring freedom to mean that *the religious organization can consider the conduct, and not just stated beliefs, of job applicants, so that the religious employer is able to decide whether an applicant is sincerely committed to the religious convictions that animate the organization* (italics mine).

Note especially that the Civil Rights Act and its subsequent interpretations allow an organization to "consider the conduct and not just stated beliefs of job applicants." As Chelsea points out there is lack of clarity as to whether this stipulation will be included in forthcoming anti-discrimination laws. In her own words:

> In most sexual orientation and gender identity nondiscrimination legislation, there is not clarity about whether religious employers sued for SOGI discrimination can base their defense off Title VII's religious exemption. Essentially, will religious employers be able to define religious identity and thus employability not just by a title (Baptist, Muslim, Baha'i) but also by faith-inspired conduct (not smoking, certain expectations of sexual behavior?). May the government decide what counts as essential to true religion?

In other words, the unsettled issue, as stated by Chelsea, is whether "existing and pending federal, state, and local sexual orientation and gender identity non-discrimination laws ought to include a clarification of the religious staffing right from Title VII to continue the protection of religious staffing for faith-based organizations, *even when it extends to employee conduct*" (italics mine).

To make this need for further clarification more concrete Chelsea considers the case of a job applicant for a position in a Catholic organization.

> What will be the consequences for religious staffing practices ... if sexual orientation and gender identity become prohibited bases of job discrimination? ... [It] is unclear what will happen if a faith-based organization decides a potential employee

is religiously unsuitable because of his same-sex marriage or other conduct or relationships related to the new protected categories. For example, if the organization is Catholic and he says he is Catholic, but the organization prizes not just a declaration of Catholic belief but a lifestyle that is compatible with the teachings of the Catholic Church, including generosity toward the poor, the cherishing of life from conception onward, and marriage as a life-long union of one man and one woman. Is its decision not to hire the applicant a (legal) employment decision based on religion or an (illegal) decision based on sexual orientation?

Chelsea speculates that "The Equal Employment Opportunity Commission will likely claim the decision is an illegal act of sexual orientation discrimination." But, "Will the courts agree?" Chelsea responds to her own question:

> In general, they [the courts] have ruled that the religious staffing exemption protects religion-based employment decisions beyond the narrow and formalistic question of whether the person claims to be of the same religion as the employer, and instead have accepted that the employer has to be free to assess the authenticity of that claim. But the courts could rule the other way, narrowing the concept of "religion" when it intersects with SOGI.

But "if the courts rule the other way," Chelsea's concern is that:

> Such a formalistic religious hiring freedom will do little to enable religious organizations to maintain a robust religious identity, to constitute a community of like-minded people whose lives are witnesses to the religious commitments the organization professes to follow.

How can Chelsea's concern be ameliorated? She suggests two possible "solutions."

> One solution: a religious organization exemption can be added. The language for the exemption, and the accompanying non-retaliation language, can be taken directly from the Employment Nondiscrimination Act (ENDA) bill that the US Senate adopted in November, 2013 (the House never took up the bill). Another solution: the addition of some words of clarification to Title VII. Those words would explain that the "religion" that religious employers are legally free to consider is more than a formalism but instead encompasses not only religious beliefs but also conduct standards rooted in those religious beliefs.

> Then religious employers who have religion-based employment policies and consistently apply them will continue to be free to build and safeguard staffs that reflect and embody the religious convictions that the organizations desire to honor.

Therefore, the bottom line for Chelsea is that "If I had to pick one area to press for accommodations for religious institutions in SOGI nondiscrimination laws, it would be this: the capacity of faith-based nonprofits who hold themselves out as explicitly religious to be able to continue to select employees who embody, in belief and practice, the religious precepts (including conduct standards) that shape their institutional DNA."

To add fuel to the controversy, Chelsea suggests that "mission-centric employment practices are essential to most organizations, not just religious ones," giving the examples of PETA and Planned Parenthood.

> Many secular employers require that their employees *adhere to conduct* aligned with their missions. For example, PETA (People for the Ethical Treatment of Animals) lists right on their job descriptions that a requirement of employment is "adherence to a healthy vegan lifestyle." It is easy to understand why it would undercut the organization's mission for a PETA employee to be seen at the local Burger King enjoying a Whopper, even when she is off the clock. Likewise, Planned Parenthood job descriptions specify that applicants must demonstrate "commitment to the goals and mission of Planned Parenthood." This would, most certainly limit a Planned Parenthood employee's ability to attend pro-life rallies on her own time, because this conduct would be inconsistent with the mission of her employer.
>
> In America, we see a diverse and differentiated spectrum of civil society organizations, many whose missions are often directly at odds with one another. Faith-based organizations need the continued protection to be able to hire individuals who embody not just the specific service-sector mission of the organization, but the faith-centric aspects of the mission as well.

Kathryn is strongly opposed to Chelsea's proposal that faith-based nonprofits who hold themselves out as explicitly religious . . . [should] be able to continue to select employees who embody, in belief and practice, the religious precepts (including conduct standards) that shape their institutional DNA." She asserts that "not only is there not a religious freedom right that would exempt religious for-profit or non-profit corporations from nondiscrimination laws, but faith-based discrimination is antithetical to the teachings of Scripture."

Relative to the teachings of Scripture, Kathryn asserts that "When Jesus says, whatever you did not do for the least of these, you did not do for me, he didn't include the caveat, 'unless the least of these are LGBT, then you're free to discriminate without guilt.'"

Going back to the beginning of this conversation, Kathryn repeats her "ideal" for a "democratic, pluralistic society" that "all members of that society must be given the equal opportunity to participate in society." Therefore, to deny LGBT persons equal access to employment possibilities at faith-based organizations wanting a "religious exemption denies them access to a large swath of public life."

Chelsea and Kathryn seem to be at an impasse relative to whether religious organizations should ever be granted exemptions to anti-discrimination laws regarding hiring practices. In that light, about halfway through their conversation, I suggested to both of them that they explore the possibility that the stipulations in the federal Religious Freedom Restoration Act (RFRA) could overcome the stalemate by finding a way to create a proper balance between protecting religious freedom and protecting LGBT rights when it comes to hiring practices. What follows reports on the results of that exploration.

RFRA AS A POSSIBLE MEANS FOR BALANCING RELIGIOUS FREEDOM AND LGBT RIGHTS RELATIVE TO HIRING PRACTICES

Chelsea appeals to the federal Religious Freedom Restoration Act (RFRA) as providing "a proper balancing test for weighing the rights of religious actors vs. the government's interests." The criteria for this "strict scrutiny" test are threefold, described by Chelsea as follows:

> The federal RFRA establishes the strict scrutiny test—if a generally applicable law "substantially burdens" one's free exercise of religion, only the existence of the government's "compelling interest" can allow the burdening of the claimant's religious freedom. In addition, the government's compelling interest has to be fulfilled in the "least restrictive means" possible.

Chelsea asserts that the purpose of the federal RFRA and the "many states enacted RFRAs" is to ensure that "the government has a sufficient reason before it can curtail religious exercise."

Kathryn also appeals to RFRAs as a means for "balancing religious freedom with the rights of others not to have their lives and well-being harmed by the religious practices of another." She provides a number of helpful examples, ranging from the obvious to the more debatable (none of which deal with hiring practices, to which we will eventually return).

> *Human Sacrifice:* Even if human sacrifice is a central tenet of your faith, that does not exempt you from laws against murder .... The government has a compelling interest in preventing its citizens from murdering each other, so even though a law against murder substantially burdens our erstwhile human sacrificer's exercise of religion, the government can prevent human sacrifice.
>
> *Jehovah's Witnesses:* The Supreme Court found that a religious belief in proselytization via the distribution of religious literature did not exempt Jehovah's Witnesses from child labor laws. Their right to practice their religion did not extend to a right to allow small children to endanger themselves by selling newspapers on the street in violation of child labor laws.
>
> *Amish:* The Amish have the religious freedom right to exempt their children from compulsory attendance laws after eighth grade, not because religious freedom automatically overrules compulsory attendance, but rather because in the balancing act between religious freedom and the well-being of others, the courts found that an eighth-grade education did not harm Amish children's ability to be fully functioning productive members of society.
>
> *Hobby Lobby:* In the Hobby Lobby case, the Supreme Court concluded that the Obamacare contraceptive mandate substantially burdened free exercise of religion without meeting the compelling government interest test.
>
> *Bob Jones University and University Religious Clubs:* "The Supreme Court has found, both the pre-RFRA *Bob Jones University v. United States* (whether Bob Jones University could receive tax exempt status and maintain racially discriminatory policies) and the post-RFRA *Christian Legal Society v. Martinez* (whether a public university's policies requiring recognized student clubs be open to all students infringed on a Christian club's religious freedom), that non-discrimination laws don't violate religious freedom. In other words, the government has a compelling interest in preventing discrimination, even if those non-discrimination policies substantially burden the exercise of religion.
>
> *Fair Housing Act and Gender Equity Laws:* [The criterion that] the government has a compelling interest in preventing discrimination, even if those non-discrimination policies

substantially burden the exercise of religion . . . is why the Fair Housing Act prohibition on race-based housing discrimination is constitutional, even if it infringes on the landlord's sincerely held religious belief that renting to an interracial couple would be participating in the couple's sinful relationship. It's also why religious colleges that receive federal funds can't opt out of Title IX gender equity rules, regardless of their beliefs about the roles of women.

So, I believe it is fair to say that both Chelsea and Kathryn agree that, in certain cases, RFRAs can be appropriate for seeking a proper balance between protecting religious freedom and the rights of persons who may be harmed by an unbounded exercise of religious freedom. But, relative to hiring practices, they disagree strongly about whether RFRAs can justify exemptions to SOGI anti-discrimination laws. I will proceed by first noting in some detail Chelsea's arguments for such exemptions relative to hiring practices in light of RFRA stipulations (italics mine, for later reference).

> A religious institution must be able to employ people who fully embody its religious mission and doctrinal practices. The ability of a religious organization to hire based on faith is central to its ability to exercise its religion without substantial burden. . . .
>
> I would argue that under a RFRA balancing inquiry, it is clear that a religious organization's religious practices are substantially burdened if they are forced to hire employees who are engaging in conduct or expressions that are in direct conflict with the doctrinal beliefs and practices of the faith-based institution. . . . I believe it is clear that there is harm being done to the faith-based organization when it is not allowed to hire employees aligned with its faith-shaped mission and practices. Along the same lines, there would be harm done to an organization like Believe Out Loud, a faith-based organization "that empowers Christians to work for lesbian, gay, bisexual, transgender, and queer (LGBTQ) equality" if they were not allowed to staff according to their faith-based mission and were expected to hire all Christians indiscriminately, including those whose religious beliefs did not support same-sex relationships or gender variant identity expressions.
>
> The next inquiry is whether there is a compelling interest in passing a SOGI employment nondiscrimination act. I believe that a case can be made that there is a compelling interest to *end workplace discrimination in the secular and governmental spheres for members of the LGBT community.*

The final inquiry in a RFRA balancing test is whether the law is achieving its compelling interest through the "least restrictive means" necessary.... *Providing a clarification that religious employers are still allowed to hire based on faith would not impinge on the capacity of LGBT people to be protected from adverse actions in the vast majority of workplaces in this country.* In fact, if the argument is that LGBT people suffer higher levels of unemployment now because they are not protected from discrimination by law, then passing such a SOGI employment nondiscrimination act with a properly tailored provision for religious organizations to hire based on religion would *still achieve the goal of protecting LGBT workers from baseless discrimination by secular and governmental employers.* And such a provision could be tailored in a way as to prevent any potential abuse: a religious employer could be required to certify that it is a religious organization that considers religion in hiring and that it would substantially burden its religious exercise if the religious organization was mandated to exercise employment practices contrary to its religious precepts and practices. This certification process could be subject to governmental inquiry as to ensure that employers were not merely claiming a pre-textual reason for SOGI discrimination, as opposed to a sincerely held and consistently practiced religious reason.

Thus, I believe that SOGI accommodations are justified for religious organizations in an employment context under a strict scrutiny balancing inquiry. Specifically, I believe that such an accommodation accomplishes beautifully the "least restrictive means" part of the test, achieving both the protection of the religious exercise of faith-based organizations and the compelling interest of preventing LGBT workplace discrimination, simultaneously. Win-win might not be the right expression. After all, some staunch LGBT advocates would rather see no religious accommodations under any circumstance. And some staunch religious leaders would rather see SOGI laws never pass under any circumstance. But balancing interests is not a zero-sum game. In fact, it isn't a game at all. Real injustices, both for LGBT people and for the religious freedom of faith-based organizations, are on the line. This may be a perfect solution to no one. But it is, or at least should be, a possible, livable solution for everyone.

Our month of electronic conversation came to a close before Kathryn was able to give a full-blown response to Chelsea's argument that RFRA stipulations allow for exemptions to SOGI anti-discrimination laws relative to hiring practices for faith-based organizations. I will, however, note one strong disagreement expressed by Kathryn, to be followed by my own personal reflections (starting with the portions of Chelsea's argument that I italicized above), hoping that all of this will provide a good starting point for ongoing conversations.

Kathryn expresses the objection that Chelsea has not adequately presented evidence that requiring faith-based organizations to abide by anti-discrimination laws regarding hiring practices will "harm" those organizations, while there is considerable evidence that LGBT persons are "harmed" by discriminatory hiring practices and other forms of discrimination against LGBT persons.

> The final question I want to address is this. Where is the harm? Ms. Langston repeatedly asserts that without laws legalizing faith-based discrimination, people of faith will be harmed. She does not, however, demonstrate any concrete examples of harm caused by banning faith-based discrimination. If she is going to assert that not being allowed to discriminate harms the practice of religion, she needs to provide some sort of evidence that the harm not only exists, she needs to explain why that harm is any different than the harm caused by prohibitions on race-based discrimination. Merely asserting it does not make it so.
>
> On the other hand, we can easily see where the harm is if faith-based discrimination against LGBT people is permitted. *People can lose their jobs or be unable to find one*, they can be refused service in restaurants and stores and their access to social services that are covered by faith-based organizations in their communities will be cut off. For LGBT young people who are expelled from faith-based colleges because of who they are, they are out tens of thousands of dollars and have the expulsion as a black mark on their record that can negatively affect their ability to transfer to a new institution and to pass background checks in the future. Those are very real harms. (Italics mine.)
>
> Now, I want to be clear, I do not believe that Ms. Langston thinks that LGBT people should end up on the streets because they are unable to find work. She seems to be genuinely concerned for the well-being of LGBT people. That said, if you are proposing a faith-based discrimination framework that is going to harm LGBT people and make it difficult for them to work and support themselves, it's necessary to demonstrate that failure to do so will bring actual harm to faith-based organizations.
>
> And so I end with that final question. Where is the harm?

Once again, there appears to be no resolution of the disagreement about whether there are any circumstances under which religious organizations should be granted "religious exemptions" to SOGI anti-discrimination laws. I wonder if some movement toward resolution may be possible if consideration is given to a distinction I will now propose.

MICRO-PLURALISM OR MACRO-PLURALISM REGARDING HIRING PRACTICES

Since this book is essentially a journalistic effort (of sorts) where I report on the differing views of conversation partners who disagree about contentious LGBT issues, I have tried to avoid personal commentary that would favor one side or the other relative to any given issue. And I will continue to do so. (The reader can decide whether or not I have been successful.) But for this thorny issue of hiring practices that significantly impact LGBT persons, I will now share some personal reflections about the disagreements between Chelsea and Kathryn regarding such hiring practices that could be interpreted as "taking sides." But it is not my intention to "take sides." Rather, my intention is to provide a perspective that could inform ongoing conversations about the disagreements between Chelsea and Kathryn that could also have implications for other aspects of our pluralistic society.

I grant the obvious fact that we Americans live in a pluralistic society relative to worldviews and ways to live out our respective worldviews. I also embrace the ideal expressed by Kathryn that all persons should *have equal opportunity to participate in American society.* But it is far from clear, at least to me, what such "equal participation" means. As I struggle with that issue, I am thinking about a possible distinction between "micro-pluralism" and "macro-pluralism" when it comes to hiring practices for all organizations, faith-based or secular. Since I have never read or heard anyone use such words, this will take some explanation.

By "micro-pluralism" relative to organizational hiring practices or membership requirements I mean an approach that adheres to the requirement that each and every organization should have an employee pool or membership that reflects its pluralistic culture. Here are two examples.

Relative to membership requirements in student clubs at institutions of higher education that warrant institutional sanction and support, a micro-pluralist approach would require that to gain institutional sanction and support, a "Christian club" would have to open its membership to interested students having other religious or secular worldview commitments. In similar fashion, this micro-pluralist approach would suggest that an organization taking a stance for or against same-sex marriage would have to employ persons who disagree with that stance.

In contrast, a "macro-pluralist" approach relative to hiring practices or membership requirements would take the position that it is acceptable for individual organizations to limit its membership or employment pool to those who share its particular worldview commitments, provided "society as a whole" encourages and supports enough diversity among such organizations to insure (1) that every citizen has an equal opportunity to participate in society by associating with available organizations that embrace his/her particular worldview; and (2) that, when it comes to services provided to citizens, there is sufficient number of diverse organizations providing a particular service to insure that every citizen has adequate access to the service. Going back to my first example above, this means that an institution of higher education should encourage, sanction, and support a diversity of student clubs, with each club allowed to stipulate membership requirements that reflects its particular worldview commitment, without favoring any particular club (what some have called "providing an "even playing field"). As I have suggested elsewhere,[1] I would add the unusual stipulation that, in order to avoid the potential "tribalism" that would be an abuse of such a micro-pluralist approach, institutional sanction and support would be granted to a given club only if that club agreed to orchestrate campus "forums for conversation" with other clubs holding different worldview commitments so that students holding to differing world views can adequately understand each other and learn from each other (a seemingly incontrovertible goal for an institution of higher education).

Relative to my second example, a macro-pluralist approach would allow organizations who take differing stances on same-sex marriage to limit their employee pool to those who share their stance, provided that when "religious employers are . . . allowed to hire based on faith, . . . [this] would not impinge on the capacity of LGBT people to be protected from adverse actions in the vast majority of workplaces in this country" (quoting Chelsea, as italicized above), and provided that granting such hiring exemptions to faith-based organizations would not deprive any LGBT person from the opportunity to obtain that service from an organization of his/her choice that is not faith-based.

From Chelsea's position, quoted at length above, which appears to me to be sympathetic to what I have called a "macro-pluralist" approach to hiring practices, I surmise that Chelsea would argue that (1) there are a sufficient number of work opportunities for members of the LGBT community in the "secular and governmental spheres" to provide ample space for participation of LGBT persons in our society in the form of employment;

---

1. Heie, "Values," 131–43.

(2) relative to any particular service needed by citizens, there is sufficient diversity in organizations providing social services to insure that every citizen has the opportunity to obtain that service from an organization of his/her choice. Therefore, if an RFRA type "strict scrutiny" test is passed, then an "exemption" to SOGI anti-discrimination laws relative to hiring practices should be granted.

But I believe it is also fair to surmise that Kathryn, who appears to embrace the "micro-pluralist" approach, at least relative to my hiring practices example, strongly objects to Chelsea's position since the employment opportunities it provides for LGBT persons are a far cry from the ideal that all persons should have *equal opportunity* to participate in American society.

In any case, it is my hope that the distinction I suggest between micro-pluralist and macro-pluralist approaches to hiring practices does not just muddy the waters but can be a springboard for ongoing conversations about the complex and contentious issue of hiring practices for organizations having a diversity of worldview commitments.

A LINGERING QUESTION: GOVERNMENT FUNDING OF FAITH-BASED ORGANIZATIONS

A thorny question that was raised earlier but never addressed asked about the appropriate nature of participation in society for those non-LGBT persons and their organizations who, based on their religious convictions, wish to provide social services that contribute to society but oppose expressions of sexual intimacy for same-sex couples. A sub-set of this question pertains to the issue of whether government should provide funding for such faith-based organizations, a question to which we now turn.

One way in which government currently funds faith-based organizations is by providing them tax-exempt status. Kathryn asserts that such tax-exemptions are appropriate only for "places of worship."

> With the exception of churches, synagogues, mosques, temples, and other places of worship, the regulation of which would violate the free exercise clause, non-profits should not be exempt from non-discrimination rules. We grant tax exempt status to non-profit entities because those entities *exist to serve the public interest* (italics mine).

Kathryn supports her position by quoting from the Supreme Court decision in *Bob Jones University v. United States*, a portion of which reads as follows:

> Charitable exemptions are justified on the basis that the exempt entity *confers a public benefit*—a benefit which the society or the community may not itself choose or be able to provide, or which supplements and advances the work of public institutions already supported by tax revenues. History buttresses logic to make clear that, to warrant exemption under § 501(c)(3), an institution must fall within a category specified in that section and must *demonstrably serve and be in harmony with the public interest*. (Italics mine.)

Kathryn adds that when tax-exemptions are given to institutions that discriminate against LGBT people, "it is forcing LGBT people to subsidize an organization from which they are barred from participating."

> To allow non-profit organizations to discriminate is to force all taxpayers, regardless of religion, to contribute to a discriminatory institution. This is more than mere religious freedom, it is the imposition of a particular religion on the populous as a whole, and indeed is forcing LGBT people to subsidize an organization from which they are barred from participating.

Chelsea has two responses to Kathryn's position on tax-exempt status for faith-based organizations. First, she points out that "Tax-exempt status does not confer governmental agreement on all the positions an organization makes," noting a number of examples:

> [T]ax-exempt status is given to groups who support gun control and those who support gun ownership, to those who still oppose abortion forty-two years after *Roe v. Wade* and to those who advocate for a woman's right to choose. Tax-exempt status does not confer governmental agreement on all the positions an organization makes.
>
> Vegetarian societies are not going to lose their tax-exempt status because they force meat-eaters to "subsidize an organization from which they are barred from participating." Likewise, LGBT advocacy groups are not going to lose their tax-exempt status because they bar from employment and/or participation individuals who affirm a different paradigm of human sexuality and human flourishing, nor should they.

Chelsea also asserts that it is "essential that faith-based organizations show their societal contributions." This comports with Kathryn's assertions (italicized above) that tax-exemptions should be reserved for organizations that "confer a public benefit" and "exist to serve the public interest."

While asserting that "Everyone eligible should be able to get respectful services," Chelsea asks a probing question: "Is there room for diversity in the way each federally supported faith-based organization provides those services in exactly the same way or can and should there be diversity, given the moral differences we have?"

Chelsea's implicit answer to her own question is that there should be room for diversity in how faith-based organizations (and secular organizations for that matter) deliver "essential services"; a diversity that allows faith-based organizations to "provide services in a distinctively faith-shaped manner."

> Policymakers need help from FBOs in seeing the connection between the essential services they provide and the religious precepts that motivate that belief. Others may need help understanding that religious exemptions in SOGIs have the aim of preserving the historic freedom for organizations to act on the core tenets of their faith—not rejecting services to anyone because of their sexual orientation or gender identity, but having the freedom to provide services in a distinctively faith-shaped manner.

TOWARD A THEOLOGY OF MUTUAL RESPECT

As should be obvious by now, although Chelsea and Kathryn agree that it is important to protect both religious freedom and LGBT rights, they appear to have irreconcilable disagreements as to how to accomplish that delicate balancing act, especially in the area of hiring practices.

Therefore, it is important to address the question of how those who disagree about the nature of that balance can show "mutual respect" for one another in the midst of their disagreements. Both Kathryn and Chelsea address this prior issue.

Kathryn asserts that "if we are going to build a theology based on mutual respect, that requires both sides to actually respect each other and to discuss our differences as equals."

Kathryn adds that "It's difficult to have [such] mutual respect when one party considers the other party's very existence to be an abomination and a sin against God," elaborating on the following position taken by some faith traditions.

> Depending on the faith tradition, this language [an "orthodox sexual ethic"] means that LGBT people are irreparably broken

because of the fall, mentally ill, willful sinners deserving of the fires of hell, abominations, depraved, reprobate people who should be "fried" as in Sodom and Gomorrah, or who should be stoned.

Kathryn concludes that for such faith traditions, this is "respect in a single direction, and LGBT people are not the recipients of that respect."

Chelsea takes issue with Kathryn's apparent "broad-stroke assumptions that all who support man-woman marriage must believe that LGBT individuals are "abominations" who should be "stoned" or "fried," adding that such assumptions "demonstrate a lack of respect for the many people who hold conservative sexual views yet deeply value that lives and human dignity of their gay and transgender neighbors," noting that "many who hold the view that same-sex relationships are not biblically supported express their views with love and compassion."

Chelsea concludes that "not everyone who opposes same-sex marriage does so with the hate and venom Kathryn alluded to. They do not have to affirm conduct they believe to be outside of God's paradigm for human flourishing to be able to affirm that all people, of every sexual orientation, race, class, or identity, are children of God, beautifully and wonderfully made."

Chelsea's conclusion can be summarized in her assertion that "respect is not the same as unconditional affirmation," elaborated as follows:

> Real respect is not based on complete affirmation of each other's opinions or worldviews, for it is easy to give respect to those with whom you agree. But rather, I am seeking a respect between people who will, most probably, not come to a common understanding of what is God's best for Christian faithfulness and human sexuality.

What steps can be taken to foster such "real respect"? Chelsea asserts that "Often, leaders in faith communities do not know about the very real challenges the LGBT community faces, especially the many young people who have been turned away by their families." Therefore, such leaders "first have to be educated about the tangible harms being done to the LGBT community."

Noting that "Many Americans, especially those over fifty, haven't ever heard the personal stories of hardship that many LGBT people face," Chelsea asserts that such education must start with "listening," and this should be a two-way street.

> For a meaningful, respectful dialogue to take place, people who have disparate views of sexuality have to be willing to come

together and really listen to one another. Proximity is usually
the best antidote to misunderstanding and enmity.

The assertion that "proximity is usually the best antidote to misunderstanding and enmity" is central to the focus of this entire book. It is my hope that ongoing conversations about anti-discrimination laws precipitated by this chapter, and all the other challenging issues addressed in the other chapters, will be characterized by such proximate respectful listening to one another. I even dare to imagine, through the eyes of faith, the possibility that such ongoing respectful conversations can model commitments of Christians to the foundational values of truth, love, and Christian unity.

7

Voices from Younger Christians

I have heard it suggested a number of times that the current controversies within Christian circles about LGBT issues will fade away in the future because of a significant generation gap; the common argument being that younger Christians are more open to affirming gay marriage and, therefore, as they move into positions of influence and leadership in Christian circles, we will someday wonder what all the fuss was about.

As a reader will soon discover, our two conversation partners for this seventh round of conversation, Matthew Lee Anderson and Isaac Sharp, two members of the "younger generation" of Christians, will argue that such a simplistic prediction is unfounded. This result emerged from their three successive postings around the following Leading Question: As a member of this younger generation, how do you view the future relative to LGBT issues in American society in general and in Christian churches in particular?

A careful reading of the postings by Matthew and Isaac will reveal that they listened carefully to one another and were able to identify significant areas of agreement and identify and illuminate areas of disagreement.

AGREEMENT ON THE FOLLY OF PREDICTING THE FUTURE

Matthew observes that "Prognosticating about the shape of the world has been an inescapable feature of our culture war politics for the past thirty years." Despite that, it is his view that "Prophecy is a game that should be reserved for either fools or saints."

Isaac concurs when he asserts that one of "the two strongest points that Matthew and I consistently reached" was that "Predictive attempts are largely folly." He elaborates with the following humorous reflection:

> ... [Matthew and I] share a justifiable reluctance to offer definitive predictions about the direction that future winds may blow. Make no mistake, I—and I would be willing to bet *we*—hedge on pronouncements on the shape of things to come out of self-interest: wagering aloud is one thing, committing forecasts to print is quite another. And the Internet would, no doubt, be all too happy to oblige in one day pointing out how wrong we were.

Despite these reservations, Matthew does point to a possible benefit of "reflecting about the future" if it "forces us to attend to what are we today, and what we do now to become the people and society we want to be." He adds, "The purpose of such visions is to evaluate our lives *today*, to determine how *we* should act now in order to bring about the ends that we deem valuable and good." Isaac concurs with Matthew's desire to focus on "today," as follows:

> Matthew ... highlighted the necessity of attending more directly to the *present* state of affairs in US Christianity rather than being caught gazing either longingly or warily down the road too far—I heartily concur.

When push came to shove, however, both Matthew and Isaac did speculate on some possible future directions relative to LGBT conversations (because I asked them to do so), even if done with some "fear and trembling."

THERE IS A "GENERATION GAP," BUT ...

Isaac presents considerable sociological evidence from polls and surveys for the existence of a generation gap relative to views on same-sex marriage, about which Matthew says: "I appreciate [this work] and largely agree with [it]," especially noting that "there is little doubt these days about a 'generation gap' on matters pertaining to human sexuality." However, as will soon be seen, a disagreement emerges as to the most adequate interpretation of some of this data. We consider first the evidence that Isaac presents.

Based on the sociological data that Isaac presents in detail in his first posting, he argues that "there is obviously something to the idea of a 'generation gap' between younger American Christians and older American Christians when it comes to the 'acceptance of homosexuality.'" But, Isaac is careful to add that "this particular trend does not, by any means, tell the whole story."

Isaac then asserts that at least a portion of the rest of story is the "rise of the nones," meaning "the phenomenon of the increasing number of predominantly younger Americans who have become less religious, when defined by institutional affiliation and 'traditional' measures of religiosity."

Isaac combines these two parts of the story as follows:

> Just as there is something to the idea of a "generation gap" within American Christianity on LGBT discussions, there is also something to the fact that younger Americans are increasingly disassociating themselves from Christianity altogether. There are, it would seem, more American Christians who favor the "acceptance of homosexuality" than ever before, and younger Christians tend toward this position in higher numbers than older Christians. But . . . there are fewer and fewer younger Americans who identify as Christian.

The thorny question is whether there is any causal relationship between these two parts of the story: Is the decrease in the number of younger Americans who identify themselves as Christian caused by their acceptance of homosexuality combined with the resistance to accepting homosexuality that they find in the many Christian churches?

Matthew reads Isaac as seeing such a causal connection: "Sharp seems to indicate that the traditional account of gay marriage is causally responsible for the abandonment of traditional Christianity." Matthew calls into question such a causal connection, noting first that "Causality is notoriously difficult to identify," and providing the following counter-example.

> If the doctrinal position of traditional churches was uniquely responsible for fragmenting religious beliefs, we might expect to see rapidly expanding youth movements in progressive, gay-affirming churches. But the Episcopalian Church USA, to pick one, has hemorrhaged its membership during the same period that the "nones" have grown.

Adding that "A full analysis of why the nones *might* be a phenomenon is well beyond the purview of [this] essay," Matthew suggests that a number of "alternate explanations are readily at hand": "The fragmentation of faith in the conditions of late modernity, the exhaustion of a moralistic therapeutic deism, the consummation of a religious atmosphere that has emphasized individualism over forms, the pervasive effects of a consumeristic mind-set that hollowed out the salability of traditional religious life."

However, despite this disagreement about how to interpret the possible connection between the data relative to a "generation gap" and the "rise of the nones," Matthew and Isaac reach strong agreement as to the implications of these two sets of data for whether the present controversies about LGBT issues will "fade away," or will persist, a topic to which I now turn.

THE PRESENT LGBT CONTROVERSIES WILL NOT FADE AWAY

As already noted, Isaac asserted that the first of the "two strongest points of agreement" [with Matthew] was that "predictive attempts are largely folly." But then, pressed by me to speculate, the second strong point of agreement that emerges is, in Isaac's words, "the unlikelihood of the 'fading of the present controversies.'" Isaac elaborates as follows:

> We doubt the efficacy of prognostication but, when pressed, we both put our chips down on the side of the probability of ongoing and, indeed, rancorous debate.

What are the reasons given for speculating that the current rancorous debate will not subside? Matthew suggests a number of reasons. First, a sociological reason:

> ... socially, many millennial evangelicals who have not changed their minds already are vastly more acquainted with the arguments for and against gay marriage than they were five years ago, and have been quickly growing accustomed to the pressures that come from being in a minority. Why should we expect those who have survived the bombardment of the past five years with their beliefs intact to change their mind in the future? All this provides some reason to question the narrative that the "generation gap" will be wide enough to avoid serious divisions and disputes within the conservative Christian world.

Matthew also presents a theological reason in terms of what he calls an "architectural doctrine of the Christian faith."

Indeed, it seems to me there are good reasons to think that more conservative millennials will continue to hold to traditional views than people might think. The gender-binary at the heart of marriage is an 'architectural doctrine' of the Christian faith: it permeates the whole of Scripture, stands beneath the traditional naming of God as Father, is necessary for explaining Christ's relationship to the church, and generates an indispensable role for Mary in salvation history. Excising the doctrine would be nearer to a theological heart transplant than cosmetic surgery.

We will seek to further unpack this "architectural doctrine" later. In the meantime, it suffices to note that Isaac finds Matthew's reasons "convincing": "Matthew convincingly suggested that it seems likely that the millennials currently holding onto a more traditional sexual ethic will continue to argue their position all the more fervently."

A third possible reason why the current debate will probably persist is based on an unusual fact that Isaac points out relative to the "ages" of the twenty-one "conversation partners" who are contributing to this eCircle: "Without exception, every previous sub-topic of conversation in this series has (ahem) a 'more senior' author presenting the more 'progressive' line of reasoning and a younger author articulating the more traditionally 'conservative' position."

Noting, accurately, that my conversation partners were "clearly chosen with the intention of having a discussion between people with opposing perspectives," Isaac suggests that "the fact that they have consistently diverged along the lines of seniority is, at the very least, intriguing if not ironic." Reflecting on this unusual age disparity, Matthew suggests that this may provide some partial evidence that "conservatives . . . [on LGBT issues] are not going away anytime soon."[1]

---

1. A point of clarification that may call into question this third reason why the LGBT controversies will not fade away consists of the following brief glimpse into some of the behind the scenes challenges I faced in assembling my twenty-one conversation partners (which Isaac and Matthew had no way of knowing). During a three-month period in the first half of 2015 when I spent a significant portion of each day recruiting conversation partners for my eCircle, I invited forty-eight persons to be conversation partners, with twenty-one accepting my invitation. The most interesting pattern that I found was that I had the greatest difficulty finding "traditionalists" able or willing to accept my invitations. The specific result that is pertinent to my intended point of clarification is that for a number of my nine sub-topics, my first invitees to present a "traditional" perspective were senior scholars who had significant name recognition and reputations for presenting strong cases for traditional positions. Although they generally applauded my eCircle project, all of these senior scholars declined my invitations, primarily citing their busyness with other commitments. But, they were very helpful in suggesting alternatives, generally younger scholars, to take their places in my

Isaac adds a final "reason" (with which Matthew concurs) why the current rancor will not subside in terms of the "power dynamics within conservative Christian institutions," which he sees as "another contributing factor in the possibility of future strife." We now turn to this important sub-theme.

THE CHANGING LANDSCAPE FOR ONGOING CONTROVERSY

Accepting my invitation to speculate, Isaac does so based on "current trends . . . in combination with personal, admittedly anecdotal, interactions with members of 'my generation.'" He foresees two "possible outcomes with respect to the 'present controversies.'"

> 1. The more "conservative" Christian institutions in the US—be they congregations, denominations, Christian colleges or other religious organizations—will continue to be the last major sites of this particular battle in the on-again-off-again culture war and, partially in response, a younger generation of LGBT persons and their friends will continue to disassociate themselves with Christianity bit by bit over time leaving leadership in the hands of those who take a more "traditional" line.

Isaac suggests that "This situation would . . . be most probable if the 'rise of the millennial nones' becomes the most dominant trend in the US religious landscape," adding that:

> The "present controversies" would, in this hypothetical situation, continue but would proceed largely at the borders of US Christianity rather than internally. In this case, we would have increasingly smaller and older Christian institutions that have clarified that they will continue to uphold the "traditional" teachings on sexuality and will, then, continue the debate as a minority position in a broader culture that disagrees.

However, Isaac foresees a second possible outcome.

> 2. As a younger generation of Christians becomes more and more accepting of LGBT persons—or are indeed themselves LGBT—the nature of the "present controversies" will become increasingly localized and, at times, more intense. Particularly when it comes to diverging from institutional leadership that supports a "traditional" sexual ethic.

---

roster of conversation partners. And that is what eventually happened, which explains at least some of the age disparity pointed out by Isaac.

Isaac suggests that "This scenario would . . . be most possible if the upward trend in the 'acceptance of homosexuality' by younger Christians outweighs the rise of continued institutional religious disassociation," adding that "The 'present controversies' may, in this case, slowly move from the center stage position they now hold to more particular sites of contestation, but they show little sign of waning."

Matthew resonates particularly with Isaac's first scenario, stating that:

> Sharp has cleanly articulated a point I was aiming at but said less elegantly. His summation that we will have "increasingly smaller and older Christian institutions that have clarified that they will continue to uphold the 'traditional' teachings on sexuality and will . . . continue the debate as a minority position in a broader culture that disagrees" distills my own thought about the likely future as effectively and efficiently as anything I have read.

Elaborating further, Matthew speculates that "Ongoing contestation, but on a plane in which conservative institutions have diminished presence and power, is the best bet about this subject I know."

Matthew then expresses concern as to whether these "increasingly smaller and older Christian institutions," when engaging with those who disagree with them about LGBT issues, can "retain . . . [their] convictions" without becoming "belligerently hostile."

> Among the many dangers for the church, and for society, that lie before us is the prospect of a conservative Christianity that retains its convictions with a more belligerently hostile, anti-modern edge than it even now has.

Matthew adds that "Confidently retaining convictions in the face of disagreement is the mark of a mature mind:[2] whether evangelicals will be able to arrive there remains to be seen" (much more about that later).

A major force that Matthew sees as contributing to smaller and older Christian institutions continuing to hold to traditional teachings on sexuality is that "advancement within conservative institutions depends upon being a traditionalist."

> While the many millennial evangelicals have become affirming, advancement within conservative institutions depends upon

---

2. Matthew's reference to a "mark of mature mind" resonated with a definition of "religious maturity" proposed by Ian Barbour: "It is by no means easy to hold beliefs for which you would be willing to die, and yet to remain open to new insights; but it is precisely such a combination of commitment and inquiry that constitutes religious maturity." Barbour, *Myths*, 138.

being a traditionalist. That will ensure institutional continuity for far longer than people might expect, even if the size of those institutions decreases.

At this point an extremely important question emerges: Will it be possible for a given Christian institution to embrace members who disagree about sexuality issues? In other words, can members of a given Christian institution "agree to disagree"? As will be reported in a later section of this chapter, both Matthew and Isaac question whether this will be possible, at least in the long run.

For the time being, one of the major reasons why "agreeing to disagree" may not be possible within a given Christian institution is because of strong disagreements about "limits on Christian diversity" and "limits on Christian orthodoxy." It is with respect to such limits that Isaac and Matthew have some significant disagreements, as we will now see.

THE LEGITIMATE RANGE OF POSSIBILITIES FOR CHRISTIAN THEOLOGY

It is now important to get the most fundamental disagreement between Isaac and Matthew out on the table. A disagreement that, as Isaac says, reflects "our divergent understandings of the legitimate range of possibilities for Christian theology." Isaac's statement of "our most fundamental disagreement" is:

> I articulated a hope that Christianity will become increasingly more open to theological positions that affirm the moral legitimacy of same-gendered sexual relationships. Matthew thinks that any such position is, in fact, an inherent theological impossibility within the bounds of Christianity. A Christian ethic that does not maintain a strict gender binary as requisite for marriage is, in his view, a contradiction in terms due to its position as "an architectural doctrine," the removal of which amounts to "a theological heart transplant."

What follows is my attempt to sort through this fundamental disagreement, drawing on the various postings from Isaac and Matthew.

THE REALITY OF CHRISTIAN DIVERSITY

Isaac observes that "Christianity, from its inception, has included a fairly wide range of theological interpretations," adding his "suggestion" that

"Catholicism, Eastern Orthodoxy, as well as the various and diverse range of Protestant denominations, all fall within the bounds of Christianity 'proper'" (while acknowledging that not all Christians will agree with his suggestion).

Given that empirical claim about the reality of Christian diversity, Isaac asserts that "The possibility of future conversation [about theological disagreements] will, I think, depend on the ability to acknowledge the reality of historic and present Christian diversity."

THE LIMITS OF CHRISTIAN DIVERSITY AND ORTHODOXY

But Isaac is not suggesting that there are no limits to the legitimacy of Christian diversity. The debatable issue is where to draw such limits, as revealed by his further reflections.

> Are there outer limits to the possibilities of diversity on theological and ethical positions still classifiable as within the realm of the Christian tradition?
> Probably.
> But I don't think that differences of opinion on, for instance, the legitimate possibilities of the gender of one's spouse put us very near the boundaries.
> I personally believe that a lot of Christians are woefully wrong about any number of things—double-predestination Calvinists, for instance. But being wrong and being "beyond the pale" are, in my humble opinion, two decidedly different things.

Here is the heart of the disagreement with Matthew. Whereas Isaac believes that "the legitimate possibilities of the gender of one's spouse" does not put Christians "near the boundaries" for legitimate Christian diversity (and, hence acceptable Christian orthodoxy), Matthew believes that allowing for same-sex marriage crosses that boundary.

Matthew acknowledges that to defend this assertion goes beyond what is possible in this current conversation (which I hope will be a springboard for ongoing conversations). He hints at his argument by suggesting that belief in the legitimacy of same-sex marriage is incoherent with "traditional orthodox formulations of God's identity," as revealed by the following excerpts from his postings:

> My concern about holding together gay marriage with traditional orthodoxy is a *doctrinal* one: it is about the way in which various intellectual positions hang together, or don't . . . .

> The question ... is whether ... "theologically traditional" organizations are internally coherent, and whether gay marriage itself has any substantive bearing on how the church speaks of and understands God, such that to affirm gay marriage implicitly—even if the advocates do not themselves recognize it immediately—commits one to doctrinal positions that depart from traditionally orthodox formulations of God's identity.
>
> These connections are elusive, and need far more work to unpack them than I could possibly provide here. But they are the kind of structural ties that I was alluding to in describing marriage as an 'architectural doctrine.' ... Showing marriage's proximity to the doctrine of God is one way to unpack that claim, and to explain *why* those who affirm gay marriage are simply incoherent in their attempt to affirm traditional views of the Trinity.

So, Isaac and Matthew are at an impasse as to whether the affirmation of gay marriage takes one "beyond the pale" of legitimate Christian theology. Therefore, the question that must now be addressed is how Christians, like Isaac and Matthew, who have such a fundamental disagreement as to what is an acceptable Christian belief about gay marriage, or any other contentious issue, should engage or disengage one another. When is "separation" called for and when can we "agree to disagree" while continuing to fellowship together as professing Christians despite such a fundamental disagreement?

WHEN IS "SEPARATION" OF PROFESSING CHRISTIANS CALLED FOR?

Isaac asserts that "separation" from other Christians who you believe have crossed the boundaries of legitimate Christian theology is warranted at both the "individual" and "institutional" level, citing the Protestant Reformation as one example of "justifiable separation."

> I do indeed think that there are points "at which separation is justified, at least among individuals." I, furthermore, believe that *institutional separation* is, in fact, justified in some cases. Though I dearly love my Catholic brothers and sisters and strive to learn from them as much as I can, as a Protestant I think that the Reformation was, for instance, one such example of "justifiable separation."

As a personal example of what Isaac believes to be "justifiable separation" at the "individual" level, Isaac first expresses his "hope that all iterations of

Christianity, both in the US and abroad, will eventually be able to come to a place where they can articulate an LGBT-affirming sexual ethic." Isaac then adds that for him to "personally identify with institutions that cannot [affirm an LGBT-affirming Christian ethic] would, at this point, be a profound violation of my own conscience."

In response to this personal example from Isaac, Matthew raises a question about Isaac's "conviction that he could not, in good conscience, align with an institution that refused to affirm gay unions in the way he deems fit."

> It simply strikes me as interesting that Sharp goes all the way by suggesting that he can only align in affirming churches rather than opening himself to aligning in churches that attempted to maintain both positions.

Isaac's response to Matthew's expression of concern is:

> My conscience indeed dictates that I can no longer personally associate with institutions in which my LGBTQ Christian brothers and sisters cannot participate as fully as I can. But I possess neither the desire nor the ability to say that these kinds of institutions are, therefore, excommunicated from the wide stream of Christian tradition. To be able to personally engage in ongoing dialogue with these institutions and their representatives will, however, depend on whether or not they can say the same thing about me.

Note carefully that Isaac is saying that although he believes that being true to his conscience dictates that he not associate with institutions that limit the participation of LGBT Christians, he does not believe that these institutions should be *excommunicated* from the Christian tradition.

But "excommunication" is just one of two extremes that Isaac wishes to avoid. The other is "irreconcilable schism."

> I do hope that Christians can delicately navigate the "present controversies" by avoiding the extremities of attempts to effectively excommunicate those viewed as heretical on the one hand, and an irreconcilable schism on the other.

Having reported on Isaac's take on "separation" and his desire to avoid two "extremes," Matthew asks why these extremes should be avoided.

> I wonder why Sharp thinks that these "extremities" are so bad. We tend to assume that because of the New Testament's obvious emphasis on unity that it should be maintained at all costs.

But, the church has always had to draw sharp doctrinal lines, if only for the sake of not confusing the world on the nature and shape of its own witness to the truth. Certainly something is lost within the possibilities that Sharp lays out: but might not something also be gained? And if not, might not division be demanded of us anyway sometimes?

If we focus on the issue of same-sex marriage, my summary, then, of a fundamental disagreement between Isaac and Matthew is that Isaac believes that affirming same-sex marriage does not take one beyond the bounds of acceptable Christian orthodoxy while Matthew believes it transgresses that boundary.

Of course, that disagreement is decisive for answering the question of whether Christians will be able to "agree to disagree" about same-sex marriage. For theological reasons, as outlined above, Matthew would answer "no," arguing that "separation" is called for. Interestingly, both Matthew and Isaac answer "no," as reported below.

CAN'T WE JUST "AGREE TO DISAGREE" ABOUT SAME-SEX MARRIAGE?

In 1992, Rodney King, the Los Angeles taxi driver who was beaten up by four LA police officers after a high speed auto chase, famously asked "Can we all get along?" Similarly, we ask whether Christians on both sides of LGBT issues can "agree to disagree" without separating into warring factions.

Both Isaac and Matthew see little hope for individual Christian "institutions, denominations or church congregations" to "agree to disagree" about same-sex marriage, at least in the long run. As Isaac puts it:

> I think that, like our convergence around the projection that the "present controversies" will not soon "fade away," Matthew and I are in agreement on another aspect of the broader future outlook for the shape of these debates within various iterations of US Christianity. When he suggests, then, that, "I suspect the 'generation gap' will not be wide enough to avoid the ongoing balkanization and fragmentation of the Protestant world," I am afraid that he is absolutely right on this one. Like Matthew, I have a hard time imagining, for instance, that it will ultimately be "feasible for institutions to somehow leave room for both positions." I don't foresee any individual denomination or congregation escaping this with the "agree to disagree" approach in place for the long haul.

Similarly, Matthew points to the problem of persons on either side of the debate questioning the motives of those who disagree with them.

> It is possible . . . that many LGBT activists will look at efforts by conservatives to be more welcoming and hospitable as a pretense, an attempt to "put a smile on hate"—as one phrase sums up the skepticism. Similarly, conservatives may treat "agreeing to disagree" as a halfway house toward full inclusion and the stigmatization within the church of conservative opinions.

The primary reason for this pessimism may be the nature of the dynamics of leadership within institutionalized Christianity pointed to previously. Consistent with his concern that affirming same-sex marriage crosses the boundary of Christian orthodoxy, Matthew questions whether Christian institutions can allow its members to "agree to disagree" while still remaining "faithful."

> The question, then, is whether it is feasible for institutions to somehow leave room for both positions [conservative and progressive]. Whether it would work, pragmatically, is dubious—but would it still be faithful? The question is pertinent to both sides of this dispute. Should those who are progressive rest content worshiping next to those they think are papering over their bigotry and hatred with religious dogmas? Or vice versa?

I will soon ask "faithful to what"?

Isaac and Matthew are both skeptical of whether "conservative and progressive Christians" who disagree about LGBT issues can maintain "close fellowship" within Christian institutions. As Isaac puts it:

> Matthew and I both agree that it will be increasingly difficult for particular institutions—colleges, denominations, non-profit organizations, etc.—to maintain close fellowship *within* their ranks across the "affirming" and "non-affirming" lines. *In-house* conversation across these divisions might possibly, I think, continue in some of these spaces for a short while longer—and I know some brave congregations that are trying. But I think that Matthew and I are also in agreement on the likelihood that this possibility will not last indefinitely.

Isaac also wonders about the viability of "meaningful conversations" between Christian institutions that take opposing stances on LGBT issues or between individual Christians "affiliated with opposing institutions."

> As these groups [colleges, denominations, non-profit organizations] are forced to make their institutional positions clear, individual Christians will affiliate or dis-affiliate with these institutions based on their personal interpretations of the ethical demands of their faith. The real question, I humbly submit, will be whether or not the two "sides" will be able to continue any meaningful conversation across institutional lines—or for that matter between individuals affiliated with opposing institutions.

An important addendum to the skepticism of both Isaac and Matthew regarding the possibility for those embedded within the "institutions" of Christianity "agreeing to disagree" about LGBT issues is the possibility, hinted at by Isaac, that there may be more room to talk about a diversity of perspectives outside of these institutions.

> ... [W]hile individual Christian institutions will likely be hard pressed to sustain a wide diversity of perspectives on these questions, I like to imagine that the broader Christian tradition might. If historical precedent is any indication, there have been divisions both as bitter and as polarizing as these throughout Christian history and many of *the warring factions have been able to still conceive of one another as Christians* (italics mine).

It is also important to add that both Matthew and Isaac "agree that there is a potential generational shift occurring in political theology" (Isaac) that "minimizes the role of legislation for the sake of social and cultural persuasion" (Matthew).

> It is likely ... that the aging donor base of the Religious Right will not be replaced by "millennials," and that their nihilistic politics will come to an end. In the best case, conservative evangelicals will jettison the resentment that has motivated them and order themselves toward a substantive, thoroughgoing account of the common good that minimizes the role of legislation for the sake of social and cultural persuasion (Matthew).
>
> I also appreciated Matthew's hypothesis that the, "the most important and interesting generational gap is not over the substance of sexual ethics, but about political theology," as well. The dubiousness of polling measures aside, it seems undeniable that there has been a decline in the popularly held, appropriately vague, loosely Protestant, widespread US civil Christianity, as well as its alleged minimum of ethical consensus—if there ever was such a thoroughgoing historical agreement in the first place. The very idea that the US could be conceptualized as a "Christian nation"—whatever that actually means—seems, mercifully,

less and less a rhetorical trope these days. Add to that a generation of Christians that is, in my experience, acutely wary of a Religious Right style, theocratically inflected, sort of politics and political theology does seem to be a place where there will be more than just a "generational gap": we may very well be in for a decisive *generational break* (Isaac).

I think that Matthew and I are in agreement that whatever happens with the future of Christianity in the US, the hopes of achieving even a minimal religious and social-ethical consensus in the electorate or of the possibility of legislating the "kingdom of God" into existence, will not be as great a temptation as for past generations. I agree with Matthew's observation that the most prominent present-day Christian conservative reform movements "have not mobilized politically as past evangelical movements have done," and would add that the notable relative absence of publicly cozy associations between current Christian leaders and those in the highest political offices is further indication of changes in the generational landscape with respect to political theology (Isaac).

Reflecting on these two addenda (as I also succumb to the folly of peering into the future), I believe that the possibility of orchestrating respectful conversations about divisive issues (like LGBT issues) that allows Christians to "agree to disagree" will be very challenging within formal "institutions" (be they religious, such as Christian organizations, churches, and denominations, or political). But I see a bit more "hope" for the possibility of Christians "agreeing to disagree" about LGBT issues then do Isaac and Matthew, at least within some churches,[3] and the case studies reported on chapter 9 will give some credence to that hope.

But if the hope on my part for more respectful conversations about LGBT issues within formal Christian institutions is not adequately realized, my experience suggests that when some Christian institutions are not comfortable, or even "open," to discussing LGBT issues, it is possible to create "safe, welcoming spaces" for such conversations in private homes and coffee shops.

I close this lengthy section with what I believe is an uncompromising prerequisite for the possibility of ongoing respectful conversations about

---

3. The Colossian Forum (TCF) has been very effective in helping a number of Christian churches to engage in respectful conversations about the contentious issues of "origins" and "human sexuality" by means of orchestrating face-to-face conversations and the production of curricular materials designed for church use. For more information, go to www.colossianforum.org. I will comment further on the excellent work of TCF in chapter 10.

LGBT issues, wherever that may occur, that will allow us to "agree to disagree," as stated by Isaac.

> I [Isaac] believe that the very possibility of ongoing dialogue between the coalescing "non-affirming" and "affirming" sides of US Christianity is predicated on *the ability to view one another as mistaken, but still Christian.*

In the next two sections, I will draw on some further reflections from Matthew and Isaac, as well as some of my own thoughts, to elaborate on this prerequisite of being able to "view one another as mistaken, but still Christian."

ASKING THE RIGHT QUESTION: IS IT "TRUE"?

To suggest that someone is "mistaken" about any issue is to believe that there is some truth about that issue. Therefore, I am encouraged by the fact that both Isaac and Matthew agree that the right question to be asked about any position on any LGBT issue is "is it true" rather than "is it popular" or "does it work."

> I [Isaac] fully, furthermore, concur with Matthew's suggestion that "is it true?" is a stronger criteria of evaluation for an ethic than either, "is it popular?" or, "does it work?"

In my estimation, making the quest for truth primary, albeit still an enormously challenging task, avoids the many dead ends that will arise if the starting point for conversation is concern about what others will think about my particular position, or how my position will be received in the broader culture within which I or a Christian organization with which I am affiliated is trying to gain or maintain respectability, or the possible unintended negative consequences that might emerge if the constituents or supporters of a Christian organization with which I am affiliated finds out about my position or questions whether Christians within my organization should even be talking about such contentious issues. To be sure, to swim upstream against such variations of making the questions "is it popular" or "does it work" primary will require a healthy dose of individual and institutional humility and courage, but there is no hope for ongoing conversations to converge on a better understanding of the truth about LGBT issues unless all those engaged in such conversations start with an unswerving commitment to "seeking after the truth."

Both Isaac and Matthew make note of an example where asking the wrong question is a dead end: the failure of progressive mainline denominations to "make it work"; "it" being the attempt to "hold together the affirmation of gay unions with the traditional core of the [Christian] faith." Some elaboration is called for.

First, Matthew points to the failure of these attempts.

> Conservative Christians have also watched carefully as progressive mainline churches have attempted, and failed, to hold together the affirmation of gay unions with the traditional core of the faith.

But, what do these failed attempts "prove"? As indicated in the following quote, Isaac suggests that while Matthew no doubt believes that the attempt of "progressive mainline denominations" to "articulate pro-LGBT Christian sexual ethic ... represents a theological *untruth*," he comes "perilously close" to saying that the fact that it hasn't "worked" is proof of its "untruth."

> I am confident that Matthew personally believes that the move by progressive mainline denominations in the past several decades to try and articulate a pro-LGBT Christian sexual ethic, indeed, represents a theological *untruth*. But I feel that, *while holding up the criteria of truth as a defense for a more conservative view of Christian sexual ethics in the face of shifting social mores*, Matthew edges toward leveling the charge that, "it simply hasn't worked," at Christian denominations who have historically taken a less conservative approach. He comes perilously close, in fact, to suggesting that the, "bitter dividing of the mainline denominations," represents *proof* of their "failed attempt," "to hold together the affirmation of gay unions with the traditional core of the faith." (Italics mine.)

As italicized above, Matthew certainly believes that his traditional view is true. But, needless to say, those holding to a nontraditional view also believe that their view is true, as Isaac states below.

> I'd be willing to bet that many were motivated by a belief that holding "together the affirmation of gay unions with the traditional core of the faith," is not only possible *but is, in fact, true*. If the decline in popularity of a more conservative position and the probability of ongoing divisiveness in the conservative Christian world over these questions are not an accurate measure of the truthfulness of a more traditional Christian sexual ethic, then the denominational schisms of the mainline ought not be gestured toward as evidence of the untruthfulness of a more progressive stance. As Matthew pointed out, whether

> something polls well should neither be celebrated nor mourned for those seeking truth.

So, we have not negated, or even ameliorated, the strong disagreements between traditionalists and nontraditionalists as to what is true relative to LGBT issues. But it is no small accomplishment to arrive at the point where the question "is it true" is primary. This is nicely summarized in Isaac's concluding reflection on Matthew's position.

> As Matthew pointed out, whether something polls well should neither be celebrated nor mourned for those seeking truth.

Of course, none of this settles the outstanding question as to whether "agreeing to disagree" about LGBT issues is a viable position for Christians or their churches or organizations to take. But it at least clarifies that the primary question about any position taken relative to LGBT issues is "Is it true?"

I return now to the question raised by Matthew as to whether Christian institutions will be "faithful" if they "somehow leave room for both positions (conservative and progressive) regarding same-sex marriage. Recall the question that Matthew posed.

> The question, then, is whether it is feasible for institutions to somehow leave room for both positions. Whether it would work, pragmatically, is dubious—but would it still be *faithful*?

I ask once again, faithful to what? I believe that the aspiration of those on both sides of the same-sex marriage issue should be to be "faithful" to the truth as they understand that truth, while at the same time being open to the possibility that they may "mistaken (embracing an untruth)." It is only this shared aspiration that will lead to a shared willingness to engage in respectful conversations with those Christians with whom they disagree about what is true.

WHO IS A "CHRISTIAN"?

The assertion by Isaac that ongoing dialogue about contentious LGBT issues will be possible only if those on both sides of these issues have the "ability to view one another as mistaken, but still Christian" not only presupposes that there is some "truth" about these matters that both sides should aspire to understand; it also assumes that both parties agree upon what it means to be a "Christian."

We are now entering a minefield. Isaac takes one modest step into this minefield in his reflections about how Christian institutions, like denominations, respond to "dissenters."

> ... [T]here have been times when some previously established institutional bodies subsequently and effectively declare that the new fellowship of dissenters are heretics beyond the pale of "true" Christianity. In such cases, there are often obvious power dynamics in play such that the established institutional leadership fears the loss of control in dictating the legitimate range of Christian belief.
>
> There have also, however, been times—generally after a sort of "cooling off" period—when the divergence of interpretations amongst Christians allows *both* for *individual* breaks with one Christian institution in favor of another that more accurately represents one's own beliefs *and* an eventual ability for *estranged institutions* to suggest things like, "*just because they are Methodists doesn't mean they aren't Christians!*" (Italics mine.)

Most of us would agree that it isn't membership in any one particular Christian denomination that makes one a "Christian." But that is a tiny first step.

Who, then, is a Christian? That is for God to judge, not me. Nevertheless, we humans who profess commitment to the Christian faith have seldom hesitated to answer that question on God's behalf. For some Christians, the criteria for "membership" in the body of Christ includes commitment to one or more of the historic Christian creeds (e.g., The Apostles' Creed). Other Christians would require adherence to a particular list of doctrinal statements, some short and some long.

Of course, the reason we are now treading in a minefield is that the sets of differing proposed "criteria for membership" within the circle of Christians are too numerous to count and are sometimes contradictory. For example, some lists of expected beliefs will include belief in a traditional view of marriage and some will allow for a nontraditional view of marriage.

How do I propose navigating this minefield? I do so by embracing a definition of what it means to be a "Christian" that allows for a Christian to take either a traditional or nontraditional view of marriage, as follows:

> I believe that someone is a Christian if he/she personally trusts in the death and resurrection of Jesus Christ as decisive for salvation and the redemption of the entire created order, and if he/she aspires to be a "follower of Jesus" by means of obedience to the two great "love commandments" taught by Jesus: love for God and love for neighbor.

Some will surely take this to be too minimalist a view of what it means to be a Christian since it allows for Christians to disagree on numerous issues, including same-sex marriage. I will be happy to discuss that with dissenters.

But it is in light of this view of what it means to be a Christian that I can embrace the view that one can be a Christian and yet be "mistaken" about many issues (among which I include same-sex marriage). And it is only my willingness to say "I may be wrong" about same-sex marriage and many other issues that opens up the possibility and desirability of having respectful conversations with other Christians who disagree with me about these issues.

But we human beings find it hard to say "I may be wrong." When I am unwilling to say that, I am failing to practice the Christian virtue of humility by not acknowledging that as a finite, fallible human being, I do not "have the mind of God." Rather, "I see through a glass darkly" (1 Cor 13:12). Therefore, I must be open to the possibility that my belief as to what is true is actually untrue.

But, then, if we as Christians can be "mistaken," where is the "unity" among Christians for which Jesus prays, as recorded in John 17:20-21? Unity among Christians is not "uniformity" of belief about every last issue. Rather it lies in a shared commitment to the "Lordship of Jesus Christ." (My minimalist description of that "Lordship" presented above is only one possible description.)

I conclude this section, rather immodestly, with my suggestion that this entire book demonstrates that Christians can disagree about LGBT issues without calling into question the authenticity of each other's Christian faith. Any reader of this book who takes the trouble to work through the multiple postings for my eCircle will see that although my conversation partners expressed strong disagreements about many LGBT issues, each one is a deeply committed Christian motivated by his/her understanding of the Christian faith.

But a formidable question still remains. Whatever the "content" of our views of what is true relative to LGBT issues, what is the best way for Christians to engage those other Christians who have different views about that truth?

A CHRISTIAN WAY TO DISAGREE

As already quoted, Matthew points us toward the danger of "conservative Christianity retaining its convictions" on LGBT issues with belligerence and hostility.

> Among the many dangers for the church, and for society, that lie before us is the prospect of a conservative Christianity that retains its convictions with a more belligerently hostile, anti-modern edge than it even now has. Confidently retaining convictions in the face of disagreement is the mark of a mature mind: whether evangelicals will be able to arrive there remains to be seen.

Of course, there is enough belligerence and hostility to go around. There is ample evidence that those who hold to nontraditional views on LGBT issues can also resort to such dreadful ways of engaging with those with whom they disagree.

In that light, Isaac wisely points us toward the need to pay as much attention to "how" we disagree as Christians as to the "content" of our disagreements.

> Regardless of the future probability of outcomes in the debates around the "present controversies [regarding LGBT issues]," it is absolutely clear, as of today, that the apparent shifting tides of consensus will not be enough to eradicate dissent. I want to propose, therefore, that US Christians ought to think about the *form* of our disagreements as much as we do the *content*. It is impossible to change the *fact* of Christian disagreement and diversity of interpretation—and if the history of the church is any indication, we are probably in for, shall we say, *vigorous* debate for the long haul—but I would like to believe that there is room for improvement in the *ways* in which we disagree.

Before considering concrete strategies suggested by both Isaac and Matthew for improving on the "ways" in which we disagree as Christians, I will draw attention for some good reasons for seeking this "better way," proposed by both Matthew and me, that are deeply informed by our respective understandings of our Christian faith commitments.

Matthew suggests the need for Christians on both sides of LGBT debates to practice extending the Christian gift of "mercy" by asking "Can there be mercy in the gay marriage debates?"

Matthew elaborates on how this need for extending mercy applies to those Christians on both sides of the gay marriage debates. First, Matthew proposes that the LGBT community must avoid responding to conservative Christians in a way that reflects a desire for a tit-for-tat approach based on the "unjust persecution and stigmatization they have received from the hands of conservative Christians."

> They [the LGBT community] have a deep and pervasive narrative about the unjust persecution and stigmatization they have received from the hands of conservative Christians. But the question before them is whether they wish to exact an eye for an eye, and narrow the range for public expression of traditional sexual ethics as much as possible, or if they will take a more lenient and capacious approach than they themselves once received.

Matthew later adds that "Whether conservative Christians deserve such magnanimous treatment is certainly an important question; but then, it may not be mercy if they did."

But Matthew also points out that "At the same time, framing the question as one of mercy requires something of conservative Christians, too."

> It demands the recognition that mercy is what is required, that the behavior of our own community throughout history toward LGBT individuals has been less exemplary than it should have been. Mercy may not be merited if conservative Christians learn nothing at all. If conservative Christians now object to the use of the law to punitively encroach upon their way of life, we should seriously reflect about our own use of similar methods in the past. It may be that quietly accepting our marginalized future is an appropriate form of political contrition, and that any purging of our past may not be complete except through such penance.

In addition to the Christian value of "mercy" that Matthew points to, I will take the liberty of adding my own rationale for Christians needing to seek a "better way" to engage one another about their disagreements regarding LGBT issues.

My commitment to fostering respectful conversation among persons who disagree with one another is based on the Christian value of love. It is a clear biblical teaching that if you aspire to be a follower of Jesus, you are called to "love your neighbor as yourself" (Mark 12:31). That assertion is obvious. What is not obvious is the particular expression of what it means to love someone who disagrees with you (about anything) that informs this present eCircle project and most of my labors over the past few years.

In brief, I believe that it is a deep expression of love for another person who disagrees with you about any issue when you provide that person with a "safe and welcoming space" to express their disagreements and you then engage that person in "respectful conversation" about your agreements and disagreements. This better way leaves no room for demonizing the person who disagrees with you or any other forms of vitriolic discourse that are so prevalent in our culture.

SUGGESTIONS FOR THE "BETTER WAY" FOR ENGAGEMENT

Matthew suggests that future conversations about LGBT issues need to be characterized by "reasonable discourse" and "persuasion" that includes an "exchange of reasons."

Matthew's suggestion comports well with my own experience trying to help people to sort through their disagreements. I have found that all too often when persons disagree they make an inadequate attempt to understand the reasons behind the other person's point of view. Those reasons often reflect the particularities of the other's social location, such as race, gender, sexual orientation, socioeconomic status, faith commitment (religious or secular), and personal biography. Getting to know the other person better by understanding the underlying reasons for his/her perspective increases the likelihood of finding some common ground and illuminating remaining differences sufficient to enable continuing conversation.

Isaac provides valuable insight on a "better way" for engagement in a lesson that he has learned.

> The possibility of finding healthier ways for US Christians to disagree on these questions [LGBT issues] will absolutely depend on the intentional diversification of *both* conversation partners *and* conversation mediums.

There is much to unpack in this valuable lesson relative to the needed "diversification" of "conversation partners" and "conversation mediums" that are suggestive of both strengths and weaknesses of my eCircle project. Let me start with Isaac's reflections on the "mediums" for conversation (what I like to call "venues"), with some of my own reflections interspersed.

First, I resonate deeply with Isaac's reflections on the dismal way in which many Christians are contributing to the "angry noise being broadcast daily" by means of the Internet and other forms of electronic communication.

> It . . . bears mentioning that the corners of the Internet where Christians often congregate are no exception to the unending dross of banal and angry noise being broadcast online daily. Conspicuous Christian online presences tend, in my experience, toward either a) reactionary responses passed virally in an echo chamber on an unending loop or b) ad hominem attacks

directed at both "the world" and each other, rivaling and even surpassing the vitriol of any other Internet comment section.

I am encouraged by the sharp contrast that Isaac draws between such online banality and "angry noise" and what I am attempting with my online eCircle, which he perceives as one attempt to diversify both "conversation partners" and "conversation mediums."

> This very blog series is, I think, one such attempt [at diversification]. By requiring longer-form pieces and multiple responses over a more sustained period of time, as well as by inviting conversation partners who will inevitably disagree but hopefully without resorting to name-calling, *Respectful Conversations* aims, it seems, for both of these measures.

Therefore, Isaac concludes that "Any attempt—like the one made in this series—to subvert these tendencies [toward banality and angry noise] through creative adaptations of available online mediums is, in my humble opinion, a worthwhile experiment."

While deeply appreciating Isaac's laudatory comments about my eCircle project, I also agree with his reflections on two significant weaknesses in my array of "conversation partners": "the striking *whiteness* of these conversations" and, to paraphrase Isaac, the fact that this is a conversation limited to "US Christians."[4]

> I firmly believe that it is incumbent upon US Christians with varying degrees of social privilege to work oh-so-very-much harder at broadening their purview of *possible conversation partners* in matters ethical and theological. Though I obviously can't speak for everyone else involved in this particular set of exchanges, I, for one, have personally noticed the striking *whiteness* of these conversations. And I am, furthermore, worried that every time I wrote "US Christianity" in one of my posts, I probably should have written "white US Christianity" as a qualifier—I admittedly assumed, after all, a primarily white audience.

For emphasis, Isaac adds that "the absence of Christians of color in debates such as these is both unconscionable and, indeed, unrepresentative.

---

4. Matthew agrees with Isaac's concern that my conversation partners were limited to US citizens. As Matthew says, "His [Isaac's] acknowledgment of the geographical limitations of the discussion is also salutatory: for as much anxiety as North American Christians have about their own peculiar situation, we need as many reminders as possible that the future of Christianity may not hinge upon us or our internal disputes."

Matthew and I, for example, are *both* straight, white, US, Protestant, Christian males."

Another valid critique of my eCircle project that Isaac presents is embedded in his assertion that the persons "most equipped" to discuss LGBT issues are the "young LGBT Christians" who are "most affected by them," adding the important observation that a further benefit of that strategy is that we would be talking more "with persons rather than about issues."

> I would be remiss in not explicitly stating that the persons *most equipped* to address the future of US Christianity as it relates to generational shifts and the "present controversies" [regarding LGBT issues] are, in my opinion, those who are most affected by them: the young LGBTQ Christians negotiating the often dire straits between a community that may malign them for their sexual/gender identity and a community that might deride them for their faith.
>
> I think that the voluntary and un-coerced presence of LGBTQ Christians in any venue of conversation about "the present controversies" is a non-negotiable necessity for more just forms of Christian theological disagreement. It is, in my experience, easier to unpardonably collapse people into mere "issues" when they aren't in the room with you. Disagree though we might, Christians should, as an absolute minimum, strive to talk *with* persons rather than about "issues."

I believe that Isaac's critiques of my array of conversation partners are valid. Although I believe I assembled an excellent array of twenty-one conversation partners, the greater diversity that he calls for is lacking (e.g., to the best of my knowledge, four of my twenty-one conversation partners identify themselves as LGBT; none are persons of color; all are US citizens).

Having said that, however, I need to reiterate a point I made in the Preface to this book: My fondest dream is that the conversations reported on in this book will not be the "end" of a conversation, but only the "beginning." In that light, it is my recommendation that those who orchestrate such ongoing conversations pay close attention to Isaac's legitimate call for greater diversification in conversation partners.

LEARNING FROM THOSE WHO DISAGREE WITH YOU

Given that the purpose of my eCircle and this book is to model respectful conversation among Christians who disagree with one another, I close this chapter with some expressions of appreciation that suggest that this goal has been accomplished admirably in the conversation between Isaac and Matthew. Here are a few reflections.

> Sharp's willingness to say in four words what I said in far too many—"[We] have no idea" where we are headed—is refreshing and important. Temptations to triumphalism beset everyone when it comes to demography, and Sharp's willingness to avoid feeding that sort of atmosphere is both gracious and wise. (Matthew)
>
> I owe Matthew a good deal of thanks for engaging with me the past few weeks as this summative hypothesis, which I have been nursing, draws as much on his contributions as it does my own. (Isaac)

Note especially Isaac's assertion above that his concluding thoughts have been influenced by what he has learned from Matthew's previous postings. This theme is continued in the following expressions of appreciation from Matthew that point not only to the importance of finding some common ground ("points of agreement") but also to the importance of "identifying crucial and important aspects of disagreement," which makes one "return to and reevaluate . . . [one's] own commitments."

> I am grateful for Sharp's thoughtful contribution to this symposium and delighted to discover so many points of agreement. In the face of such divides, that is worth holding on to indeed.
>
> Finding unexpected sources of agreement is a rewarding part of any good dialogue. But identifying crucial and important aspects of disagreement is equally thrilling, even if it is far less appreciated. Most of the time in discussions like this, people tend to get lost in confusion and miscommunication and never make their way to the happy shores of clear-eyed, uncompromising differences of opinion. Such disagreements, though, are often genuine sources of creativity and promise. Forcing ourselves to find new reasons to offer in hopes of persuading makes us return to and reevaluate our own commitments, and gives us again the possibility of changing our minds or renewing our confidence.

8

Churches and the LGBT Community

There is enormous diversity in how Christian churches and their pastors respond to LGBT persons that cannot be easily categorized. Yet, as a starting point for this conversation, it is recognized that many of these responses are variations of the following general positions:

- Welcoming but not affirming.
- Welcoming and affirming.
- Accepting, without taking a position relative to "welcoming" and/or "affirming" because the theological issues are "disputed matters" and we agree to allow disagreement (what will later be called a "Third Way").

In extending invitations to three conversation partners, I tried my best to match each partner with one of the general categories above. As will soon be seen, that was too simple an approach. For one problem, as one of my conversation partners (Weldon Nisly) noted, there are possible positions other than those that fit nicely into one of these three categories: "I am aware that the three 'positions' proclaimed by Chris, Tim, and I, do not embrace all 'positions' in the church. Some beloved sisters and brothers in the Church wouldn't readily engage this Respectful Conversation much less engage with LGBTQ members." But I think it is fair to say that my three conversation partners fit the above categories "close enough" to at least start a robust conversation.

The overarching Leading Question that each conversation partner was asked to address was: How do you recommend that churches engage with LGBT individuals and why?

For the sake of context, it is important to note the particular church setting for each of our conversation partners. I will also present a summary response to the Leading Question for each of my conversation partners, gleaned from their various postings, with the understanding that some of the themes pointed to in these summary statements will be elaborated upon when I attempt to sort through agreements and disagreements

Chris Schutte, who says that "my own position is likely a variation on the theme of welcoming but not affirming," is Rector of Christ Church Phoenix. He was ordained in The Episcopal Church (TEC) in 2002. Chris notes the schism in the global Anglican communion that was precipitated in 2003 when "Gene Robinson, a partnered gay man, was elected and consecrated as the bishop of New Hampshire."

> This set off a conflict that has resulted in many Americans leaving TEC, and has brought the global Anglican Communion to the brink of schism. In the course of my ministry, I've spent quite a bit of time praying, studying, and listening—listening to the voices of LGBT individuals both in my congregations and in the broader church, and listening to angry, frustrated, and confused straight people, some affirming and others running the gamut between compassionately non-affirming and outright homophobic, as they try to reconcile faithful Christian living with the reality of LGBT people in our midst. I've also listened to the voices of Anglicans around the globe, many of whom, for an array of cultural and theological reasons, stridently oppose any move toward LGBT acceptance, whether in the church or society.

Chris "chose to leave TEC in 2007," but explains that "I didn't leave TEC because of 'homosexuality,' but rather because TEC had grown apart from historic and global Christianity, and, by aligning myself with the Anglicans in the Global South, I was aligning myself not only with historic Christianity, but also with our ecumenical partners in Roman Catholicism, Eastern Orthodoxy, and the burgeoning evangelical and charismatic groups around the world."

Christ Church Phoenix began in 2007 under the oversight of the Anglican Church of Uganda, and is now a part of the Anglican Church in North America. As Chris reports, "The official policy of Christ Church Phoenix relative to LGBT persons is to affirm the dignity of every human person regardless of sexual orientation and to live in a culture of safety in which we can share our deepest pains and hurts free from shame. In our new members' class we teach, in accordance with the canons of our denomination, that the sacrament of Holy Matrimony is to be a lifelong covenant between a man and a woman, and, in order to serve in leadership, one must share this conviction. We teach our youth and parents that Christ Church is a 'safe place' to struggle with sexual identity issues."

Chris's summary response to the Leading Question is:

> I remain convinced that the biblical prohibitions of sexual intimacy between two people of the same gender do, in fact, apply to our modern construct of same-sex relationships....
>
> Theologically, as the church has reflected on marriage over the millennia, the radical difference—yet profound compatibility and procreative potential—of a man and a woman has been an essential component of our understanding of marriage, as has the image of the church as Christ's bride, with the consummation of redemption likened to a wedding feast. Altering our understanding of marriage in such a way that removes gender as a factor would strike at the heart of how we think about what it means that God created us "male and female" in his image, and the mystery that "a man shall leave his mother, and a woman leave her home, and the two shall become one flesh." Again, I simply can't embrace a theology of marriage, which I think that we all agree must be the context for sexual intimacy, that eliminates gender difference and also removes the potential for childbearing.
>
> So, how to balance the radical welcome of Jesus with the biblical prohibition against sexual intimacy outside of heterosexual marriage? In the case of the Samaritan woman, the woman caught in adultery, and Zacchaeus, Jesus never affirmed their behavior (namely serial marriage, adultery, and financial malfeasance), but he did affirm them. That was Jesus' priority—seeking and saving the lost. It strikes me that, at its best, this is what it might mean to be "welcoming but not affirming"—always mindful that the outcast, especially those rejected by our religious authorities (who look and dress and talk like me), are the ones that Jesus sought, first seeing broken hearts and bodies rather than sinful behavior. Yet, it also means that when Jesus shows up in our lives, we can't stay the same; moving toward the new creation with Jesus requires reordering our lives.

Weldon Nisly was called to be pastor of Seattle Mennonite Church in early 1995, where he served as lead pastor until he retired from pastoral ministry in late 2013. His retirement ministry is committed to Contemplative Just Peacebuilding, developing a more comprehensive model for peacemaking and envisioning a paradigm shift from Just War to Just Peace. He performed a same-sex marriage in 2004, followed by a discipline process with the Pacific Northwest Mennonite Conference Pastoral Leadership Team, who suspended his ordination credentials in 2005. In the Mennonite Church polity, regional Conferences have primary responsibility for ordination in collaboration with the congregation. Having his ordination credential suspended meant it was acknowledged that Weldon continued as pastor of Seattle Mennonite Church but without recognition by the Mennonite Church. Further discernment by the Conference led to Weldon's ordination credentials being restored in 2006. Seattle Mennonite Church engaged in an extensive discernment from 2007–2010, when the congregation decided by consensus to become a "welcoming and affirming" church (http://www.seattlemennonite.org/about/welcome-statement/).

Weldon's summary response to the Leading Question is:

> . . . My encouragement is for church members to truly engage with sisters and brothers who are LGBTQ. At least in the Mennonite Church, the struggle has often been "heterosexuals" talking and deciding about "homosexuals" rather than engaging sisters and brothers who are LGBTQ. Great pain has been suffered by being othered rather than engaged. To engage the other begins with deep listening, particularly for those with privilege and power. Failure to listen to and engage those we label "homosexual" has also caused the church great harm and loss of the gifts of members and the wholeness of the body of Christ.
>
> I am committed to being "welcoming and affirming" from a personal and pastoral perspective, but I don't consider my pastoral approach to be a "position" called "welcoming and affirming." It is a calling I have lived and grown into over four decades of ministry. I have found that being faithful to our calling is to live a trajectory of continuity and change, forged in its share of confrontation and conflict. Along the Way, God surprises and changes us in ways that lead us a step beyond where we are or want to go. Yet God's surprises are consistent with the trajectory of our lives and life together. The Way of continuity and change leads us into the wonder of paradox (the impossible that God makes possible) and the beauty of mystery (the endlessly knowable yet never fully knowable God). In the church, all are welcome in paradox and mystery!

> ... We will listen to what God sets before us and trust God to lead us faithfully as a church. Along the way we will search the Scriptures and explore how to be faithful spiritual-sexual beings by being spiritually discerning and communally compassionate.

Tim Otto is an Associate Pastor at the Church of the Sojourners in San Francisco. Sojourners is a "live together" intentional church community. While it has no official denominational affiliation, it has ties with many Mennonite congregations and understands itself to be part of the Anabaptist tradition. As Tim reports, "Shortly after it's beginning in 1988, Sojourners had a conversation about LGBT inclusion and decided that it would not take an official position on the morality of same-sex relationships. At the time, a primary focus of the church was ministry to Salvadoran refugees. We decided that for practical reasons we would not affirm same-sex unions since we believed it would create a distraction from our primary ministry. This meant that gay members would need to remain celibate. Recently, we've realized that we want to revisit that policy, and we will begin a new conversation about LGBT inclusion starting September of 2016."

Tim's summary response to the Leading Question is:

> Rather than treat LGBT Christians as a sexuality to be affirmed or disciplined, churches should walk with LGBT people with curiosity. Churches should ask the same question of an LGBT member it asks of all its members: how is God at work in this person's life and how can we cooperate with that?
>
> Churches should model the difficult practice of loving each other in spite of differences—differences like affirming vs. non-affirming. This is preferable to demanding doctrinal correctness (on either side) concerning a small aspect of sexual ethics: something that affects around 3 percent of the population, a topic on which there are six explicit verses in the Bible.
>
> Practically this means allowing for differences of belief and action on both sides. LGBT people—acting with a clear conscience—should be able to marry the same sex, transition genders, and be leaders in a congregation. On the other hand, an affirming theology should not be officially adopted by the church. Non-affirming members should be free to hold dissenting opinions. Just as many churches tolerate a range of opinions concerning pacifism and just war (and whether it is permissible to serve in the military), churches should allow members to hold and practice different beliefs on this topic.
>
> ... The church should adopt a "third-way" stance not just because the reasons this argument gets so heated are misguided

(though they often are). This is a chance for the church to witness to a beautiful and important aspect of the gospel: that because of Christ people who disagree over important things can still live together in peace.

Chris, Weldon, and Tim did an admirable job in identifying their agreements and disagreements in response to my Leading Question. I first note two major areas of agreement.

AGREEMENT: SOME CHURCHES HAVE DONE GREAT HARM

In the sub-section titled "Churches Can Be Brutal" in Chapter 1, I shared heartbreaking stories of the pain experienced by some gay Christians, including the following horrific account from an anonymous reader of my eCircle.

> I am very old now, well into my sixties. I tried the ex-gay and celibacy paths for at least ten years between about age thirteen and age twenty-three years. Then four or five decades on from back then.
>
> All that heartache could not, in the end, be worth it. I should have been one of those guys who hung himself in the rafters of the empty garage in the abandoned house next door, or perhaps who found a wild moment to jump from the college bell tower or high rise science buildings. Instead, I just doggedly went on and on and on.
>
> Life has just about been like a forced prisoner of war march, or perhaps in shallower extent like the Native American trails of tears.

Chris, Weldon, and Tim all agree that the Christian Church has too often been the cause of great pain to gay Christians. Tim recounts his own painful experience as a gay Christian within the church:

> I grew up in the conservative church, and because it didn't distinguish between orientation and behavior, I grew up loathing myself. It is difficult to communicate the cost of this. It contributed to significant sadness and self-destructive behaviors aimed at medicating my self-hate. The same church that caused such pain is telling me that I'm not allowed to enter into a bodily, healing, reciprocal relationship of covenanted, faithful love. That is hard to take. It doesn't *feel* like Christ's love. It doesn't *feel* like mercy.

Chris confesses his "own blindness and indifference to LGBT people, the uncharitable thoughts, prejudice, and even contempt for LGBT people and their allies that I, and my brothers and sisters in Christ, have shown." Chris also resonates with Weldon's take on the great harm that has been done to the church because of the deep pain it has inflicted on many LGBT Christians.

> I'm also in agreement with my brothers [Weldon and Tim] that the church, both individual Christians and corporate church bodies, has caused deep pain to LGBT people, both inside and outside of the church, which has caused, to use Weldon's words, "the church great harm and loss of the gifts of members and the wholeness of the body of Christ."

Chris also contrasts the "horrible persecution from Christians" that many LGBT individuals have experienced with the manner in which Jesus engaged with "the outcast, the marginalized, and the excluded."

> As I read the Gospels, I'm struck that Jesus seemed to delight in pursuing, loving, and restoring the outcast, the marginalized, and the excluded. Historically, LGBT individuals have experienced horrible persecution from Christians, even, and perhaps especially, from Christian leaders. This persecution, while considerably lessened recently in many sectors of contemporary American society, still exists, though often much more subtly, in enclaves of conservative American Christianity. It is also brutally, often murderously, present in certain societies throughout the world—many of which, disturbingly, are largely "Christian." So, LGBT individuals who experience profound rejection, and even violence, at the hands of religious leaders are the kinds of people Jesus was keenly interested in pursuing. Whether the woman at the well with her five husbands plus the one who wasn't, the woman caught in adultery whose accusers slowly slipped aside, or Zacchaeus, who dishonestly accumulated vast amounts of wealth (that's a sin, right?), Jesus' radical welcome saw past their behavior, looked at their hearts, and loved them. So this practice of not only welcoming but actively pursuing those broken-hearted, beat-up, and vulnerable divine-image bearers for whom Christ was pleased to die seems thoroughly biblical, and the implications for how the church engages with the LGBT community are profound.

Weldon also sees an important area of agreement "in the pain we bear and sorrow we share over how the church inflicts pain on sisters and brothers who are LGBT."

> Tim, you very graciously unpacked your vision for the church navigating this conflicted territory and noted the "many casualties" this conflict has cost the church: "We've ruptured families, churches, and denominations. We've hurt sexual minorities and alienated sincere Christians . . . . We've eviscerated the gospel witness that because of Jesus we can be reconciled not only to God, but with one another." Chris, you lamented that "LGBT individuals have experienced horrible persecution from Christians . . . [and] have experienced profound rejection, and even violence, at the hands of religious leaders." You both express a clear word that stands as a strong critique of the pain inflicted on our LGBT sisters and brothers by the church. I am grateful for and share the way you contrast such violent rejection of LGBT members with "Jesus' radical welcome" and loving relationship with oppressed and marginalized people throughout the Gospels.
>
> I also know that the pain I bear as an older white male heterosexual pastor encountering oppressive violence toward LGBT members, or even toward me as a welcoming and affirming pastor, is miniscule compared to the pain borne by sisters and brothers who are victimized by such violence. In a comment not directed at either of you but from long painful experience in the church, I find it incomprehensible and unconscionable that "homosexuality" is deemed to be sin justifying the egregious sin of violence against sisters and brothers we categorically consider "other." That flies in the face of all that is Jesus and the Gospels. What really is *sin* in this conflict?

All of the above reflections on how the church has too often done great harm to LGBT Christians comport well with the agreement expressed by Eve Tushnet and Justin Lee in Chapter 1 that "Gay People Take Priority Over Gay Issues." The nature of such prioritization will become clearer as we consider a second major area of agreement between Chris, Weldon, and Tim.

AGREEMENT: GUIDELINES FOR "ENGAGEMENT" WITH LGBT CHRISTIANS

Weldon calls for "engagement" with LGBT Christians: "My encouragement is for church members to truly *engage with* sisters and brothers who are LGBTQ. At least in the Mennonite Church, the struggle has often been "heterosexuals" talking and deciding *about* "homosexuals" rather than engaging sisters and brothers who are LGBTQ. "Great pain has been suffered by being othered rather than engaged."

Chris concurs, saying that he "resonated deeply with . . . Weldon's exhortation to 'engage with' rather than 'talking and deciding about' our LGBT brothers and sisters."

Tim also heartily agrees with the need for "engagement" with LGBT Christians" in his response to Weldon: "There is so much of what you say that I agree with, especially (since something like this was my opening line) that 'church members [should] truly engage with sisters and brothers who are LGBTQ.'"

Three dimensions of such "engagement" with LGBT Christians emerge from further postings.

CREATING "SAFE PLACES" FOR LGBT CHRISTIANS

In his definition of a "safe place," Tim reminds us that "safe" does not mean "comfortable."

> I'm sympathetic with the drive to provide a "safe," affirming place for LGBT Christians. But I don't think "safe" means "comfortable." *Safe means something like, "A place where we are all allowed to speak the truth as we see it, and we can all try to hear it, because we know ourselves to be—above all—beloved by God."* Safe means a place where truth is spoken and welcomed. (Italics mine.)

Chris also points to the need for church to be a "a safe space within which [LGBT Christians can] . . . share the deepest pains and struggles in their lives." This need to have a "safe place" for sharing one's deepest pains and struggles suggests a second dimension of "engagement" with LGBT Christians, the need for careful listening. At the same time, Chris asserts that "I also need to make sure that my congregation, and, to extent that I have influence, my denomination, never becomes a safe haven for homophobia."

LISTENING TO THE STORIES OF LGBT CHRISTIANS

Chris reports that he encourages his parishioners to "listen to the stories of LGBT people, especially those who have been raised in the church," adding that "I also urge them to consider carefully the evangelistic and pastoral consequences of engaging in defensive, reactionary, and often ignorant rhetoric on the 'culture war' issues of same-sex marriage and LGBT rights."

Furthermore, Chris asserts that "not listening to LGBT people, both within and outside of the church, has had, and will continue to have, disastrous consequences for the witness and ministry of the church."

Tim expresses agreement with Chris' call for listening to LGBT Christians: "Chris, you also echo this sentiment [the need for engagement] when you say that you "encourage ... parishioners to listen to the stories of LGBT people, especially those who have been raised in the church."

Weldon also points us toward the need for careful listening when he asserts that "sexual minorities" are "crying to be heard": "There are vulnerable sexual minorities in every culture, country, race, and religion crying to be heard and held as fully human rather than hated and harmed."

"WALKING WITH" LGBT CHRISTIANS

Careful "listening" is only a starting point for a journey with LGBT Christians, a first step for "walking with" brothers and sisters in Christ. Weldon beautifully portrays the essence of this deeper journey of "walking with" (being "present with") an LGBT Christian in his story of engagement with a close pastoral friend who "came out" to him as gay.

> Over the years we spent long hours in conversation about being married, being a pastor, and being gay in the Mennonite Church when it wasn't safe to "come out" in the church. Through our friendship and with others in the church, I learned much about sexuality, including "homosexuality." *I listened to and walked with* many people in pain—pain often inflicted by sisters and brothers in the church. I made a covenant with God that I will seek to *be present with* people in pain without adding to their pain, especially from a place of privilege and power. (Italics mine.)

Chris expresses appreciation for Weldon's commitment to "be present with people in pain without adding to their pain," adding that this commitment, which Chris views as being "shaped" by "the pacifist convictions of Mennonites," does seem to "capture Jesus' words that he is 'gentle, and humble of heart' (Matt 11:29)." Chris concludes that "The church is desperate for more gentle, humble pastors."

Tim also expressed appreciation for the "truth nugget" contained in Weldon's statement that "I made a covenant with God that I will seek to be present with people in pain without adding to their pain, especially from a place of privilege and power."

Tim also affirms Weldon's call for Christians to "walk with" their LGBT brothers and sisters in Christ, while adding an extremely important suggestion as to a pivotal question that should be a focus of such "walking with": "how is God at work in this person's life and how can we cooperate with that?"

> Rather than treat LGBT Christians as a sexuality to be affirmed or disciplined, churches should walk with LGBT people with curiosity. Churches should ask the same question of an LGBT member it asks of all its members: how is God at work in this person's life and how can we cooperate with that?[1]

Tim then adds the provocative suggestion that if one focuses on this question of how God is working in the life of an LGBT Christian with whom one is "walking," the answer may not be easily categorized as "conservative" or "liberal." Rather the advice to be given to that particular LGBT Christian at this time in his/her life may be an expression of "what faithfulness looks like in a given situation."

> My own opinion is that having curiosity about what God is doing in the life of a gay Christian may mean encouraging someone towards either a "liberal" or a "conservative" perspective. For instance, I can imagine Christians coming alongside "Kent" and observing that "Like many oppressed minorities you've fetishized and idolized the goods of the majority culture. As much as you obsess over getting married, your driven relationship with "Sam" seems destructive for you both. You may want to give yourself to celibacy, and to welcoming the healing love of God." Or, for "Emily" it might mean reflecting, "Growing up in a fundamentalist home, it seems like you've internalized a self-loathing toward your body in general and your gay sexuality in particular. As 'Amy' loves you bodily, it seems like a source of

---

1. This suggestion from Tim is similar to Justin Lee's proposal, as reported in chapter 1, that churches must help gay Christians address some "bigger questions" (beyond "what the Bible says about same-sex sex"), such as "Where is my place in the church? What is my vocation? What does my future look like? If I'm single the rest of my life, what happens when I get old? Who will take care of me?"

> grace and healing for you. We'd like to support you in marrying her."
>
> In this model, "Scripture" or "justice" do not become rigid dictates which reduce the Christian life to an exercise in painting by numbers. Rather, the life of faith requires *faith* that the Holy Spirit is available and will show us (yes through Scripture, and the demands of justice, and tradition, and the gifts of pastoral discernment, and other things as well) what faithfulness looks like in a given situation.

This provocative suggestion came too late in the month-long conversation to allow for responses from Weldon or Chris. I suspect this would not be an area of agreement. More conversation is obviously needed. From my perspective that ongoing conversation should include recognition of the importance of "getting to know someone well on a personal level" (as a result of "walking with" that person) before you can adequately understand what God is currently doing in that person's life and how you may be able to "cooperate with" what God is doing.

Of course, since Tim's provocative suggestion also brings into play the question of how Scripture should inform Christian living, ongoing conversation will require a return to the topic of "Biblical Understandings" (first dealt with in chapter 2), about which Chris, Weldon, and Tim have some significant disagreements, as will soon be reported. But we will first consider the issue of how well these "ideal" guidelines for engagement with LGBT individuals, work, or not, "on the ground" when pastors carry out their responsibilities.

CHALLENGES FOR PASTORAL CARE FOR LGBT CHRISTIANS

Weldon asks a number of practical questions about pastoral care for LGBT Christians, the first three of which are:

> How do you as a pastor hold together the views of those who feel strongly about "exclusion" and "inclusion" of LGBT members? Do you see these as parallel opposing views? In other words, how do you encourage members to agree to disagree and still be church together?

Weldon then reports on his own struggles with these three questions.

> My great struggle with these questions is twofold. On the one hand I believe the church must be able to "agree to disagree"

on many if not most matters over which there is disagreement. In the Mennonite Church we worked out a method for "agreeing and disagreeing in love." It has not found a clear consistent place in the church but I believe we have been able to embody it on many important matters without being fully aware of it. Are there limits to how far and on what concerns our disagreements can be embraced and still maintain the unity of the body? On the other hand, my deeper struggle is that our differences often are not parallel disagreements. And they certainly are not parallel harms or hurt. I do not see how the hurt a member may feel who holds the traditional view if LGBT members are included is equivalent to the harm done to an LGBT member who is excluded as a member or from marriage or ministry in the church. It really matters who is being harmed and what violence is being down to whom and with what manner of privilege and power are marshalled to harm another member of the body.

Since third-way churches intentionally promote fellowship between those who disagree about "exclusion" or "inclusion" of LGBT members, Tim's response to Weldon's first set of questions is particularly relevant.

The church I'm part of has been a "Third Way" church in that we've allowed for both views but have asked LGBT people to bear the burden of being Third Way by remaining celibate. I'd like us to continue as a Third Way church, but would like for a change in policy so that non-affirming Christians bear the burden of the disagreement since they are the people of privilege in this situation (we hope to begin such a conversation in the Fall [of 2016]). Practically this would mean allowing LGBT Christians to marry and serve in leadership.

I recently interviewed Ken Wilson, a pastor of a Third Way church in which this is being practiced.[2] I asked him questions similar to the one's you've addressed to me. He answered, in part that it's been his experience that people from conservative backgrounds really have to get it. They have to buy into Romans 14 [A passage in which Paul exhorts Christians to welcome one another in the face of "disputable matters"]. They have to let go of their privilege in order to follow this path. And some can do it and some can't. But that's true of many things in Christianity. How many conservative Christians are obeying the gospel commands of radical discipleship in the realms of materialism, and

---

2. For an elaboration of the way in which Ken Wilson envisions his church being a "third-way" church, see Wilson, *A Letter to my Congregation*.

> greed, and other areas of life? So the fact that it's not easy for people to do, doesn't mean it's not the right thing to do.
>
> I agree. I also think it is crucial for a congregation to see that having important differences of opinion, and yet continuing to live in love and unity is an important witness of what it means to be a people of peace, a people who call Jesus Lord. It is no great accomplishment (although given our sin it is still an accomplishment!) to get a group of similar people to live in unity. But if we can live in love and peace across differences, then we have something worth sharing with others.

But Tim acknowledges the stress that some LGBT persons can experience in a third-way church when other members favor "exclusion" of LGBT members, likening this stress to Post Traumatic Stress Disorder.

> For some LGBT people, going to a third-way church, a church in which some people might condemn same-sex relations, gender-transition, etc., may trigger PTSD symptoms. For such people, I recommend a "welcoming and affirming" church.

But Tim's caveat follows.

> But for most of us, church shouldn't be an exercise in relating to "people like me." Rather, it ought to be a place where we engage the difficult practice of relating to people who, in all kinds of ways, are unlike ourselves. To say that most LGBT people can't hack a church in which people disagree with us is ultimately patronizing, and its own kind of prejudice.

Weldon asks Chris how his "welcoming but not affirming" church deals with the issues of membership and ministry for LGBT Christians. Chris responds by outlining what his church teaches about sexuality.

> Being a hierarchical church, our national denomination is clear that we uphold the historic Christian understanding of marriage as a lifelong covenant between a man and a woman. So, I'm not permitted to perform same-sex marriages....
>
> In my preaching I roughly follow the Revised Common Lectionary, so, when assigned texts deal with issues of marriage and sexuality, I'll preach on it. For example, last October the assigned Gospel reading was Mark 10:2–12. It's true that there are a lot more texts on compassion, mercy, forgiveness, grace, and justice, so my people generally hear more about these topics than on topics specifically relating to sexuality. I'll often mention LGBT people as groups who tend to be marginalized and beaten down, thus especially close to God's heart.

> Also, in our new members' class, we walk through the Book of Common Prayer, which, of course, includes the liturgy for Holy Matrimony.... As I teach about marriage, I also try to articulate my "welcoming but not affirming" posture toward LGBT people. When someone joins our church, they know that our intention is to uphold the historic Christian teaching and practice on marriage, all the while welcoming any who might come. Finally, our youth minister occasionally teaches on issues related to sexuality, and he's been clear with both the youth and their parents that our congregation is a safe place to wrestle through issues of sexual identity.

Weldon shared his overarching response to the questions he posed to Chris and Tim about marriage and ministry.

> The most frequent way I faced that kind of question [about "marriage or ministry"] was when someone was drawn to Seattle Mennonite Church but had real reservations about pacifism and our peace theology. My approach was always one of welcome, come and worship with us, be in relationship with us as a community of faith and live into your question. Yes, who we are and what we proclaim is deeply grounded in the nonviolent love of Jesus Christ, that is what you will hear and what we strive to live together. I am confident the Spirit will give you clarity in due time—clarity that grows into and shares our commitment to the nonviolent love of Jesus Christ or clarity that you are called to another spiritual home. If it is the latter, and you truly do not share this way of Jesus, as your pastor, I will prayerfully help you find the spiritual home where you are called to be. I have helped more than one person find another spiritual home.

Chris posed some penetrating questions to Tim about what he views as particular challenges for third-way churches. He wonders about "how many non-affirming parents would feel comfortable if their children began to struggle with sexual identity issues at a Third Way church." He also questions whether "a non-affirming pastor [or a 'non-affirming youth pastor'] could be effective at a Third Way congregation." He calls into question the possibility of such effectiveness, as follows.

> I find Tim's paradigm of a "Third Way" church intriguing. However, it seems to me that, at the very least, the pastor of such a church would need be able to support same-sex relationships, as pastors are involved in marriage preparation, marriage counseling, and other pastoral initiatives to strengthen and support marriages. If the pastor felt uncomfortable with a gay couple

getting married, it would be nearly impossible for him or her to minister effectively.

Tim responds to Chris's question by drawing on an analogy with how disagreements are worked out in a "family."

> In regard to your question about how a Third Way would work out if the pastor opposed gay marriage, in my context we'd work it out as if we were a family (which isn't always great!). It might be something like: Malcolm would talk with Pastor Sally about his desire to marry his boyfriend and Sally would explain why she doesn't bless gay marriages but also (having had this conversation twice already) that she knows a nearby pastor who will do it, and that in spite of not doing the wedding she still loves Malcolm to pieces (which he already knows, because she visited him faithfully when he was in the hospital).
> Of course there is always the possibility that Malcolm will stomp off in a rage declaring that Sally doesn't *really* love him. Or Sally might capitulate and seethe with resentment while she conducts the ceremony. But hey, that's how we Anabaptists do business. Or hopefully, *family*.
> But I don't know how it would work in a different setting. Putting up the hood on the Book of Common Prayer to mess with its engine sounds daunting. And the fact that you all think of marriage as a sacrament between a man and woman . . . do sacraments even have a latch for the hood?

So many questions, so little time. There is an obvious need for ongoing conversation about the specific challenges for pastors and their churches as they seek to care for LGBT individuals.

OTHER QUESTIONS BEGGING FOR ONGOING CONVERSATION

WHAT ABOUT THE GLOBAL SOUTH?

As is well known, Christians in the Global South generally embrace the traditional view of marriage, some to the point of calling for harsh penalties for LGBT individuals. Chris reflects on this as follows.

> I've also spent time listening to the concerns of my brothers and sisters in the Global South, agreeing with them on the importance of upholding the traditional Christian understanding of marriage, yet also sharing my concerns about legislation that

might result in the imprisonment, or even death, of openly gay or lesbian people.

In a later posting, Chris reiterates his "strong opposition to the 'anti-gay' laws that have been in the news recently in many countries in Africa." But he adds a reflection on a possible analogy with the issue of polygamy to suggest that when same-sex married couples come to faith in Christ, there may be a good argument for the continuation of that union of marriage, "especially [for] a couple who are raising children."

> I should be clear that I've been quite open about my strong opposition to the "anti-gay" laws that have been in the news recently in many countries in Africa. I've also spent time with some of these brothers and sisters, seeking to understand their perspective, all the while sharing my concerns. It's interesting that Tim raised the issue of polygamy. Among our brothers and sisters in Africa, there seems to be a consensus that, when a man in multiple marriages comes to faith in Christ, it would be a greater wrong to insist that he simply choose one wife, thus exposing the others to deep shame and vulnerability, than to remain in an arrangement that is less than God's intention but does honor and protect his wives. So, the man is allowed to maintain the marriages, yet, he is prohibited from serving in church leadership. I wonder if, ironically, this pastoral solution might be roughly applicable to a man or woman in a same-sex marriage who may come to faith in Christ, especially a couple who are raising children.

Tim has some reflections on Chris's view that "taking a welcoming but not affirming stance [is] . . . standing in solidarity with the Global South." Tim first points to differing "cultural factors" in the West and Global South that could lead to contrary views about the "most humane thing to do" relative to both homosexuality and polygamy (which seems to echo, at least in part, Chris's view as to how to respond to same-sex married couples who are raising children).

> *There are confounding cultural factors on both sides, that make this a fraught issue.* My Old Testament professor Ellen Davis tells the story of teaching a seminary class in South Sudan. The topic of homosexuality came up and her students expressed their inability to understand permissive Western attitudes toward same-sex relationships. She then asked them, "How many of you think polygamous marriage is acceptable?" About half the hands went up. She responded, "Westerners find that incomprehensible."

> Having lived in Uganda as a kid (and having visited as an adult), I became sympathetic towards some of the arguments for having more than one wife. The cultural context is so different, that in certain situations, it seems like the most humane thing to do. I believe that if those in the Global South understood the way we construct same-sex relationships, and the intense loneliness of people in our fragmented society, that they would be more sympathetic toward same-sex relationships.

Tim then presents a deep concern that "The Global South seems posed to repeat some of the destructive church divisions that have taken place in the West."

> Although in places like Uganda public opinion is solidly against LGBT affirmation, there is a growing group of LGBT advocates and an increasingly visible population of sexual minorities. Eventually the church, in places like Uganda, will have to face the same questions we've faced.
>
> And so the important question is, "can we find a way to live together in peace on this, or is division inevitable?" If we can find a "third way" then I think we will have done the hard work that might serve our brothers and sisters from the Global South. And if not, then I suspect that like us, they will experience the same damnable rupture of unity and love.

Further conversation is needed relative to the above reflections regarding the stance of the Global South relative to LGBT persons and issues.

WHY HAS "HOMOSEXUALITY" BECOME A DEFINING AND DIVIDING ISSUE FOR THE CHRISTIAN CHURCH?

Weldon poses this probing question, drawing a contrast with his experience of how the Mennonite Church has dealt with the issues of "women in leadership and divorce and remarriage."

> Why is "homosexuality" a church defining and dividing matter when other highly conflicted issues don't necessarily define or divide us? In the Mennonite Church women in leadership and divorce and remarriage have been contended over the past four decades as has "homosexuality." Ironically, my ministry has precisely coincided with and engaged these three concerns and changes in the church. Yet we have found a way to navigate the contentious waters of women in leadership and divorce and remarriage in ways that honor the authority of Scripture, the

faithfulness of the church, and the integrity of pastoral leadership. We have done so with clarity and honesty, recognizing differences without resorting to discipline to keep members in line or out of the church. What are the differences in the differences we have on these matters? What are the limits of difference and on what "issues" that the church can tolerate and still be the church together?[3]

To add fuel to the fire, I add the following personal reflection. I find no uncertainty or ambiguity in what the Bible teaches about greed: it is sin. Biblical exhortations to be generous to others, especially the poor and marginalized, are legion. Yet, I have never attended a church where anyone has suggested that to become a member of the church or to share in the ministry of the church, a Christian must demonstrate that he/she is not "greedy."[4] Why do we treat homosexuality differently?

Tim's answer to the question of why homosexuality has become a defining and dividing issue for the Christian church is that this issue is accompanied by "supercharged emotions."

> ... this debate should not divide the church. My conservative Bible professor used to quote the helpful adage, "In essentials unity, in non-essentials liberty, in all things charity." This is a non-essential matter that feels essential because of the supercharged emotions that accompany it. It is a clash of conservative and liberal presuppositions that are more products of culture than of Christ's teachings.

---

3. Weldon adds a further note as to how the Mennonite Church has navigated the issue of divorce and remarriage: "The Mennonite Church has found a way to hold members who are divorced with compassion while upholding our confessional commitment to lifelong marriage. I have accompanied many couples who have made a marriage covenant with God and each other. About half of these marriage partners had been previously married. Yet we have found a faithful way to uphold lifelong marriage while caring for divorced members and blessing remarriages in the church. This path of exceptional healing and healing exception, is manifested in remarriages that are healthy and happy. They also become faithful members and leaders in the church."

4. One might be tempted to suggest that those deciding on church membership should ask to see income tax returns. I am not proposing such an impersonal strategy. But, if Tim is correct, as I believe he is, that an important question to be asked of all church members is "How is God working in your life and how can we cooperate with that?," then an appropriate time may present itself when two Christians who have developed a close personal relationship of mutual understanding and trust talk about their respective charitable contribution practices. Based on the same foundation of having formed a caring personal relationship, these same two persons may also be poised to have a respectful conversation about disagreements regarding LGBT issues.

Tim elaborates as follows by suggesting that the "disgust" that many Christians "feel" about homosexuality may be culturally conditioned rather than "a God-given moral compass meant to help them tell right from wrong." In his own heartfelt and provocative words:

> Growing up in this culture, even though I'm gay, I sometimes feel disgust at things like the sight of men kissing. But I believe I was taught this feeling. Some cultures, after all, regard men holding hands or even kissing as normal. The fact that I feel somewhat differently about women engaging in public displays of affection makes me think that this sense isn't directly from God.
>
> Being gay I often—in place of disgust—feel joy at the sight of two men kissing. Joy is another core human emotion. The longest stretch of joy I ever felt came from being infatuated with another guy. I loved being loved. I loved loving. It is tempting to take this feeling as a sign of approval from God. Jesuit priest and philosopher Pierre Teilhard de Chardin wrote that "Joy is the infallible sign of the presence of God."
>
> This is the problem. One person's disgust collides with another's joy. Disgust, designed to protect us from ingesting harmful food from which we get sick or die, is a potent and powerful emotion. Joy, on the other hand, taps into our brain's reward centers and sends the command: you've done something right! Do it again!
>
> One side thinks, "Given the obvious sinfulness (read: the disgust I feel) of same-sex relationships, those people have forsaken what it means to be Christian." The other side thinks, "Those people are so opposed to human flourishing (read: the joy I feel), they're clearly the self-righteous religious leaders Jesus would have condemned."
>
> So let's begin by taking a deep breath. The Christian doctrine of sin teaches that our feelings can deceive us. Disgust might help us detect sin or it might be a sign of a Pharisee heart. On the other hand, our culture tends toward an idolatry of romantic love so our joy may be in the service of worshipping a false god.
>
> At the very least, let's humbly admit that our feelings may influence how we think about this. Given the powerful emotions associated with this topic, we tend to feel that being right about this question (either affirming or non-affirming) is central to faith. In fact, there is good reason to believe this is an important matter but ultimately peripheral to an orthodox Christianity. There is good reason for a "respectful conversation."

Chris expressed appreciation for Tim's recognition of the "culturally conditioned nature of our emotions," adding that this insight is "similar" to Weldon's "affirmation of the importance of experience in applying the truth of Scripture to a given context."

> I also appreciated Tim's observations on the importance of recognizing the culturally conditioned nature of our emotions, whether disgust or joy, and that, biblically, "our feelings can deceive us." Weldon similarly affirms the importance of experience in applying the truth of Scripture to a given context, noting that "'experience' alone does not constitute the church's faithful profession or practice," but that 'experience' is essential to being church."

This raises the contested issue as to the relationship between one's "experience" and one's understanding of biblical teachings, a topic to which we will eventually turn. In the meantime, I consider Weldon's own radical response to his question as to why homosexuality has become such a defining issue for the Christian church. Weldon suggests that the reasons for this are "rooted in two 'issues' deeper than 'homosexuality': our "fear of our own sexuality," which makes us "even more afraid of same-sex sexuality"; and the issue of who in the church has the "power" to decide and enforce decisions about homosexuality.

> I have yet to hear a coherent explanation of why "homosexuality" is our greatest church defining and dividing "issue" for the past half century.
>
> I believe our reasons for it being church defining and dividing are rooted in "issues" deeper than "homosexuality." What I have long known and often said as a pastor, is that for most matters we fight over in the church, "the issue is not the issue." What is identified as the "issue" is often a manifestation of and triggered by much deeper matters we deny or don't want to face.
>
> I see two deeper "issues" that drive this conflict and divide us. First, the church has a tragic history with sexuality—being embodied sexual humans created in God's image. Our fears and fantasies about being sexual bodies are projected onto "homosexuality" rather than faced forthrightly . . . . Our persistent denial or refusal to face these profound sexual matters in ourselves and in human relationship in the church tends to be projected onto "others" who are not "us." Our projection is manifested as control over the "other" to keep them away so we aren't reminded of something we need to face in ourselves. If we are afraid of our own sexuality, we are even more afraid of

same-sex sexuality. In other words, we have both an obsession with sexuality and aversion to sexuality that subverts the centrality of sexuality in human life and relationship . . . . These matters desperately need the church's fullest attention. Our obsessive focus on "homosexuality" has not and will not help us find *the way forward*.

This segues into the second deeper issue we face in the church over sexuality, which is power. At one level, a central "issue" in this controversy is over authority—authority of Scripture, authority of church leaders, authority of the church, and our own personal authority. All of those embody multiple levels of meaning worthy of unpacking. That too is more than this conversation can bear. More to the point here, underneath these struggles with authority is the deeper "issue" of power. Who decides and how are decisions enacted and enforced? Equally important is who doesn't have power and who is the recipient of what is enacted and enforced?

The power for "exclusion" and the power for "inclusion" are opposing forces, to be sure. But they are not parallel approaches or access to power; they do not have parallel strategic or substantive purposes.

From the beginning a decade ago, our Inclusive Mennonite Pastors effort has been invitational and formational rather than dominating and disciplinary. We don't demand that everyone agree and act with us. We don't threaten to take our congregations and leave the denomination if those who exclude LGBTQ members remain in the denomination. We don't have and wouldn't use power to discipline and dismember congregations or pastors who are "exclusive." We believe we can be and must be the church together even with these differences.

As Weldon sees it, the problem created by the church not addressing these two deeper issues is that it "subverts faithful exploration of the fullness and beauty of what it means to be wholly/holy spiritual-sexual beings created in God's image."

The church's obsession with "homosexuality" has subverted faithful exploration of the fullness and beauty of what it means to be wholly/holy spiritual-sexual beings created in God's image. Sexuality is not the antithesis of but deeply interwoven with spirituality. Sexual identity is complex and diverse with nuanced identities across a spectrum. We are created by God and are children of God—which takes us into the deep intersection and integration of our spiritual-sexual being.

It is in light of this conviction that Weldon decided many years ago that he would "refrain from making 'homosexuality' be the defining, consuming, or dividing issue of the church," but would pursue a challenging path involving a "search of Scriptures" and a communal exploration of "how to be faithful spiritual-sexual beings by being spiritually discerning and communally compassionate."

> When I was called to be pastor of Seattle Mennonite Church over two decades ago, I shared with the congregation my pastoral commitment to refrain from making "homosexuality" be the defining, consuming, or dividing issue of the church. I also shared my sense that this congregation would not exist without being in some way inclusive of LGBTQ members. We will *listen to what God sets before us* and trust God to lead us faithfully as a church. Along the way we will search the Scriptures and explore how to be faithful spiritual-sexual beings by being spiritually discerning and communally compassionate. We will remain committed to our beloved Mennonite Church, knowing that the majority of Mennonites will continue to reject the Way we are being led.

Of course, there is much contention among Christians about what will result from such a "search of Scriptures," including significant disagreements among Chris, Weldon, and Tim, a topic to which we will soon turn. But, first, there is another lingering question that has already been hinted at a number of times.

WHAT IS THE ROLE OF POWER AND PRIVILEGE WHEN THE CHURCH ENGAGES LGBT CHRISTIANS?

Based on his belief that same-sex orientation is "a creation-based biological-sexual determination that all humans are born with," Weldon questions the right of a "sexual majority" to have the power that "prevents a sister or brother who is a sexual minority from fully living their identity and calling."

> Given a creation-based biological-sexual determination that all humans are born with, I find it equally incomprehensible for a sexual majority to impose control that prevents a sister or brother who is a sexual minority from fully living their identity and calling, including the covenant love of sacramental marriage. God created us in God's image as wholly-holy spiritual-sexual beings and created us to be in relationship. Yes, that has many manifestations, of which marriage is a primary human

relationship. That truth and reality, not who is having sex with whom, is the heart of the matter.

Tim expresses the same concern when he refers to the "privilege and power" that are at times "marshalled to harm another member of the body [of Christ]."

We ran out of time before anyone could elaborate on this concern. It raises huge questions as to the nature of church governance, including the decision-making prerogatives, or not, of pastors as well as those charged with local church authority (e.g., the Consistory in my church, a member of the Reformed Church in America) and national church bodies (e.g., the Reformed Church in America denomination). I will share my reflections on these thorny "governance" issues in my concluding chapter 10.

BIBLICAL UNDERSTANDINGS (REVISITED)

Chapter 2 reported in depth on the agreements and disagreements between two biblical scholars, Mark Strauss and Jim Brownson, as to what the Bible teaches regarding same-sex marriage, with Mark taking the traditional position that marriage should be reserved for a man and a woman and Jim taking the nontraditional position that Scriptures allow for same-sex marriage as a lifelong, monogamous covenant.

While Chris, Weldon, and Tim are not professional biblical scholars, their education for pastoral ministry obviously included a healthy dose of biblical and theological studies, and they bring to bear perspectives on LGBT persons and issues that are deeply informed by their "pastoral care in the trenches" that deserve careful attention as a complement to the perspectives of biblical scholars working in the academy. Therefore this section will revisit "biblical understandings" as seen through the eyes of three pastors, with some mention made of connections with the perspectives of Mark and Jim reported in chapter 2.

BIBLICAL AUTHORITY AND BIBLICAL INTERPRETATION

Chris, Weldon, and Tim agree with Mark and Jim that the Bible is "authoritative" for Christians, while also agreeing that the central issue when considering LGBT issues is that of biblical interpretation. As Tim puts it, "The debate over same-sex relationships and the Bible is not one about Scripture's *authority*, but of Scripture's *interpretation*."

Chris agrees with this assertion by Tim, but with the caveat that "not all interpretations of scripture are equally valid." I believe that the other four conversation partners would surely embrace Chris's caveat in light of their arguments for the adequacy, or not, of differing interpretations of relevant biblical passages.

While affirming that the central issue when considering LGBT issues is that of "biblical interpretation," Tim expresses concern that "some people, as they move towards the affirming side [relative to same-sex marriage], will be tempted to dismiss Scripture out of hand rather than seize the chance to examine how to best interpret Scripture." Tim is also "troubled" by his "inability to completely articulate a way of interpreting Scripture that avoids the dangers of literalism, while retaining something to which we must submit."

> Reading Scripture (I'm in 1 Samuel in my read-through-the-Bible plan) I find it to be a different book than the one described by most evangelicals. So I resonate with critiques like Peter Enn's *The Bible Tells me So*[5] and Christian Smith's *The Bible Made Impossible*.[6] But both of those books falter in terms of a positive proposal for how we *should* interpret Scripture. I don't feel completely adrift in this regard, but it troubles me. I want to keep thinking and talking with others about how to understand the Bible as an authoritative narrative.

We will soon turn to Tim's effort to find a "middle way" between "biblical literalism" and "dismissing Scripture out of hand."

CONTEXT IS IMPORTANT

As reported in chapter 2, both Mark and Jim agreed that "the Bible is contextually given." I believe that Chris, Weldon, and Tim would all agree, although their interpretations of the significance of the context of a given biblical passage related to LGBT issues will differ. For example, Tim poses a question that reflects his understanding of the context for selected passages in the Old Testament that prohibit same-sex relationships.

> A reader of Scripture, *seeking to submit herself to the authority of Scripture*, might ask questions like the following with integrity: Since the primary expression of same-sex relationships in the

5. Enns, *The Bible Tells Me So*.
6. Smith, *The Bible Made Impossible*.

first century was older men with thirteen- to seventeen-year-old boys, could it be that Scripture is condemning that practice rather than modern day relationships of equals?

It is important at this point to recall my report in chapter 1 on Justin Lee's assertion that consideration of the "context" of biblical passages should focus on the "context of people's lives."

> Justin asserts that a mistake he made in his early dealings with LGBT persons and issues is that he "tried to interpret Scripture in a vacuum rather than in the context of people's lives," adding that "when hurting people's lives are involved, a compelling Scriptural argument in the *abstract* is not enough."

THE CREATION NARRATIVE IN GENESIS 1-2

While recognizing the importance of context in biblical interpretation, especially in interpreting those "texts of terror" that possibly refer to "cultic, non-consensual, or exploitative sex," Chris asserts that "we can't avoid these passages" or separate them from the "creation narratives of Genesis 1-2."

> I want to be careful here, because, truly, passages from Genesis 19, Leviticus 18 and 22, Romans 1, 1 Corinthians 6, and 1 Timothy 1, have been used as "texts of terror" (often known among the LGBT community as "clobber passages") in the lives of many LGBT people. We must reject using these passages, isolated from their context (a context which is, ultimately, the whole Bible, at the heart of which is the gospel), to put guilt and shame on anyone. However, we also can't avoid these passages, which, while possibly referring to cultic, non-consensual, or exploitative sex, simply can't, with integrity, be reduced so narrowly, and separated from the creation narrative(s) of Genesis 1-2. We enter dangerous territory when we say things like, "Well, if Paul had only known . . ."

Chris adds that "Changing our understanding of marriage and sexuality, however, touches on core understandings of creation, the fall, redemption, and even the doctrine of God" (which is similar to Matthew Anderson's position regarding the "Doctrine of God," as reported in chapter 7).

Weldon notes that the traditional view of the significance of the Creation account in Genesis 1-2 is that "God's creation of male and female somehow means 'homosexuality' is not of creation and is 'disordered,'" adding that he wonders about the effect on this traditional' view of current debates about whether sexual orientation has biological causation.

> Finally, I find it surprising that none of us directly addressed the traditional creation question, where God's creation of male and female somehow means "homosexuality" is not of creation and is "disordered." My sense is that arguments over "birth" versus "choice" claims for LGBT orientation have diminished as awareness, experience, and scientific evidence grows that indicates considerable biological factors and nuanced diversity in sexual orientation. However, I have spent my pastoral years in congregations where that wasn't disputed. So I am wondering if or how that is still a matter of contention across our churches?

Tim reflects as follows on the "traditional" view that "homosexuality is not of creation" but is "disordered."

> I contend that God's ideal pattern (as revealed in the Genesis account) is that of male and female joining together in marriage. Based on this, the Christian tradition has labeled same-sex coupling as a "disorder," a non-conformity with God's will, and therefore a sin. But just because something deviates from the ideal, it isn't necessarily a sin.
>
> ... If someone is born colorblind, we don't say, "Well, since you can't do it as God designed, you probably shouldn't try to see at all." So too with a same-sex orientation, I think it is possible to say, "Well, it is not God's ideal, but love sexually as you can, and enter into the beautiful Christian story of faithful covenant keeping." With this perspective I think we can still affirm "core understandings of creation, the fall, redemption, and even the doctrine of God" without condemning LGBT Christians who chose to commit to someone of the same sex, with a steadfast and costly love.

Weldon also suggests that "Marriage is more complex and problematic in the Bible and the church than we acknowledge," noting that "polygamy, patriarchy, and property have a troubling marriage history."

Chris's response to this complexity regarding marriage pointed to by Weldon follows:

> As I said in my first post, the creation narrative, Jesus' affirmation of the creation narrative, Paul's echoes of the creation narrative in Romans 1, and, finally, the hope of the ultimate renewal of creation (or, to use another N. T. Wright-ism, "putting the world to rights"), convinces me that God's intention for

> sexual intimacy is within a covenantal relationship between a man and a woman. Weldon rightly points out that marriage in Scripture is problematic due to . . . "polygamy, patriarchy, and property." However, this is a far cry from the radical equality envisioned in Genesis 1-2, and, post-Resurrection, Ascension, and Pentecost, a far cry from Paul commanding husbands to love their wives, "as Christ loved the church" (Ephesians 5:25). In other words, God's creative intention is clear in Genesis 1-2, but the fall puts everything out of whack, and then Jesus' life, death, resurrection, and ascension begins to put things back together. The redemptive arc on marriage is clear—a first-century Roman or Jewish husband called to love his wife as Christ loved the church simply cannot revert to the "polygamy, patriarchy, and property" paradigm, but is rather thrust forward to the new creation, which finds it roots in Eden.

While agreeing with Chris that "the new creation has its roots in Eden," Tim notes that "a tree can look a lot different than its roots," further suggesting that the key Creation teaching is that "It is not good that the man should be alone" (Gen 2:18), which may provide "an opening for gay marriage."

> One of the few things we know about the new creation is that "At the resurrection people will neither marry nor be given in marriage" (Matt 22:30). In the New Testament we already see a considerable de-emphasis on the traditional family. Jesus and Paul both seem to be single. Paul recommends that single people remain single unless they are "not practicing self-control" (1 Corinthians 7:9). Marriage, in this view, doesn't seem freighted with all the theological weight we tend to ascribe to it, but is a rather plain solution to God's compassionate observation, "It is not good that the man should be alone" (Gen 2:18).
>
> Since that is the most plainly stated biblical purpose of marriage (rather than the speculative, and sometimes beautiful theories about how its real purpose is to mirror the unity-in-diversity of the Trinity) I see an opening for gay marriage.

Along similar lines, one of our eCircle readers responds to Chris as follows: "You bring up the creation narrative as though the Garden were normative rather than the beginning of the wonderful diversity described in Revelation."

We obviously have some disagreements about how to interpret the Genesis 1-2 creation account.

BENEATH THE SURFACE OF BIBLICAL RULES

There is also disagreement about the nature of "biblical rules," those many prescriptions and proscriptions for human behavior contained in the Bible.

First, note Tim's commentary on the assertion of "conservatives" that because "there are six verses about same-sex relations and they all speak against it," "Anyone ... who denies that Scripture speaks against homosexuality is engaged in rationalizations for a cherished yet sinful behavior."

> At its most simplistic, this view sees the Bible as a kind of moral encyclopedia—pick an ethical question, look up the entries about it, obey the answer. But a few quick tests reveal the inadequacy of this view. Is it okay to wear clothes that blend fabrics? Have multiple wives? Eat road kill? Look up the verses. The answers are: no, maybe, no. Perhaps more disturbing, look for the verse that says definitively that slave-holding is a sin. It is not there.

Tim asserts that "What needs to change is the way we understand the nature of Scripture."

> The Bible is more a storybook than a morality textbook....
> I think literalist approaches to Scripture make Christianity into a "paint by numbers exercise rather than an adventure in faith."

Tim views "the whole LGBT question" as "an opportunity to move beyond a simplistic, modernist view of Scripture in which the Bible is a divine morality hotline."

Weldon expresses agreement with Tim's concern about "the Bible being wrongly used as a "moral encyclopedia," noting his appreciation for Tim "reminding us that the Bible is 'more a storybook than a morality textbook,'" but also pointing out that the Bible contains "much good moral instruction."

> I concur that the Bible is the living Word of God not a moral code or rule book. In interpreting and living God's Word we find much good moral instruction but not a moral weapon.

While agreeing with Tim that "Scripture is, primarily 'storied' rather than legal," Chris expresses a concern.

> However, the "mystery novel" analogy only works up to a point. For example, a first-time reader of Scripture might be shocked by Jesus' teaching about the Sabbath and the Spirit's work incorporating Gentiles into God's people "apart from the Law."

> However, as modern readers, we know how the canonical story ends, and, as a result, also catch a glimpse of how the cosmic story ends.

Neither Tim nor Weldon had an opportunity to respond to Chris's concern. More conversation is obviously needed.

In the meantime, there is enough concern expressed here as to how to interpret the "moral instruction" in the Bible to warrant further reflection about the nature of its moral prescriptions and proscriptions, about which Chris, Weldon, and Tim provide further commentary, and for which both Jim Brownson and Mark Strauss provide a good starting point.

Although Jim and Mark used different terminology, as reported in chapter 2, they agreed that "the moral logic of the Bible focuses on the purposes of commandments." In Jim's words, "we need to probe the 'moral logic' of the commands and prohibitions of Scripture, asking not only *what* they say, but also *why they say* what they do."

Since both Tim and Chris reflect on biblical passages related to the issues of "Sabbath observance" and the "inclusion of Gentiles within the Christian fold" (which will soon be seen to be interrelated issues), what follows will be an attempt to "dig beneath" the surface of the relevant biblical commandments to identify "purpose."

Tim notes that although Sabbath observance was grounded in the Creation, it was "set aside in order to include the Gentiles."

> If *anything, ever, in the history of theological teaching*, was grounded in creation it was Sabbath. Sabbath-keeping is embedded in the Ten Commandments and Israel's law. Yet passages like Romans 14 and Galatians 4 seem to put Sabbath-keeping aside in order to include the Gentiles.

But Tim asserts that it was not just for the sake of including the Gentiles that strict Sabbath observance was set aside. As he also says, elaborating on his earlier assertion that "the Bible is more a storybook than a morality textbook."

> The Bible . . . is a story in which Jesus sets aside Sabbath laws related to harvesting and claims that "The Sabbath was made for humankind, and not humankind for the Sabbath" (Mark 2:27). It is a story in which the early church sets aside biblical prophecy that the Gentiles would learn the law from Israel (Isa 2:3, Mic 4:2) and deem the law an unnecessary burden (Acts 15:10–11).

The teaching of Mark 2:27 seems to point to the "purpose" of the Sabbath focusing on human flourishing, and its original means for observance can be altered when it hinders such human flourishing. Tim then asks: "If such a foundational understanding of creation [as calling for strict Sabbath observance relative to harvesting] was put aside to include us, shouldn't we hesitate a little at insisting that LGBT people need to follow a heterosexual norm because it is grounded in creation?"

Tim also reflects on "the Jerusalem council's decision (Acts 15) to set aside the law concerning circumcision for the Gentiles."

> I think it is telling that when James cites Scripture to back up the decision [to set aside the law concerning circumcision for the Gentiles], he says, "'the words of the prophets agree with this,' not 'this agrees with the words of the prophets'" .... Seeing God at work, by help of the Spirit, is a key to truthful discernment. Scripture plays a key role in checking what we perceive the Spirit to be doing, but this is not as simple as we are sometimes led to believe.
>
> In Acts 15 James cites a scriptural passage that is not a simple proof text. It is a remix of Scripture meant to help the community locate itself in the story of God and affirm the work that God is doing .... There was good scriptural support for the idea that Gentiles should be circumcised. The Covenant of Circumcision was an "everlasting" one (Gen 17:1-7) and other passages see Israel blessing the Gentiles as it teaches them the law (Isa 2:3, Mic 4:2)—which would have been understood as requiring circumcision. But James, by using Amos and throwing in snippets of Jeremiah and Isaiah and some words of his own, claims that the prophets foresee the rebuilding of Israel so that "all other peoples may seek the Lord" (Acts 15:17).

It appears that the "purpose" of setting aside the law concerning circumcision for Gentiles is to promote the human flourishing of Gentiles by enabling them to be included as people of God, an expression, as Tim adds, "of God's mercy and love being preeminent."

Based on this approach to Scripture as "improvisation," Tim once again wonders about the possibility of drawing an analogy relative to LGBT inclusion.

> The Christian life as improvisation also provides warrant for taking Gentile inclusion as a possible analogy for LGBT inclusion. If we were to ask evangelical Christians the question, "Who do you think is the most 'far off' from God group of people you know? The people most plagued by idolatry and sexual immorality?" I think many would answer "the gay community." That is, of course, exactly how the Jews thought of Gentiles. And our

full inclusion is more of a miracle than most of us Gentiles will ever admit.

Chris disagrees with the analogy that Tim wishes to draw between Gentile inclusion and LGBT inclusion. While acknowledging that "Sabbath and food laws were set aside for Gentile converts (and Jewish believers who felt so led)," Chris argues that "sexual morality was, if anything, made more challenging for both Jew and Gentile in the New Covenant."

> Tim asked about the early Christians' decision to put aside the Sabbath for Gentile converts, suggesting that, since the Sabbath, which is so central to the creation narrative, was set aside in the New Covenant, the male-female sexual union might also be set aside. My response is that Jesus, The Acts of the Apostles, Paul, and the author of the Letter to the Hebrews each speak about the Sabbath, namely how the coming of Jesus changes how God's people understand and experience the Sabbath. Jesus violated the Sabbath prohibitions of gleaning and healing, demonstrating that in God's kingdom pursuing shalom is always acceptable. In Acts 15, the apostles set aside Sabbath regulations, which had become ethno-cultural identity markers, for Gentile converts. In Romans 14, Paul specifically mentions those who "esteem one day better than another" as worthy of welcome and honor, all the while insisting that the one for whom "all days are alike" are worthy of equal welcome (Rom 14:5–6). The Letter to the Hebrews recasts the Sabbath in eschatological terms, writing that, "a Sabbath rest remains for the people of God" (Heb 4:9). Again, while the Sabbath and food laws were set aside for Gentile converts (and Jewish believers who felt so led), sexual morality was, if anything, made more challenging for both Jew and Gentile in the New Covenant. Thus I see no ground in setting aside the historic Christian understanding of marriage and sexuality, as it is rooted in the creation narrative, was strengthened by Jesus himself, and then affirmed by Paul.

Once again, a significant disagreement has emerged, which points to the need for more conversation.

THE WAY FORWARD

It is obvious from the above report that, despite areas of agreement between Chris, Weldon and Tim, significant disagreements persist, especially relative to "biblical understandings," which call for ongoing conversations.

Hopefully, that conversation can be informed by the following reflections from our conversation partners as to a possible way forward.

THE PRIMACY OF "LOVING MUTUAL RELATIONSHIP" FOR HUMAN FLOURISHING

Tim issues a clarion call for all pastors to "envision a pastoral way forward." As he seeks to identify the contours of such a way forward, he starts with a crucial question:

> Could we agree that "human flourishing" is one of God's intentions for all humans and that it has something (everything) to do with being in loving mutual relationship?

Weldon adds that "God created us to be in relationship."

> God created us in God's image as wholly-holy spiritual-sexual beings and created us to be in relationship. Yes, that has many manifestations, of which marriage is a primary human relationship. That truth and reality, not who is having sex with whom, is the heart of the matter.

For Weldon, this focus on "being in relationship" informs his "hope" that the church will go beyond "engaging with LGBT members" to establishing "full mutuality."

> My hope is for a church living beyond "engaging with LGBT members" into full mutuality that welcomes, embraces, and honors all people on the same basis as valued and essential members of the body of Christ. The Apostle Paul's beautiful body language of being one body with many members is dependent on difference honoring difference, not dominating or dismembering difference (1 Cor 12:12ff.)

Chris also points us to the importance of "flourishing relationships," adding that we do "more harm than good" if we do not "create space" for LGBT Christians to have such relationships.

> If we refuse to create space for LGBT Christians to flourish relationally, only telling them what they can't do, we unwittingly wind up doing more harm than good.

Of course, even if there is agreement that "loving mutual relationship" is essential for "human flourishing," the huge question remains as to appropriate forms for such "loving mutual relationships" for all Christians, including

LGBT Christians, a topic that was addressed in depth by Eve Tushnet and Justin Lee in chapter 1, and which is also addressed by our current conversation partners.

PROMOTING NEGLECTED FORMS OF GIVING AND RECEIVING LOVE

As reported in chapter 1, Eve Tushnet believes that gay Christians are called to a life of celibacy, while Justin Lee believes that same-sex marriage is appropriate for gay Christians. But they agree on the primacy of "loving mutual relationships," and that such relationships are "not all about sex." Whereas Justin believes that gay Christians should not be denied the intimacy of the loving mutual relationship of marriage, Eve points us toward nonsexual and much neglected forms of "giving and receiving love": Friendship, service, and celibate partnerships.

Chris echoes Eve's proposal by also calling for "the church to create space for creative, non-sexual, expressions of love and intimacy for those LGBT brothers and sisters within the church."

> As I've grappled with a way forward in engaging with LGBT people, I've been helped and challenged by the work of Wesley Hill, Eve Tushnet, and our conversation partner Tim Otto. Their lives and writing have, generally, assumed that sexual orientation is fairly fixed, and challenged the church to rethink how we conceive of loving, intimate relationships. If the church is asking gay and lesbian people to refrain from sexual intimacy, are we ready to create space for other expressions of love and intimacy?
>
> I'm left in a place, then, of affirming the historic Christian teaching on marriage and sexuality while seeking to embrace LGBT people outside of the church and create space for creative, non-sexual, expressions of love and intimacy for those LGBT brothers and sisters within the church. This is not a comfortable position, to be sure, but one rooted in biblical, theological, and pastoral reflection that I believe is necessary "for such a time as this."

So, while I believe it is fair to say that Chris, Weldon, Tim, Eve, and Justin agree on the primacy of "loving mutual relationship" for human flourishing," there is disagreement as to whether same-sex marriage is appropriate. But, at a minimum, one aspect of a way forward is for all churches to focus much more on the "neglected forms of giving and receiving love" that are now largely unrecognized and unsupported in our churches.

GETTING TO KNOW OUR LGBT BROTHERS AND SISTERS IN CHRIST BY LISTENING TO THEIR STORIES

As reported in chapter 1, this aspect of a way forward has already been proposed by Eve Tushnet and Justin Lee. Weldon adds a reflection on what they have learned by such careful listening and observing the exemplary Christian lives of many LGBT Christians.

> [I have been blessed to see Jesus] . . . in sisters and brothers who are LGBTQ being passionate and compassionate disciples of Jesus, committed to a church that ostracizes them, serving faithfully in congregational leadership roles within a denomination that rejects them for their sexual identity.

Tim adds the provocative suggestion:

> As we see the Spirit in gay couples animating hospitality, service to the local church, and generally blessing others, I think there is good reason to re-assess our view of same-sex acts as necessarily sinful.

On a personal note, I believe that the importance of "getting to know" LGBT Christians cannot be overstated. When we see the manner in which LGBT friends who we have come to know personally faithfully live out their Christian faith commitments, that may cause us to rethink our present "biblical understanding." I am not suggesting that "experience" trumps Scripture. But I am suggesting that when we observe splendid expressions of Christian faithfulness on the part of LGBT Christians, that ought to compel us to revisit the Bible with "fresh eyes." Whether that is possible is an aspect of a possible way forward to which we now turn.

IS A NEW "HERMENEUTICAL PARADIGM" POSSIBLE?

Relative to his call to seek a way forward, Weldon says that he does not "expect substantial disagreement [about interpreting "select texts" dealing with same-sex matters] . . . to be reconciled" (at least in the near future, I would add).

> I say that select texts will not help us find a way forward. I am not saying disregard these texts but I am saying that traditional interpretations of these texts are not the only interpretations and not the only or even the best texts to help us find *The Way forward*. After forty years I do not expect the substantial disagreement over those texts to be reconciled.

In another posting, Weldon repeats this concern, but with the important addition that "the real conflict we face . . . is deeper than differing interpretations of these select texts; it is in substantially differing (even mutually exclusive) approaches to scripture and interpretive paradigms."

> [W]e will not find the way forward in the church based on a few select texts held to settle the matter and over which we are and will remain deeply divided. I say this for two reasons. One, is that in over forty years of experience in this conflict in the Mennonite Church, arguments over these select Scriptures have not contributed to further revelation, resolution, or reconciliation. Second, I believe the real conflict we face, mostly without acknowledging or addressing it, is deeper than differing interpretations of these select texts; it is in substantially differing (even mutually exclusive) approaches to Scripture and interpretive paradigms. These are fundamental hermeneutical questions the church must face and address before we can find our way on the sexuality matters. Differing paradigms of biblical interpretation may be the primary confession and clarification we have to name and embody before we can cease dividing over "homosexuality" in our churches. Then we may even be able to agree to disagree in love and unity in Christ who has already made us one.

Chris agrees that "the primary issue [that needs to be addressed in ongoing conversation] is . . . our hermeneutical paradigms." Chris then suggests two questions that must be addressed in this future conversation.

> In thinking about issues to which each of us need to give more thought in this continuing conversation, I believe that the primary issue is, as Weldon expressed in his second post, our hermeneutical paradigms. How do we read, interpret, and then apply scripture to our given pastoral contexts? From this crucial question flows several others. For example, what is the role of the historic and global church, versus the local congregation, in discerning the Spirit's leading in and through Scripture? Another question that comes to mind is the criteria for breaking fellowship. How do we balance Jesus' prayer for unity and Paul's consistent admonitions to "be of one mind" (see, for example, Romans 15:5, 2 Corinthians 13:11, and Philippians 2:2) with both Paul's and John's pastoral practice of expelling brothers and sisters who transgress doctrinal and/or ethical boundaries?

Chris adds: "I still believe that the burden of proof is on those who argue for an affirming position, so I think that my affirming brothers and sisters need to do work on a theology of marriage that would include same-sex couples."

Chris also suggests that this ongoing conversation needs to take into account the "asymmetry" (my word, not his) in the nature of biblical texts dealing with same-sex relationships and those texts dealing with "other conflicted matters in the church."

> The dominant traditional argument is that the Bible condemns "homosexuality" as sin in a few texts with no positive references, so the matter is settled in Scripture. It is also unparalleled with other conflicted matters in the church, where great change has grown out of great controversy (e.g., slavery, divorce and remarriage, women in leadership) where numerous texts overwhelmingly portray one stance while a few texts hint of a different possibility.

Chris further elaborates on this "asymmetry," appealing to the position taken by Mennonite biblical scholar Willard Swartley.[7]

> After doing the exegesis of the texts directly related to same-sex intimacy, [Swartley] demonstrates that the church's "evolution" on pacifism, slavery, and woman in leadership are consistent with the New Testament, especially taking into consideration the "redemptive arc" of God's kingdom, while that same arc simply wouldn't work for same-sex relationships.

Chris's question (above) about "the criteria for breaking fellowship" in light of disagreements over same-sex relationships is an important question in the search for new "hermeneutical paradigms" raises a possible deeper theological issue pointed to by a distinction made by Weldon.

> When I was in seminary a Mennonite anthropologist theologian from an evangelical seminary presented a "bounded set" and "centered set" model. A "bounded set" entity emphasizes boundaries and rules (violations bring discipline or dismissal). A "centered set" entity emphasizes direction (centering) and discernment (context) in a dynamic way. I and most members grew up in a "bounded set" church they couldn't live with and have found new life and faith in a "centered set" church.

---

7. Swartley, *Homosexuality*.

IS THERE PROMISE IN A "CENTERED-SET" APPROACH TO DOING THEOLOGY?

It appears to me that this is an important question that needs to be addressed in the possible search for a new "hermeneutical paradigm" for dealing with same-sex relationships, although I have little clarity as to how to begin responding.

As I have summarized in another book,[8] this distinction has been proposed by Roger Olson in his reflections about the nature of evangelicalism.[9] Olson's view is that "the question is not who is 'in' and who is 'out' [of evangelicalism], but who is nearer the center and who is moving away from it." Olson adds that "people gathered around the center or toward it are authentically evangelical; people or institutions moving away from it or with their backs turned against it are of questionable evangelical status."

R. Albert Mohler has a problem with Olson's distinction between a centered-set and bounded-set view of evangelicalism, suggesting that "the moment the center is defined, boundaries necessarily appear."[10]

A possible way to navigate this disagreement is to note that Olson's position is dynamic, focusing on "movement" relative to a defined center. He notes that for the centered-set view, "the constructive task of theology is always open; there are no closed once for all systems of theology,"[11] adding the following reflection about the centered-set notion of "orthodoxy": "consistent and steady movement toward truth, guided by Scripture and tradition critically received, does make one orthodox."[12] In that light, it is possible to acknowledge "boundaries," but these boundaries are not fixed. Rather they are defined in terms of proximity to the center and movement toward or away from the center.

I hope that the question of the adequacy, or not, of this centered-set approach to doing theology, and its possible connection, if any, to the search for new "hermeneutical paradigms" for interpreting the Bible, especially relative to same-sex relationships, will be addressed by biblical scholars and pastors (such as Jim Brownson, Mark Strauss, Chris, Weldon, and Tim). Although I am "in way over my head here," what follows are some of my amateurish reflections.

---

8. Heie, *A Future*, 7–8.
9. Olson, *Reformed*, 59–60.
10. Mohler, "Confessional Evangelicalism," 76.
11. Olson, *Reformed*, 55.
12. Ibid., 203.

I find the centered-set approach to doing theology attractive because it avoids the temptation to make one's views on same-sex relationship a "boundary" litmus test as to the authenticity of one's Christian commitment. Rather, it allows for a diversity of perspectives on this issue (as have been presented by Jim, Mark, Chris, Weldon, and Tim), as long as one holds to a "center," which I have defined as "participation in God's project of reconciliation,"[13] And the centered-set view embraces a "dynamic" view of Christian living that I believe is evident in the reflections of Chris, Weldon, and Tim that are reported on in this chapter, and, as will be seen, in the case study reports in the next chapter.

TO WHAT EXTENT IS "FEAR" INHIBITING OR DRIVING THE CONVERSATION ABOUT LGBT ISSUES?

Weldon opens up a big can of worms with his apt observation that "fear drives our political culture today and fear drives much of our ecclesial culture today."

As Weldon said about this observation, "that . . . is far more than I can address here." Time did not allow Chris, Weldon, or Tim to comment or elaborate on this perceived problem. But I will report on some of my experience.

In brief, my experience with a number of institutions of Christian higher education is that there is great hesitancy to even talk about LGBT issues. In some cases that reflects a genuine belief that the Bible is clear that same-sex relationships are inappropriate for Christians. (So, if the issue is "settled," there is no need for further conversation.) But in other cases this hesitancy reflects palpable fear that those who support the institution, either financially or providing a good pool of students, will diminish or withdraw their support if these constituents found out that "we are actually talking about these issues."

As a result of this fear on the part of such Christian educational institutions, the ironic result is that the conversations that are needed have sometimes been driven "underground," taking place in "safe places' like private homes and coffee shops. I have been involved in such off-campus "safe conversations." That is ironic, at best, since the overarching purpose of any educational institution should be to "seek after Truth." One is tempted to think that some Christian educational institutions are willing to embrace that overarching purpose only to the extent that is doesn't alienate their constituents.

13. Heie, *A Future*, xi, 137–38.

Fear is also a major driving force in the reluctance of many churches (or church denominations) to host open, respectful conversations about LGBT issues. Will just having such conversations cause church members to "find another church" or cause denominational schism? The casualty of such "fear" in churches, church denominations and Christian educational institutions is the search for Truth. Until such fear is overcome, there is no way forward.

Well, there are some complex and controversial reflections on possible "ways forward" regarding LGBT people and issues that beg for considerable ongoing conversation.[14]

RESPECTFUL CONVERSATION TOWARD TRUTH AND CHRISTIAN UNITY

As far as I can tell, a prayer that Jesus uttered that has yet to be answered is his prayer for Christian unity recorded in John 17. Tim shared some reflections on this elusive ideal of Christian unity.

CHRISTIAN UNITY IS AN "ESSENTIAL"

First, in the midst of contentious debates about what is "essential" to the Christian faith, including whether a particular view on same-sex relationships is "essential," Tim unambiguously points to the "essential" nature of Christian unity, quoting from John 17.

> Just before Christ goes to the cross Jesus prays for his disciples, in what one enthusiastic preacher called "Christ's most important instructions, in the last huddle, before the big play." He prays that his followers might "become completely one, so that the world may know that you have sent me and have loved them even as you have loved me" (John 17:23). He prays that they "may be one, as we are one" (17:22).

Note carefully Tim's noticing that the often overlooked teaching of Jesus in this prayer that "Christian unity" has the potential to be our greatest witness to those who do not share our Christian faith (all too seldom mentioned in the voluminous literature on Christian apologetics). Tim elaborates

---

14. Weldon suggest that such ongoing conversation should give "renewed attention" to "three bodies": "the body of Scripture, the human body, and the body of Christ," and he recommends four books for consideration: Schneider, *The Revelatory Text*; Johnson, *The Revelatory Body*; Farley, *Just Love*; and Bradshaw, ed., *The Way Forward*?

beautifully on the core of that "prophetic witness," the demonstration of "unity in difference" or a "fellowship of differences," showing those who do not share our Christian faith that "we can live with one another across . . . dividing lines."

> We desperately need a way beyond the endless splintering of Protestantism. We need to model a way of unity in difference if the world is ever going to believe that the Messiah has come. I hope that all sides can devote more passion and energy toward finding a way of unity for the church.
>
> As our world suffers conflict, I doubt our best witness is to "get it right" and separate from those who are "wrong." Our most prophetic witness will be as we bridge divisions of race, class, gender, and the liberal versus conservative chasm. If we can live with each other in love and peace across those dividing lines, then we will have something to offer the world that others will know as "good news."
>
> I also think it is crucial for a congregation to see that having important differences of opinion, and yet continuing to live in love and unity, is an important witness of what it means to be a people of peace, a people who call Jesus Lord. It is no great accomplishment (although given our sin it is still an accomplishment!) to get a group of similar people to live in unity. But if we can live in love and peace across differences, then we have something worth sharing with others.

Of course, a significant question remains, raised by Weldon: "Are there limits to how far and on what concerns our disagreements can be embraced and still maintain the unity of the body?" In response, Tim allows for the possible need for "division," but asserts that "the criteria for Christian division ought to be very high," defined in terms of an adequate definition of "heresy," which he believes would allow for either an "affirming or non-affirming" view of same-sex relationships.

> [T]he criteria for Christian division ought to be very high. The clearest case for division is when someone persists in heresy. What constitutes heresy? Theologian Steve Harmon defines it this way, "A heretic is someone whose account of the Christian story is so dangerously inadequate that's really an altogether different story than the biblical story of the Triune God." Justin S. Holcomb, Episcopal Priest and author of *Know the Heretics*, writes "The apostles were not afraid to denounce heresy.

If a teaching or practice threatened *the gospel's integrity*, they strongly condemned it . . ." [emphasis mine].[15] Writing in the evangelical magazine *Christianity Today* he commends the creeds as a guide to identifying heresy and writes, "If a believer genuinely accepts the Nicene Creed, they should not be dubbed a heretic."[16]

Clearly, by these definitions, one can hold either an affirming or non-affirming view, without being a heretic.

Chris "totally agree[s]" with Tim when he says "that anyone who affirms Nicene orthodoxy ought not be labeled a heretic. But Chris adds the caveat that "for Paul, the proper ordering of sexual relationships within the church was important enough to expel a brother from fellowship."

> I totally agree that anyone who affirms Nicene orthodoxy ought not be labelled a heretic, and, to the extent that an affirming Christian can honestly affirm the creed in its plain sense, he or she is not, technically, a heretic. However, Paul chided the Corinthians for allowing a man to have a sexual relationship with his step-mother (1 Cor 5:1–5), going so far as demanding that he be expelled from the community. In this case, it wasn't a doctrinal issue, but a specific sexual relationship that, according to Paul, was not only destroying the integrity of the community, but also its witness to the world. So, while it may not be proper for a non-affirming Christian to declare affirming Christians as heretics, it is instructive that, for Paul, the proper ordering of sexual relationships within the church was important enough to expel a brother from fellowship.

More conversation is called for.

THE QUEST FOR TRUTH

No Christian would argue that Christians should "unite" around a set of beliefs that are false. Therefore, the quest for Christian unity will always be of "one piece" with the quest for truth about the matter at hand, including same-sex relationships. Tim expresses his appreciation to both Chris and Weldon for their evident commitment to seeking truth in the midst of their disagreements.

> As I've experienced conflict in the community in which I live, I've reflected on Stanley Hauerwas's comment that we need to

15. Holcomb, "Why You Shouldn't," 42.
16. Ibid., 45.

> *tell* one another the truth—but perhaps even more—we must want to *hear* truth. I appreciate both of you for speaking truth and I hope I have the will to hear it.
>
> Chris and Weldon, I feel like both of you have entered this conversation in a non-anxious way that helps us toward truth rather than further alienation. Thank you for the generous spirit (Spirit?) you've both exhibited in this; it has been an honor to participate in this dialogue with you.

But, as an LGBT reader points out in response to one of Chris's postings, if the quest for truth is paramount, then this quest requires that those in conversation be willing to believe that "LGBTQ people are telling the truth about their own lives and happiness."

> I appreciate your honesty and careful thought, but what I don't think you understand is that in addition to wanting to share "deepest pains and struggles," we also want to worship in churches that are open to and acknowledging of our greatest joys and our loving relationships. This unwillingness of the church to believe that LGBTQ people are telling the truth about their own lives and happiness is core to the paternalistic stances that continue to drive them out of the church.

RESPECTFUL CONVERSATION AS A MEANS FOR SEEKING TRUTH AND CHRISTIAN UNITY

If seeking truth and Christian unity are paramount for Christians, which is a major thesis in this book, then the question remains as to the best means for seeking those ideals. As I have already argued, providing a safe, welcoming space, as a deep expression of love, for those who disagree with you to express their disagreements is a necessary starting point. But that starting point must be followed by ongoing conversations about initial areas of agreement and disagreement. The following reflections from Chris, Weldon, and Tim point to the need for such ongoing conversations, and close this chapter.

> [In my church] we've worked hard at reconciliation and we've come to a place of appreciating each other across differences. Although I may disagree with others on many topics, I've come to believe that *I need their perspective*. I've come to see the profound wisdom of philosopher David Hume's observation that "Truth springs from an argument among friends." (Tim)

Having stated the disagreements . . . I must say that I have a great deal of respect for both Tim and Weldon, and, in their stories, I see each of them longing to be faithful to Jesus. (Chris)

I hope that the above is a helpful "last word," which, ideally, is not the last word at all, but rather the last word in a specific conversation, which is a part of a much larger and ongoing conversation to which we are called, continually, to participate. (Chris)

My first response [after the first set of postings] is to thank you, Chris and Tim, for your passionate personal and pastoral posts. I am grateful for you, for the clarity of your conviction, and for your contribution to this conversation. I am eager to share a second and third round of this conversation with you. . . . Not knowing each other poses a distance that has a relational downside for such an important conversation. But it may also foster a kind of generosity of spirit toward each other as an upside to our conversation. (Weldon)

9

Case Study Conversations about LGBT People and Issues

Conversations about LGBT people and issues at Christian institutions of higher education and within Christian churches and denominations have often been vitriolic, with those having strong disagreements too often not showing respect for one another.

In that light, it is important to pay close attention to the results of in-depth "discernment" processes that a number of Christian institutions have navigated, hopefully learning from what has worked well and what has not worked so well. This chapter highlights the results of three case studies, one featuring a Christian university and two featuring churches/denominations within two different Christian traditions.

The Leading Questions posed to Julie Morgan, professor of Communication studies at Eastern University were: How has Eastern University engaged LGBT issues? How were LGBT students involved in your conversations and what were the results of their involvement? What lessons have you learned as to ways for Christians to talk respectfully to one another about their disagreements? What worked well? What didn't work at all?

The Leading Questions posed to both Jeff Lincicome, Senior Pastor, Sammamish Presbyterian Church (Washington) and Jessica Schrock Ringenberg, Pastor, Zion Mennonite Church (Archbold, Ohio) were: How has your church engaged LGBT issues? Did this engagement lead to an official church position? How have you navigated denominational expectations as your church has discussed LGBT issues? What lessons have you learned as to ways for Christians to talk respectfully to one another about their disagreements? What worked well? What didn't work at all?

I will set the stage for reporting on the thematic highlights of this three-way conversation by quoting Julie, Jeff, and Jessica regarding three dimensions of their respective institutional discernment endeavors regarding LGBT people and issues: the *context* for seeking discernment, including the reason they began a discernment process; the actual discernment *process*; and the *results*, actual or projected, of the discernment process. I quote them at length to capture the rich nuances and dynamism of their respective discernment endeavors.

Eastern University

Context: The discernment process at Eastern was initiated as a result of a strong negative reaction on campus to a petition their president signed. Julie describes this as follows:

> In June of 2014, the President of Eastern University, Robert Duffett, signed a petition (along with about 150 other key leaders of faith-based organizations) asking President Obama for exemption to the proposed executive order concerning federal contractors and the gay, lesbian, bisexual, and transgender community. Specifically, the religious leaders wanted explicit language providing for religious freedom, which would allow faith-based organizations to use their understanding of their doctrine as the basis for their policies and treatment of those identifying as homosexual.
>
> Perhaps unanticipated, many in the Eastern community reacted strongly to President Duffett's support of the petition. While some agreed with Duffett, others felt that his support stood in contrast to the university's mission of "faith, reason, and justice." Around 1,000 Eastern community members signed a petition asking President Duffett to rescind his support of the letter to President Obama.
>
> By the end of the summer, President Duffett was ready to address faculty, staff, and administration in his state-of-the-university address. In his address, he faced the crisis head on. He explained that his motivation had been to protect religious freedom but admitted that the impact caused many in the community pain. He apologized for causing the pain, and explained

that he was setting up a task force to engage the community on human sexuality. In setting up the task force, Duffett tried to balance the membership with equal representation from conservative and progressive faculty, administration, and students.

The president charged the Human Sexuality Task Force (HSTF) to complete a three-step process: (1) planning a dialogue process/conversation on human sexuality, (2) implementing the process/conversation, and (3) drawing implications about what EU should be and become as a Christian university based on the process/conversation.

Process: The discernment process began when "a call was sent to the entire Eastern community, asking for groups (academic departments, groups, and so forth) to propose speakers for the spring, with the HSTF providing financial support to bring invited speakers to campus." Julie describes the continuation of the process as follows, including some self-assessments as to "what worked well" and "what did not work well."

> . . . in all, about twenty different departments and student groups proposed events.
>
> Perhaps the most meaningful for LGBT students was an event sponsored by Refuge, a student-led group supporting those who are LGBT. The event focused on "Stories of Courage and Healing: Experiences of LGBTQ Eastern Alumni." The keynote alum who spoke said that he was impressed with the lineup of speakers. But he also noted that he only saw one other LGBT person as an invited speaker—and that person presented a celibate lifestyle approach.
>
> From the first event, we learned that students perceive feedback differently than faculty. A well-known evangelical speaker presented the traditional perspective of marriage, adding that homosexuality was a moral distortion, not unlike the propensity for pedophilia. During the question/answer session, the conversation was lively. Some faculty were questioning the speaker's interpretation of Scripture, asking about the acceptance of divorce, and so forth. From a faculty perspective, the event was an academic event and deserved truth-seeking critique. In survey responses after the event, the students were astonished at the "bad behavior" of faculty. They felt that faculty did not show kindness/respect toward the speaker. They felt that faculty usurped all the question/answer time, without an opportunity for students to participate.
>
> Based on that feedback, we adjusted the question/answer sessions. In all subsequent events, we asked for students to

participate first (at least three students first), before a faculty member could chime in. This provided some balance to the power difference of student versus faculty.

I don't think we could have been as successful at engaging LGBT students if it had not been for Refuge. Their tireless involvement opened a better channel of communication with LGBT students, and with the HSTF.

... Eastern is a diverse community of Christian denominations, from Quakers to Catholics, Baptists to Presbyterians, Episcopalians to non-denominationals, all employed full-time .... Learning to talk about differences in a community of diversity should be simple, right? It was anything but simple. Perhaps if the topic was less culturally relevant, it would have been easier. But in this case, fear seemed to be a common thread.

Those who are more conservative in their perspective expressed fear. They were afraid to appear on the wrong side of human rights, and felt that the more progressive voices would shame them. Those who were more progressive also expressed fear. They worried that expressing a progressive opinion in an evangelical organization could cost them their jobs. Students said they were afraid to speak out of fear that if their opinions were different than their professors their grades would suffer.

It did not seem to matter if a person was conservative, progressive, student, faculty—all expressed fear that their perspective would cost them in some way. Of course, those who are LGBT were the most afraid to participate since the current policies at Eastern are not inclusive. The current policy is that one may identify as LGBT, but they cannot be in a romantic relationship and cannot be married. In one survey, an LGBT faculty/staff member said the following:

> The worst part? For ten years, this has been an unsafe place for me to be who I am. People's commitment to conservative doctrine often comes at the expense of people. So my perpetual fear of repercussions should I be truly myself has alienated me from people who would find me disposable should they know who I am.

How does one have a conversation when fear is a common thread? How do we engage in a conversation that is so deeply personal and divisive?

Perhaps one of the most valuable lessons of this process is the need to build relationships. Two of the most outspoken members of our community (one progressive, one conservative), and both of whom served on the HSTF, have modeled a relationship of friendship and engagement. At a bi-annual faculty workshop, the HSTF showed a videotaped segment of the two, modeling listening, and allowing each to arrive at his or her own conclusion. While they deeply disagree with each other, they listen well and build on a relationship of trust.

... Without a doubt, one of the chief reasons the dialogue process was such a success was due to the leadership of the HSTF. Faculty were selected to serve on this task force because they represented diversity of opinion, and because they were held in high regard in the community. Two students (one representing a conservative opinion, the other a progressive) also served as *equal* members of the Task Force. Faculty and administration members of the Task Force specifically asked for their input at every turn.

The leadership provided by the HSTF to the community was greatly influenced by one of the co-chairs, a retired faculty member, well-respected by all. Her emphasis on an inclusive process and modeling it during every meeting (typical meetings lasted more than two hours) set the tone for the HSTF, and the community. Trickle down leadership at its best.

Another highlight of the process was both the number and variety of events offered in just two semesters. With about three months to host events during a semester (not scheduling events during the first few and last few weeks of each semester), about ten events were held each semester. Again, the events were sponsored and moderated by a wide variety of departments and groups. For a group to say that their opinion was not included, actually meant that they did not propose a speaker or panel during either semester. A critical motivator of the HSTF was to provide variety from the community. No one wanted it to appear that "one side" was favored over another.

Finally, some faculty offered incentives for their students to attend events. Truthfully, I was not a proponent of offering extra credit to get students to participate. I just wanted them to come because they wanted to be involved. But like the company that offers a drawing at a company picnic, the incentives worked. We saw record student attendance at almost every event. At the forum for student discernment, one student said,

> I was homeschooled my whole life. I lived in a bubble. Last semester, one of my friends dragged me to one of the events for extra credit. It changed my whole outlook. I learned so much and my perspective was changed.

Providing incentives for students to engage in the discussion was valuable. Becoming better informed, about all perspectives, fits with the mission of Christian higher education.

... it is worth mentioning some aspects that were not as successful. What lessons did we learn from our process?

First, because of current policies at Eastern, no faculty, staff, or administrators on the HSTF were LGBT. In one of the discernment forums, a number of students raised issues of justice. If the process is to dialogue about human sexuality, the absence of the LGBT voice cannot go unnoticed. As a result of the feedback, the HSTF surveyed current and former employees about their experiences at Eastern. While the stories gathered matter, they do not begin to substitute for actual representation and inclusion.

Another lesson learned was the timing of events. While a few events were held during normal work hours, most were held at night. Unfortunately, that meant that many faculty were unable to participate. And when they did, it was often picking events that already represented their perspective. Holding the events at night worked best for students, for the speakers, and for reserving precious large-room space. Trying to schedule the events during the day would mean competing for space, competing against other classes, and/or competing against athletic events; thus, this was not a solution either. We taped every event and uploaded the videos to the HSTF website. Not an ideal solution, but it was an effort to allow all community members to hear the speakers.

Finally, the last lesson. At various points, each group felt that their perspective did not matter. It seemed that some believed that it was useless to share their opinions. For some, they feared that no minds would be changed. Was "changing minds" the point of the dialogue? If the rhetoric of the process turned into war rhetoric, with one side winning, the other side losing; if the process turned into counting the number of "soldiers" on each team, then the point of the dialogue was lost. Entering into conversation, with genuine care, has the possibility to change an individual. The dialogue was not about "winning souls," it was about defining who we are as a community.

Result: The discernment process at Eastern is not competed. As Julie reports:

The HSTF was appointed by the president and given three directives. The third directive was to draw out implications about what EU should be and become as a Christian university

> based on the process/conversation. After long deliberations, the members of the HSTF have identified areas of agreement and remaining areas of disagreement regarding these implications. This points to the need for ongoing dialogue. As a basis for this ongoing dialogue, the HSTF formulated [a] statement intended to create a safe and welcoming space for ongoing respectful conversations.
>
> History tells us that ideological purity often leads to violence and scapegoating. Knowing that Eastern finds itself at a cultural crossroad where differing opinions have deep personal and institutional consequences, the University's community standards and operational policies must emphasize that all who come under the umbrella of its authority deserve to be honored by respectful language and fair judgments, whether they are LGBTQ members of the community or persons who hold to the long history of traditional teachings on sexuality. Open conversation must be a priority where discussants combine honesty with humility, difference with compassion, engagement of issues with close listening. When all agree to stand together in the tension, no one is silenced. This is a matter of Christian hospitality and of academic integrity.

In summary, the process of "figuring it out" at Eastern is still not completed. Julie notes that although the process of "figuring it out" at Eastern is still not completed, she hopes that "we can find middle ground," while acknowledging a fear of negative consequences if Eastern decides to become "more inclusive."

> I hope that we can find middle ground for our community. Jeff [Lincicome] seems to have found a way to balance his need to continue his journey, while acknowledging the differences within his community. Embracing that diversity is unique. There is growing fear within our community that if we become more inclusive (and Eastern is historically more inclusive), those who hold a traditional view of marriage will be viewed as hateful. Finding a way to include all perspectives within the community requires commitment and creativity. We are working towards that goal. The decisions we make today have the potential to determine the future survival of our university.

Julie does anticipate that the final result of this discernment process may cause Eastern to "lose members," but that does not mean the process was a "failure."

> I also can imagine that each of us [Julie, Jeff, and Jessica] must be willing to lose members as a result of this process and not call the process a failure. That will hurt, but I'm not sure it can be avoided. We must treat those who choose to leave because of we've become "too _____" as believers still on their journey as we all are and not judge or try to convince them to stay. Convince them to continue to seek Christ and to be Christlike.

The Board of Trustees has formed a sub-committee to consider a report that the HSTF shared with the Eastern community and submitted to the President. It was anticipated that the Board would act on this report in early 2017.

Sammamish Presbyterian Church

Context: As Jeff Lincicome reports, the need to initiate a discernment process at SPC was at least partially influenced by an external pressure: "For us, Washington State's legalization of gay marriage forced our hand somewhat to make a decision regarding these issues." Jeff adds the following additional contextual elements.

> SPC is a member of the Presbyterian Church (USA) nestled in the foothills of the Cascade Mountains, a growing suburb of Seattle. The church itself has been in existence for close to thirty years and is filled with both founding members and newcomers (including many young families) across the faith experience spectrum. It's ethos and roots are squarely evangelical, with Jesus Christ (hopefully) at the center of everything we say and do, and with a high value on the study of Scripture and the proclamation of the gospel through word and deed. Sammamish is located in the shadow of both Microsoft and Amazon, and both the city and our church are filled with some of the brightest, fastest moving, decisive people I've ever met. It is a creative, inquisitive, and fun place to do ministry.
>
> As a member of the Presbyterian Church (USA), however, we ran into a challenge a few years ago as the polity of the church changed. In 2011, the General Assembly of the PC(USA) opened up the option for governing bodies to ordain noncelibate homosexual persons to the role of Pastor, Elder and Deacon (the three ordained offices in our church). Fast forward a few years—in 2014, the General Assembly voted to make it possible for pastors and governing bodies in states where gay marriage was legal to perform and host gay weddings within

their churches. While these decisions were open-ended—pastors, churches and governing bodies could choose to adopt these standards or not—it suddenly made a decades-long discussion in the national church a very local and immediate one—What are we, SPC, going to choose to do?

For some churches, this conversation was a slam dunk. As a pastor, I saw colleagues in my Presbytery and around the nation make speedy and somewhat easy decisions regarding these matters, as they led congregations that were mostly unanimous in their understanding and belief regarding these issues. Congregations came out as either "for" or "against," many with very gracious postures towards the other perspective; others, not so much.

What I didn't see, however, was what I hoped for—a position somewhere in the middle. . . . So what do we do? How do we make the biggest decision our church family would make in a generation (which in my opinion, it is) and be both faithful to God and faithful to each other?

Process: Jeff provides the following report on the discernment process.

In early 2012, I asked the Session of SPC (what we call our Elder Board) to appoint a Denominational Study Group, to enter a season of study and conversation on the topic of homosexuality and the church, in the hopes of both keeping the Session abreast of the changing landscape of the PC(USA) and if necessary, make recommendations as to what we should do. This Study Group of seven people (myself included) was put together by me (the Senior Pastor) and was made up of seasoned, faithful members, both women and men, of various ages and stages in life.

There were three criteria for being in this group, 1) They had to have done their own scriptural study of this issue and could faithfully articulate their viewpoints. The group was purposely diverse—made up of three members I knew fell on the traditional side and three members on the more progressive side of this discussion (with me mostly in the middle); 2) They had to be pro-SPC. In other words, I wanted people in this group that weren't just interested in the debate of theological ideas, but were interested in the health of this church family as well. They needed to have a vested interest in this body of believers and want the best for it; 3) They could play well with others. I wanted people I knew were team players, who, while they had strong convictions, had a proven track record of listening and caring for others, even in the midst of disagreement. With that in mind, the Session approved this ragtag bunch, and we started meeting in July of 2012. I thought (we all thought) we would meet for about year.

We were wrong.

For almost three years, this group met at least once a month, eating dinner together, getting to know each other, praying for each other, reading Scripture together, digesting articles, books, and YouTube talks from all sides of the issue. And while we most certainly became the resident experts on the subject of homosexuality and the church, what we realized through this process was that what we REALLY became was not just experts, but family. In fact, family became an important metaphor for our group (which next to the "body of Christ" is the second most used metaphor in the Scriptures regarding the church—we aren't called "brothers and sisters" for nothing!). And while our study and conversation was eye opening, what we came to see most of all was a new set of family values—that just as we would never think of throwing someone out of our nuclear family for a difference of opinion, we would never turn away from each other as a church family as well, just because we saw things differently on these issues. And so we met and fell more and more in love with each other as we studied and prayed on this difficult issue.

For the record, not one person in the study group had a change of conviction on homosexuality and the church. But together we did have a change of heart—we went from trying to win each other around an issue of faith and practice, to being committed to each other and loving each other like the family God believes that we are. With that in mind, we worked hard on a process to bring our congregation on board with what these family values looked like.

How did we do it?

We started by drafting a statement of core beliefs that were ultimately approved by the Session. These Core Beliefs began with fifteen "WE BELIEVE" statements that we could agree upon and hold fast to as followers of Jesus Christ and members of the same church family. It was a powerful reminder to us of how much we hold in common. These were then followed up by four "SOME OF US BELIEVE" Statements, articulating the differences we share regarding homosexuality, ordination and marriage. Compared to what we had in common, these differences seemed paltry and unimportant. At the end we included a final set of "WE BELIEVE" Statements that I will share with you here

> *BUT TOGETHER WE BELIEVE in a God who is bigger than our differences and is not threatened by this conversation.*
>
> *WE BELIEVE in a God who knits us together as a CHRIST-CENTERED MISSION MINDED FAMILY. WE BELIEVE God has a story to tell through us in this season, through the way we love each other, the way we pursue truth mixed with grace together, and the way we bear witness to Jesus Christ.*

> Through all of this, as our study group educated our congregation on the various Christian perspectives regarding homosexuality, as we had open dialogues (we called them "Family Meetings") where people could express their thoughts and convictions, as we non-anxiously modeled healthy dialogue and conversation, we saw people catch the vision that whatever the decision was to be made by the Session and the Pastors, what holds us together is bigger and more important than what tears us apart. While the issue of homosexuality and the church is an important one, it need not be a defining one; a discipleship issue at its core, not a salvation one.

I asked Jeff whether SPC would do anything "differently" if they could carry out the discernment process again. Jeff responded:

> The assignment for this round of entries was to look back on ourselves and our processes and ask, "Would you have done anything different if you did it again?" The answer is, "Of course!" It is impossible to go through a discernment process and not see how you could have alleviated some of the struggle, shortcut some of the hours spent, or taken advantage of some of the opportunities missed.

In particular, Jeff says that he would have involved the entire congregation in the conversation at an earlier stage, not just after the "hard work" had been done by the seven-person study group, although he adds that "once we started the public conversation," the "large majority" of the "hundreds of our people involved in the conversations" said that they "felt heard and honored in the process."

> I know in the case of SPC, in hindsight we could have had better communication with our congregation throughout the process itself. I am so impressed by Jessica and her church's approach [see the next case study below] involving their entire church

throughout the process, as well as Julie and Eastern's ability to have the entire university community take part in discussions during their discernment. As I look back now, our strategy was a little like Willy Wonka—lock yourself up in a Chocolate Factory for a few years until you come out with something to show to the world. While we did a good job at inviting our congregation into the conversation once we had done the hard work, I will admit we could have done a better job at bringing them along all along. That being said, once we started the public conversation, we had hundreds of our people involved in the conversations and, for the large majority, the feedback was that they felt heard and honored in the process.

Result: the final result of the discernment process at SPC is described by Jeff as follows.

> The long and the short of it is that in April of 2015, our Session voted by an 11–6 margin to allow the possibility of both same-sex marriage within our church walls as well as a married gay person to be eligible for ordained ministry at SPC. They also passed a unanimous vote of approval for our pastors to follow their own consciences in considering whether or not to perform same-sex marriage ceremonies. None of our elder board felt the need to step down after these decisions, but in fact were convicted by the unity of Spirit we felt in our common life and mission together.

In a profound letter that Jeff sent to his congregation after this decision by the Session, Jeff emphasizes that although he "cannot in good conscience perform same-sex marriages," he supports the position SPC has taken that another one of their pastors can, in accordance with his conscience, perform same-sex marriages within the church, since "at SPC . . . we agree on the essentials of the gospel, and can disagree on the non-essentials, and this is a non-essential in my book."

> . . . if you disagree with these decisions, it doesn't mean there isn't a place for you at SPC. I know that for a fact, because there is a place for me.
> I'd love to tell you my story. As your pastor, I have spent more time these past three years studying this issue than anything else. I have prayed, scoured the Scriptures, talked to those who see things from a different perspective (as well as talking with those who don't!), read books, thought long and hard, and prayed again. Fortunately for me, SPC is filled with faithful people who worship together, serve together, and act like a

family—and yet hold different scriptural perspectives on this issue. Because of that, SPC has been a wonderful seedbed for my own spiritual growth and discovery. I have grown immensely in my faith from having this conversation with you, and I have God and you to thank for that.

For myself, I have decided (at this point) that I still cannot in good conscience perform same-sex marriages. While I can see the fruit of the Spirit that is often born out of these relationships, and understand (and even agree) with many of the scriptural understandings that can lead to blessing these relationships (I have outlined these in detail in our all-church family conversations), I am still not at a place where I can personally perform these marriages in an official manner. This has to do with my own ongoing wrestling with the different levels of scriptural teaching and the relative newness of this discussion in my own life and in the church universal. Because of these factors and until I have resolved it for myself, I cannot in good conscience preside. Maybe someday, but not now.

However, that is not true among all of my colleagues. While Pastor Kay holds perspective similar to my own, Pastor Austin is in a place where he can officially bless and perform these marriages, out of his own attempt to faithfully read Scripture.

I support his ability to preside at same-sex marriages, and support SPC's ability to host them. Why? Because in the end, I believe that as followers of Jesus Christ, we can disagree on a good many things and still be the body of Christ and the family of faith, and that goes for this issue as well. I take Paul's counsel in Romans 14 to heart:

> One person considers one day more sacred than another; another considers every day alike. Each of them should be fully convinced in their own mind. Whoever regards one day as special does so to the Lord. Whoever eats meat does so to the Lord, for they give thanks to God; and whoever abstains does so to the Lord and gives thanks to God. For none of us lives for ourselves alone, and none of us dies for ourselves alone. If we live, we live for the Lord; and if we die, we die for the Lord. So, whether we live or die, we belong to the Lord. For this very reason, Christ died and returned to life so that he might be the Lord of both the dead and the living (5–9).

In this discussion of personal piety and freedom, Paul gives us a great rule, "In essentials unity, in non-essentials liberty, in all things charity" (to quote St. Augustine). And while some will say that these issues at hand regarding homosexuality are essential to faith and life, as I have prayed, discussed, read Scripture and pondered, I don't think this is an essential, core belief that must be adhered to for faith in the life of the church, and our Session through their vote has agreed.

Consequently, I am comfortable being the Senior Pastor of a church that allows same sex marriage ceremonies to occur even if I personally will not perform them. How can I do that? Because at SPC, I believe we agree on the central tenets of the gospel, and can disagree on the non-essentials, and this is a non-essential in my book.

Jeff notes that about 10 percent of the church families left SPC as a result of this decision by the Session. But he adds that even those who left expressed "thanks to SPC because of the process," and "others have come to join our church, too, specifically because of the way they saw we handled and processed this conversation as a church."

Since the day we made that decision, of course we have seen some families leave (around 10 percent is our best guess estimate), which is to be expected with any big decision. But what has been so encouraging to me is that even those who have gone have made it a point to express their thanks for SPC and for the process itself, and didn't burn the house down when they left. :) Since then, others have come to join our church, too, specifically because of the way they saw we handled and processed this conversation as a church. Some SPC'ers have privately expressed their gratitude to me regarding the outcome, but have kindly not celebrated too loudly, being sensitive to their brothers and sisters who are struggling. Other SPC'ers have told me that while they may not agree with the decision, the process and the commitment to the family as a whole was far more important to them and they felt there is still a place for them to stand at SPC. I have never been more proud of our church—family values at its very best.

Zion Mennonite Church

Context: The need for Zion to initiate a discernment process was significantly driven by the existence of conflict and debate about LGBT relationships within other Mennonite institutions. As Jessica Schrock Ringenberg put it:

Case Study Conversations about LGBT People and Issues

In truth we pastors did not want to have this conversation, because of the apparently paralyzing nature of it. However, as our conference, Ohio Conference of Mennonite Church USA, became consumed by the conflict regarding the decisions of another MC USA Conference, Mountain States Mennonite Conference, and their decision to license a woman in a covenanted same-sex relationship toward ordination and the decision of Eastern Mennonite University to consider changing its hiring policy, to include those in LGBTQ relationships, it became immediately clear that conversation had to take place.

Jessica goes on the describe other aspects of the context at Zion.

Zion Mennonite Church in Archbold, Ohio is a unique congregation, not only within its location in the rural farming community of Northwest Ohio, but for its role within Ohio Conference of Mennonite Church USA.

In order to be in Mennonite Church USA, you must be a member of a Conference, you cannot simply be a congregation on your own within MC USA. There are roughly twenty conferences in MC USA. Conferences are responsible for holding the credentials of clergy. Ohio Conference of Mennonite Church USA, is arguably one of the most conservative conferences in Mennonite Church USA.

Our congregation, Zion, is just one of several Mennonite Church's [sic] within a twenty mile radius, each church taking on a very different flavor and attitude over what it means to be Mennonite or Anabaptist. We have approximately 300 "regular attendees," which these days means we have regular attendance of approximately 190 people.

Zion is unique when compared to many of the other churches (not just Mennonite churches) in the area, in that many of our congregants have moved into Northwest Ohio from "outside." While the majority of people who live in Northwest Ohio are lifelong residents, with families who go back generations, Zion has many people, mostly professionals, myself included, who have moved to the area due to work in the local businesses. However, while we have many people who have moved into the community, our congregation has not really changed much in twenty years. We have people come and go, but for the most part we are a consistent body of believers.

This has created an interesting dynamic within our congregation. While we are perceived as mostly affluent and well educated, we do have congregants who are lifelong residents, with deep ties to the community, a community that is very traditional and very conservative. However, the majority of those who find themselves *in leadership* within our congregation tend to be the well-educated and relatively well-traveled segment of our congregation.

Zion would describe herself as a fiercely Anabaptist Mennonite congregation, with deep roots in the Mennonite Church and strong connections to the Mennonite Church's institutions of higher education and because of this Zion has become known within the community and the Conference as the "Progressive/Liberal" congregation, although not everyone within the congregation would agree.

Historically an Anabaptist form of leadership is highly communal and places great value in "the priesthood of all believers." Zion's leadership culture in particular has a very strong desire to make decisions as a body, and not simply have pastors speak for the entire group.

Early on, Pastor Jeff Kauffman and myself began to recognize the extent to which the congregation wanted to make a firm decision, "taking a stand" on the wide range of issues pertaining to LGBTQ. These issue would include the whole range from whether we open our doors to simply accepting LGBTQ people in our midst, to affirming, to empowering for leadership, marrying, and ordaining.

However, as quickly as the anxious desires to "take a stand" one way or another were coming into the office, so was our realization that people within the congregation had no idea that the [people within the] congregation were not in agreement with each other. There was an interesting dynamic that was in play, where people could not fathom that others within the congregation were not in the same place as they were.

We pastors even found that as we discussed the variety of directions and nuances of Christian faithfulness and human sexuality that we were not totally in agreement. Which meant the more people insisted that we as pastoral leadership needed to take a stand and tell people where the church stood, the more we realized that we were heading towards an impossibly messy outcome.

Process: Jessica describes the "two-part conversation" that the pastors at SPC initiated.

First of all, our decision was to manage a congregational "conversation" in a way that modeled humility and love, in much the same way that we Anabaptist Mennonites believe that Jesus embodied selflessness as described by the Apostle Paul in Philippians 2:5–11.

Secondly, we decided that we needed to somehow remove the "heat" of the topic and place it within the larger context of who Mennonite Church USA is, and who we as Zion Mennonite Church say we are. We also believed it was important to place the concept of the absoluteness of scriptural authority within its own context and within the context of who we as a community of believers are called to be.

So we pastors designed our two part conversation, emphasizing the word "conversation." The purpose of these conversations were to allow the congregation to be able to hear each other, and in particular hear where there was disagreement. We emphasized that this was not going to be a debate, there was not going to be decision making, no voting. Listening to each other was the point.

This emphasis on not making a decision or not debating or discerning was frustrating to most people. They didn't understand the point of meeting if we weren't going to make a decision. Anxiety continued to grow, but we pastors strongly emphasized the need for all people to be in attendance if they wanted to be heard, which again, is a key piece of what we understand to be Anabaptist Mennonite community centered leadership.

The first conversation essentially set the context of the greater conversation. We were very intentional about setting up a context within the greater vision of the MC USA as well Zion's own priorities. We also believed that our conversation had to be set within the context of our biblical understanding of faithfulness for all.

As people arrived we knew they were going to sit with like-minded individuals, so we let them. At the center of each table was a pile of card stock cut-outs of fruit. We then began a devotional time reading from Galatians 5:22–26. We then encouraged each person to choose a picture of a fruit from the center of the table and write which fruit of the Spirit they most wanted/needed to be evident in themselves during these conversations. They were instructed to write their choice on the fruit. We then asked them to move to tables with others who chose the same fruits on their pictures. Apples sat with apples, bananas with bananas, etc. The purpose of this was to get the congregation to sit with those they normally would not sit with.

We then had an intentional time of community building around the tables, with simple non-threatening questions.

After establishing the context within community and Scripture we were able begin the primary purpose of the first conversation which was to slow the congregation down and help them peel back the layers of their assumptions concerning "morality," the Bible, and how they *use* Scripture.

We wanted people to stop and ask the question "how do we know what we know to be true or believe to be true?" And more importantly, if it is true, why do other people claim different "truths"?

Each person was invited into an exercise, basically using the concept of the Wesleyan Quadrilateral. They were invited to see how we determine ethical decisions as really just a process of prioritizing sources of authority in our lives. They were given an exercise to help break down why/how we know what we know. They were asked what is the highest authority in your life (Scripture, Tradition, Reason, Experience) and how do you rank the different sources of authority? The list of every controversial issue (women in ministry, money, the poor, sabbath, war, slavery, alcohol, sex, etc.) was given to them to rank based upon their first gut reaction. For example, MONEY. Jesus would not make a very good financial advisor. In fact he says to sell everything and give it to the poor, but still people who say they have a very high view of scriptural authority somehow manage a way around Jesus' words concerning greed. How do they get there? What sources of authority do they use to subvert Jesus' own words in Scripture?

Finally, after sorting out the variety of truth sources for decision making we approached how we read, interpret, and apply the Bible. As Anabaptist Mennonites we would say that Jesus is the radical center of our faith and therefore the central lens through which we read the Bible. "If the Scripture doesn't agree, Jesus is the referee."

Reading Scripture through Jesus is the assumed standard for MC USA and its sister institutions, but often we have found that there are people within the Mennonite Church who still practice a "flat-Bible" reading of scripture. Discussing the differences of how Scripture can be read was key (and eye opening to some) in our being able to say how it is possible that two people can hold a high view of scriptural authority and come out at very different interpretations.

The purpose of the first conversation was to set a tone of humility and mutual respect for the second conversation. Only after setting the stage through the first conversation were we able to approach the conversation on issues related to the LGBTQ community with a different Spirit and posture.

That is why it was essential that people could not attend the second conversation if they were not a part of the first. We did not want people to jump into such a sensitive conversation without context of the previous conversation or without the relationships already built around the table. Which is why people were asked to sit at the same table to engage the next conversation.

The second conversation began with visual reports of how people responded to the truth sources exercise. It quickly became obvious that we were all over the map in terms of how we weighed scripture in each circumstance. There was only one of 103 surveys returned that claimed to have a consistent use of Scripture as their ultimate authority. Likewise, people were all over the map in regards to their hermeneutics.

With that in mind we centered ourselves on Romans 12 and then we began to discuss: 1) Greatest challenge as a youth? 2) What is your first memory of dealing with the issues related to LGBTQ community? 3) What Scriptures come to mind when you consider the issues related to LGBTQ community?

We then asked each person around the table to independently fill out the boxes of the continuum from Clyde Kratz, Conference Minister of Virginia Mennonite Conference's "Ethical Views of Homosexuality" continuum, adapted from L. R. Holben's *What Christians Think about Homosexuality: Six Representative Views.*[1]

The continuum represented a range of responses from condemnation, promise of healing, costly discipleship, pastoral accommodation, affirmation, and liberation. The purpose of this exercise and the purpose of this continuum, once again was to slow the congregation down from a knee-jerk response, and recognize the variety of responses one may have toward issues related to the LGBTQ community. We strongly encouraged people to not just circle a column but to individually consider the nuances.

We then asked the congregation to consider: 1) What did you learn about yourself in filling out this form? 2) Does this reflect the degree to which you hold yourself accountable on other ethical issues? 3) Does this reflect the degree to which you seek to be held accountable to the church?

---

1. Holben, *What Christians Think About Homosexuality.*

> As we compiled the results from people's forms we pastors were somewhat surprised. We had imagined the congregation would mostly be somewhere in the center of the continuum, but the congregation was actually evenly spread along five categories, with only a couple being represented in "condemnation."

Jessica reports that throughout the two conversations there was no provision for "open mic time" since that would hinder having "dialogue" based on "commitment to a relationship" and the pastors did not state their positions "from the microphone" since to do so would inhibit dialogue.

> Keeping it a conversation between people was a key aspect of the way we managed the conversation. We wanted dialogue not debate. For this reason we purposefully did not allow for open mic time. We did not want people to be able to make blanket statements to the entire group, without a commitment to a relationship with those who may be hurt.
>
> We pastors also made the decision to not state our "positions" from the microphone. We wanted to maintain dialogue and not debate. Knowing that our congregation was divided, we did not want to give people the opportunity to interpret anything we would say through their own filters. We have been very open with anyone who wants to have conversations with us, which means they must make the initiative. We feel as though this is a model for the congregation.

Result: Zion is committed to continuing their discernment process. Jessica suggests that as they do so, they will try to model "the central role Scripture played in the discernment period for SPC" and would further encourage the "diversity of opinion as demonstrated by Eastern."

> I think when Zion is finally at a place, emotionally, where we can engage the next steps of discernment, it would take into account the intense Scripture study demonstrated by SPC, and diversity of opinion as demonstrated by Eastern.

However, remembering that SPC initially modeled respectful and loving dialogue within a small group (their seven person study group), Jessica wonders how well that will work "with [an] . . . entire congregation."

> I wonder however, what such a process of engagement with Scripture and community would look like if one were to do it with the entire congregation, rather than simply a small group of people. Would it be possible to cultivate the trust and value of

"the other" as SPC was able to do with the small group of people who met.

Recall, however, Jeff's report that when the conversation was eventually opened up to the entire congregation at SPC, many members expressed appreciation for having been "heard."

The above extended narratives about the discernment processes at Eastern, SPC and Zion should be of significant help to other Christian institutions of higher education or churches that are in various stages of seeking discernment regarding LGBT issues or are contemplating initiating such a discernment process. In what follows, I hope that further help will be provided by my attempting to identify some common themes from which "common ground" has emerged from the three case studies (repeating a few of the above direct quotes for emphasis). I start with the importance that Julie, Jeff, and Jessica attach to "context."

INSTITUTIONAL CONTEXT IS CRITICAL

Julie eloquently asserts that the discernment process for each institution must be developed in ways that are "culturally appropriate," reflecting the nature of the "local faith community."

> I hold both [Jeff and Jessica] in high regard for taking such a thoughtful approach to the conversation. Each had deep knowledge of the culture of their particular community and found ways to open opportunities for dialogue within culturally-appropriate ways. We all face different internal and external pressures; I believe each congregation pressed into the difficult conversation in a way that was unique to their individual community identities. Effective communication and solutions we seek through communication must be local. Even though we all may recognize and celebrate the universal and eternal truth of Christ, how we understand and live out that truth must occur at the level of the local community. Figuring out "what it means" and "how to do it" is the role of the local faith community.
>
> Both Jeff and Jessica took approaches that were consistent within their cultures, i.e., their local communities of faith.

Julie adds that the process for each local faith community, while "unique," must create "safety, authenticity, and accountability."

> What has risen for me as I've reviewed all three cases as summarized in the essays is that there is no one right way to process

these difficult issues. How local communities create safety, authenticity and accountability will be unique.

Because the contours of the discernment process should reflect the local context, Jessica acknowledges that "I am having a very difficult time speaking critically into a context [Eastern University or SPC] and process in which I am not fully engaged." She insightfully notes the difficulty in understanding any group of people when she is "not part of their community" (including "our LGBTQ brothers and sisters"), suggesting, however, that, in any case, "Christ's gospel" should be reflected within each given context.

> I will never fully understand our LGBTQ brothers and sisters, because I am not a part of their community. I will never fully understand my Eastern or Sammamish brothers or sisters for the same reason, but I can recognize that Christ's gospel is incarnational and should always fully represent within its context.

Jeff adds the valuable insight that locating a conversation about a contentious topic within the context of a particular Christian tradition (e.g., Mennonite) that has talked about that topic before can lessen anxiety

> Jessica . . . , one of the things I really appreciated about the process you and your colleague . . . took your congregation through was the way you located the conversation in the broader Mennonite context. It seems to me that any time we can say, "This conversation is natural because our ancestors have done this before us," it lowers people's anxiety and puts the congregation in a hopeful, positive frame of mind. That positioning unlocks the past (our theological tradition) in order to unlock the future (our congregation's path going forward).

Granted that each context for a discernment process is unique, does that uniqueness extend to the "purpose" that each institution envisions for the discernment process? Julie, Jeff, and Jessica share a number of reflections about "purpose."

WHAT IS THE "PURPOSE" FOR ENTERING INTO A DISCERNMENT PROCESS

IS THE PURPOSE TO "TAKE A STAND"; TO "MAKE A DECISION"?

Sometimes the context of an institution requires that a "decision" relative to LGBT relationships be made as soon as possible. As Jeff noted in the case of his church (SPC), "For us, Washington State's legalization of gay marriage forced our hand somewhat to make a decision regarding these issues." And, as reported above, SPC did reach a decision after a very careful and thorough discernment process.

Similar external pressures were experienced at Eastern University, as reported by Julie.

> Eastern University faces a great deal of pressure to figure out our policy on marriage, and same-sex benefits. Will we lose our accreditation? Will some (or all) of our professional programs lose their accreditations? Will our students lose federal funding? If we change our policy, will we have to leave the Council for Christian Colleges and Universities (CCCU)? And, if we have to leave the CCCU, what does that actually mean?

Zion Mennonite also experienced some "external pressures" to reach a decision, albeit from within its own Christian tradition—its denomination (Mennonite Church USA), and the Mennonite Ohio Conference to which it belongs. Jessica reports that their "denomination" doesn't officially take a "stance toward the LGBT community," because the denomination "strongly desires to maintain relationship and community dialogue." However, "there are many within our denomination who do not value such a posture." Furthermore, within the Ohio Conference there is a "strong voice ... that says we should take a strong traditional stance against the acceptance of LGBTQ relationships."

Within that context, Jessica reports that many in the Zion congregation wanted to "make a firm decision" that takes "a stand."

> Early on, Pastor Jeff Kauffman and myself began to recognize the extent to which the congregation wanted to make a firm decision, "taking a stand" on the wide range of issues pertaining to LGBTQ. These issues would include the whole range from whether we open our doors to simply accepting LGBTQ people in our midst, to affirming, to empowering for leadership, marrying, and ordaining.

However, Zion decided that the purpose for its discernment process would not be to "take a stand." In addition to the fact that deciding to not take a stand fit well with the denominational desire of Mennonite Church USA to "maintain relationship and community dialogue," it was also influenced by a discovery that the call to "take a stand" on the part of "many in the Zion congregation" was accompanied by a failure on the part of many congregants to realize that other members may disagree with them about LGBT issues

> ... as quickly as the anxious desires to "take a stand" one way or another were coming into the office, so was our realization that people within the congregation had no idea that the congregation was not in agreement with each other. There was an interesting dynamic that was in play, where people could not fathom that others within the congregation were not in the same place as they were.

Furthermore, the pastors "were not totally in agreement."

> We pastors even found that as we discussed the variety of directions and nuances of Christian faithfulness and human sexuality that we were not totally in agreement. Which meant the more people insisted that we as pastoral leadership needed to take a stand and tell people where the church stood, the more we realized that we were heading towards an impossibly messy outcome.

When congregants were eventually asked to situate themselves on a continuum of possible responses to LGBT relationships (condemnation, promise of healing, costly discipleship, pastoral accommodation, affirmation, and liberation), it was found that "If we were to take a black and white look at the continuum in terms of 'conservative v. liberal' our congregation was split 50/50," which affirmed the earlier conclusion of the pastor's that defining the purpose of the conversation as "taking a stance" would have been an "impossible way forward."

Therefore, the pastors developed a "way forward" around the purpose of allowing "the congregation "to be able to hear each other, and in particular hear where there was disagreement."

> So we pastors designed our two-part conversation, emphasizing the word "conversation." The purpose of these conversations were to allow the congregation to be able to hear each other, and in particular hear where there was disagreement. We emphasized that this was not going to be a debate, there was not going to be decision-making, no voting. Listening to each other was the point.

However, as Jessica reports, "most people" found this approach "frustrating."

> This emphasis on not making a decision or not debating or discerning was frustrating to most people. They didn't understand the point of meeting if we weren't going to make a decision. Anxiety continued to grow, but we pastors strongly emphasized the need for all people to be in attendance if they wanted to be heard, which again, is a key piece of what we understand to be Anabaptist Mennonite community-centered leadership.

Jessica reports that despite the initial frustration she believes that this process "was a success, simply because the anxiety within the congregation disappeared."

> We did lose people from not declaring a stand, but I believe the fact they left had more to do with their lack of significant relationships within the body more than their disagreement with our approach. This conversation took place two years ago and since then we have only had one flare-up of anxiety surrounding our denominational convention. Without fail, those people who since this conversation have expressed anxiety over the denominational conflict, when asked, 100 percent of them did not participate in the two conversations. People on both ends of the spectrum have told us that it was very valuable, important and well done.
>
> While it may seem to some that not making a decision was not "direct enough" we feel as though directly walking into the potential for conflict and exposing the tensions around the subject dissolved the growing anxiety within the congregation. People were given a voice and they heard each other. This happened two years ago, and we feel it has freed our congregation from the conflict that we see paralyzing so many churches around us.

However, Jessica does acknowledge and "regret" that this approach of not taking a church-wide stance failed to "communicate . . . a unified message" to "our LGBTQ people within our congregation and community."

> My only regret was our inability to communicate to our LGBTQ people within our congregation and community a unified message. We have always been a welcoming congregation and we continue to be, which is probably why we are "progressive" for our community and conference. But I cannot tell my dear neighbor when she asks where Zion "stands" on the issue, because we don't. I can tell her that everyone across the spectrum in our congregation (I have talked to) says the church is for everyone. I can tell her that she and her wife are welcome at the Lord's table, but I cannot tell her the nuances of what that means

> for us as a congregation or for her as a part of our body, but she is a welcomed part of our body.

In Jeff's reflections on the approach to discernment taken by Zion, he expressed appreciation for the fact that the pastors at Zion "didn't mandate a certain ideology or position, or expect people to see things as you do," adding that "As a leader, that is often very hard to do. Instead, you provided room at the table for everyone to be where they were at and make their own discoveries. That inductive type of teaching and learning is the best kind, in my opinion." However, Jeff adds that the fact that "no official decision that was made on the subject of LGBTQ inclusion" could "rear its head later on."

> If I were to offer one critique it would be that there was no official decision that was made on the subject of LGBTQ inclusion. While no decision is essentially a decision (for the status quo), I wonder if this will just rear its head later on and if in fact the anxiety is still underground since there is still no official position of the church on the issue. For us, Washington State's legalization of gay marriage forced our hand somewhat to make a decision regarding these issues. While I don't believe Ohio has that same state law in place, I wonder down the road if (or likely, when) it does, if Zion will have to face this issue again . . . . If I was in your position, I may have made a similar leadership move, but I wonder if this issue is done for your church family. All that being said, I so admire the process you went through, especially the way you dealt with an anxious issue and neutralized it, all the while growing your congregation in love, grace, and truth.

The above account of how Zion did not choose "to take stand" as the purpose if its discernment process seems to me to fit well with the focus in the Mennonite tradition on the central importance of "relationships" and encouraging "community dialogue."

I believe it is fair to conclude from the above reflections that external factors can dictate the need for an institution to decide that "a stance must be taken"; "a decision must be made." But, as later reflections will reveal, an external requirement that "a stance must be taken" should be viewed as an opportunity to pursue a much more fundamental purpose. But before laying bare that more fundamental purpose, I will consider the agreement among Julie, Jeff and, Jessica about what should NOT be a purpose for the discernment process

"CHANGING MINDS" IS NOT THE FUNDAMENTAL PURPOSE

A careful reading of the reports from Julie, Jeff, and Jessica on the discernment processes at Eastern, SPC, and Zion reveal that they were not driven by a desire to "change the minds" of members of their respective institutions.[2]

Before presenting the fundamental purpose that I believe Julie, Jeff, and Jessica embraced in their respective discernment processes, I will briefly interject my own view as to why "changing minds" should not be the fundamental purpose: Although all participants in the discernment process should desire to gain a better understanding of the truth relative to LGBT issues and this process could change minds, this is not a contest between two teams where each team hopes to add people to "their side" for the purpose of "winning." Rather, as we aspire to gain a better understanding as to the truth about LGBT issues, we should use a process that emphasizes Christians loving each other, including their LGBT members, and exemplifies "Christian unity" in the midst of strong disagreements.

Hopefully, the following further reflections on "the most fundamental purpose" will help us to better understand how to live that way, personally and within the Christian institutions to which we belong.

THE FUNDAMENTAL PURPOSE IS TO "CHANGE HEARTS"

Jeff eloquently points us towards another purpose other than "changing minds." The fundamental purpose of "changing hearts."

> For the record, not one person in the study group [at SPC] had a change of conviction on homosexuality and the church. But together we did have a change of heart—we went from trying to win each other around an issue of faith and practice, to being committed to each other and loving each other like the family God believes that we are. With that in mind, we worked hard on a process to bring our congregation on board with what these family values looked like.

---

2. Although Julie reports that if Eastern had used pre-process and post-process questionnaires, it would have been "interesting" to find out "how much we have changed our opinions."

Note Jeff's suggestion that the "change in heart" that he hopes for is that all SPC members become "committed to each other and loving each other like . . . family. . . ."

In the remainder of this section, I add that one dimension of such commitment and love for each other is openness to "changing one's perspective on a person who disagrees with you." I base this addition on the differing positions that two Mennonite scholars have taken as to the nature of a "genuine conversation" about disagreements.

Michael King summarizes his view of a "genuine conversation" between persons who disagree as "involving a mutual quest for treasures in our own and the other's viewpoint. The first move is to make as clear as I can why I hold this position . . . and why you might find in it treasure to value in your own quest for truth." The second move is to see the value in the other's view . . . and to grow in my own understanding by incorporating as much of the other's perspective as I can without losing the integrity of my own convictions."[3]

Carolyn Schrock-Shenk proposes that the hope to find mutual treasure in a conversation on an issue as volatile as homosexuality may be unrealistic. Rather her attenuated view of what make a conversation "genuine" is as follows.

> Does one need to be open to changing one's perspective or conviction about an issue? In my view that readiness is the ideal, but it is rarely realistic, especially in relation to issues as charged as homosexuality. I have come to believe that a minimum requirement for genuine conversation is a readiness to change or modify one's perspective about the *person or persons* holding the opposite point of view[4]

As I have written elsewhere, changing one's perspective about someone who disagrees with you is no small accomplishment.

> . . . it is no small thing if, at a minimum, those taking opposite sides in this debate [about homosexuality] at least modify their perspectives on those who disagree with them as a result of dialogue . . . those Christians taking opposite sides on this volatile issue may come to see that those on the other side of this volatile issue are also deeply committed Christians, with whom they can have fellowship despite disagreements about homosexuality. Attaining that sort of "unity in fellowship" (not uniformity in beliefs about homosexuality) would be no small accomplishment

---

3. King, "Conversations," 153, paraphrasing King, ed., *Stumbling*, 26.
4. Schrock-Shenk, "Foreword," 15.

in those Christian denominations that threaten to split over the homosexuality issue[5]

In the section that follows it will become clear that Julie, Jeff, and Jessica agree that the possibility of changing your perspective about someone who disagrees with you, as a critical dimension of a "change in heart" about that person, is enhanced when you seek to enter into a "personal relationship of mutual trust" with that person.

THE CENTRALITY OF "BUILDING RELATIONSHIPS OF MUTUAL TRUST"

Recall Julie's observation that from her experience at Eastern, the best way to overcome the "common thread of fear" that pervaded the Eastern community at the beginning of their discernment process was to seek to establish "relationships of trust."

Recall also Jeff's focus on the centrality of building relationships of mutual trust in his reflections on the manner in which almost three years of group meetings led to the emergence of a "family" in which we "fell more and more in love with one another." I repeat his important observation.

> For almost three years, this group met at least once a month, eating dinner together, getting to know each other, praying for each other, reading Scripture together, digesting articles, books, and YouTube talks from all sides of the issue together. And while we most certainly became the resident experts on the subject of homosexuality and the church, what we realized through this process was that what we REALLY became was not just experts, but family. In fact, family became an important metaphor for our group (which next to the "body of Christ" is the second most used metaphor in the Scriptures regarding the church—we aren't called "brothers and sisters" for nothing!). And while our study and conversation was eye opening, what we came to see most of all was a new set of family values—that just as we would never think of throwing someone out of our nuclear family for a difference of opinion, we would never turn away from each other as a church family as well, just because we saw things differently on these issues. And so we met and fell more and more in love with each other as we studied and prayed on this difficult issue.

---

5. Heie, "Coming Alongside," 188.

Jeff elaborates on some of the "lessons learned" during this long discernment process, which again points to the centrality of building relationships of "trust," which takes time.

> Engaging in LGBT issues as a church requires a long, slow road. Don't rush it! While some in the family are wanting to fling open the doors, there are others who are afraid of what that will look like. It takes time, conversation, patience, love, more patience, and time . . . .
>
> When engaging in LGBT issues as a church, it is imperative to find common ground. How easy it is to let things divide us when, in reality, there is so much that unites us! . . . What do we stand on together? What is our rock?
>
> When engaging in LGBT issues in the church, you must trust your conversation partners. To have these conversations requires vulnerability and trust. Neither of those things happen overnight, but if I can get to the place where I know the other loves me, hears me, disagrees with me, and loves me anyway, I am a lot closer to being a family that listens to the Spirit and works together for resolution.
>
> When engaging in LGBT issues in the church, humility is a must. In my opinion, we all need to just admit that we are at least 10 percent heretical. One day when we stand before a loving God, I'm convinced that none of us will have it all right—we will certainly learn a few things we got wrong! Because of that, we need to hold our interpretations somewhat loosely, be willing to listen, learn and respect the insights of others. When engaging in LGBT issues in the church, we must see "agreeing to disagree agreeably" as an expression of living out the gospel and as a witness to the world. We live in a world that unfortunately sees the church as fractured and unable to get along. What a witness we present when we can give ground to each other and work things out rather than rush to divorce court!
>
> Finally, when engaging in LGBT issues in the church, pastors need to lead by example. Too often (and I felt this pressure, too), pastors are expected to make their theological convictions the expectation for the entire church. "Strong leadership" is equated to a puffed-up chest and a "not on my watch" sort of posture. Instead, it seems to me that the pastor's job is to shepherd their flock to listen together to God's Spirit through God's Word and his people, to encourage the community to lean in towards each other in love and trust, rather than fear. This posture starts with the pastor, and we are called to model that spirit of generosity, grace, and enthusiasm with joy.

Case Study Conversations about LGBT People and Issues

Recall also Jessica's explanation regarding Zion's requirement that congregants attend both of their conversations, with the first conversation intended to "set a tone of humility and respect for the second conversation," which avoided people "jumping" into "a sensitive conversation without the relationships already built around the table." Jessica has much more to say about the centrality of building relationships of mutual trust.

First, Jessica points to the importance of holding to both "convictions" and "relationships."

> I am proud of our congregation's ability to delicately hold their convictions, while holding even tighter to our relationships. In the words of Palmer Becker, as Anabaptist Mennonites we believe that "Jesus is the center of our faith. Community is the center of our lives. Reconciliation is the center of our work." I believe that it is only within authentic, loving, Christ-centered community that we can hold strong disagreements within the tension of an even stronger love and greater respect for each other.

The centrality of relationships is also emphasized when Jessica notes that the members Zion lost when they didn't declare a "stance" was primarily because these members lacked "significant relationships" within the church.

> We did lose people from not declaring a stand, but I believe the fact they left had more to do with their lack of significant relationships within the body more than their disagreement with our approach.

Another way of talking about the centrality of relationships is to focus on the importance of "community." Jessica does both in her commendation of the processes at both Eastern and SPC.

> ... I highly value the role relationships and community played in both processes held by Eastern University and Sammamish. I think what I highly respect from both processes was the ability to bring both sides together to do intentional and longer processed work.
>
> Again, the beauty of both of your processes was in your ability to bring people from across the spectrum together to dialogue in order to better understand one another, which it sounds like the community became more important than the "stance."

Jessica expands on the importance of "community" in noting that in her reading of the processes at Eastern and SPC, "the health of the community was the highest good."

> I find the fullest and most beautiful example within both processes was the ability for people from both "sides" of the spectrum of responses being able to maintain and grow relationship regardless of opinion and that in the end the health of the community was the highest good. And by that I mean that if one member of the body is hurting, the whole body is hurting.
>
> I believe it is this way of being community that is a sign of God's new covenant in Christ. If we, the church, are to be the sign of the new covenant, God's new people pointing toward the kingdom of God, we have to be able to exemplify a new way of behaving. We have to be so intriguing to the watching world that they want to ask questions and hopefully be inspired to join along.

Jessica adds that in stark contrast to a "bumper sticker mentality," a "critique" of the beliefs of others "must always take place in the context of community and relationship."

> I think we live in a "bumper sticker" mentality kind of world, where we can too easily question authority or give our advice without the context of relationship, history or without the risk of accountability.
>
> I believe that critique must always belong in the context of community and relationship.

Finally, Jessica suggests that since building significant relationships takes a lot of time, the discernment process should not be rushed.

> I also value the in-depth way that SPC allowed their process to grow into a longer forum in which family-like relationships were formed. This could not have happened had the church felt like they were in a hurry to move immediately.

Julie again affirms the "centrality of relationships," adding a painful personal story of "critique" that was not given within the context of a "relationship." But she also raises the crucial issue of the willingness, or not, of extending the sphere of relationships to "people who have a different sexual orientation or gender identity."

> What is the motivation to engage in this dialogue? I think both Jeff and Jessica correctly point to the centrality of relationships in the process. Regardless of the context, whether university or

church, we see relationships as central to living well in the body of Christ.

Recently, my co-author and I submitted a chapter for an edited book that included a discussion of the dialogue on human sexuality. The copy editor for the book took real issue with our discussion and make editorial comments throughout the chapter, including, "Gay sex is a sin. No discussion needed." The comments were mean-spirited and inappropriate from the copy editor. In reflection, I think it was easy for the copy editor to make the comments because she doesn't have any relationship with me or my co-author. I want to believe that it was easier to write these comments to strangers, than to friends.

How does our motivation change when we are in relationship with people who have a different sexual orientation or gender identity? Perhaps we learn, as Justin Lee reminds us, that people are more than just sex. Perhaps we are more motivated to listen to one another when we are motivated by our love for one another.

In a later posting, Julie again emphasizes the importance of building "relationships with those who are LGBTQ," adding that a limitation of the discernment process at Eastern was that their policies did not allow faculty and staff who were LGBT to serve on their Human Sexuality Task Force.

> ... another key aspect in evaluating these models [for discernment] was relationships with those who are LGBTQ. The motivation to re-evaluate our understanding of Scripture is informed by our relationships with others. When we know same-sex married couples, committed to one another, raising children, who seem to be blessed by God, we are challenged to evaluate our understanding of Scripture. Because of our policies at Eastern, one of our limitations was actually including faculty/staff who are LGBT on the task force. Without their voices at the table, our committee discussions, and ultimately our recommendations, will be under-represented by this group.

This failure to adequately build relationships with the LGBTQ individuals at Eastern was also a problem at SPC and Zion. But before elaborating on that, I will recapitulate the above stream of thought.

Julie, Jeff, and Jessica agree that rather than seeking to "change minds," the fundamental purpose of the discernment process ought to be to "change hearts" toward commitment to and love for each other, which includes openness to changing your perspective on someone who disagrees with you. They then also agree that the path toward changing your perspective on someone who disagrees with you is to build a "personal relationship of trust" with that person.

Of course, there is a marvelous by-product of emphasizing the building of personal relationships of mutual trust with those who disagree with you about LGBT issues: you will be more open to listening empathetically to someone with whom you have developed a relationship of mutual trust; thereby opening of the possibility of collectively gaining a better understanding of the truth regarding LGBT issues.

But such empathetic listening must include everyone, which did not occur adequately at Eastern, SPC, and Zion. Julie, Jeff, and Jessica agreed that a weakness in the discernment process at all three of their institutions was a failure to adequately listen to the voices and stories of the LGBT members of their communities.

LISTENING TO ONE ANOTHER, INCLUDING LGBT CHRISTIANS

Julie, Jeff, and Jessica all agree that "building relationships within a community" requires "listening to one another." As Jessica says about the "two-part conversation" at Zion, "Listening to one another was the point."

> So we pastors designed our two-part conversation, emphasizing the word "conversation." The purpose of these conversations were to allow the congregation to be able to hear each other, and in particular hear where there was disagreement. We emphasized that this was not going to be a debate, there was not going to be decision-making, no voting. Listening to each other was the point.

As already reported, Jessica adds that this focus on "listening to each other" lessened anxiety within the congregation because "People were given a voice and they heard each other."

> While it may seem to some that not making a decision was not "direct enough" we feel as though directly walking into the potential for conflict and exposing the tensions around the subject dissolved the growing anxiety within the congregation. People were given a voice and they heard each other. This happened two years ago, and we feel it has freed our congregation from the conflict that we see paralyzing so many churches around us.

While the discernment process at all three institutions involved considerable "listening to one another," not everyone had the opportunity to speak and be heard. Notably, as the following snippets will reveal, LGBT members of these communities were too often not given a voice, and, therefore, were not heard. Recall the following stark contrast between what LGBT students at Eastern found "most meaningful" and the actual list of invited speakers.

> Perhaps the most meaningful for LGBT students was an event sponsored by Refuge, a student-led group supporting those who are LGBT. The event focused on,"Stories of Courage and Healing: Experiences of LGBTQ Eastern Alumni." The keynote alum who spoke said that he was impressed with the lineup of speakers. But he also noted that he only saw one other LGBT person as an invited speaker—and that person presented a celibate lifestyle approach.

Recall also Julie's observation about the lack of LGBT voices on the Human Sexuality Task Force (HSTF) at Eastern.

> ... because of current policies at Eastern, no faculty, staff, or administrators on the HSTF were LGBT. In one of the discernment forums, a number of students raised issues of justice. If the process is to dialogue about human sexuality, the absence of the LGBT voice cannot go unnoticed. As a result of the feedback, the HSTF surveyed current and former employees about their experiences at Eastern. While the stories gathered matter, they do not begin to substitute for actual representation and inclusion.

In commenting on Julia's report on the discernment process at Eastern, Jeff points out the destructive effect of not feeling "valued" when the "perspectives" of any community group (LGBT members or other groups) are not given a hearing.

> I also hear your concern on the disappointment of different groups not feeling like their perspectives mattered. In the end, it seems to me that what people need to know the most is that they are heard, valued, and have a place to stand in the community.

In further agreeing with Jessica's concern about "not having . . . LGBT voices at the table," Jeff points to the provocative possibility that this is "natural."

> It is against my nature to criticize other people's stories, especially when the circumstances are such that each community is just doing the best they can in the wake of anxiety and crisis. That being said, I would share your critique of not having the ability to have LGBT voices at the table when making these big decisions. I suppose in some ways this is natural—if the question to

> be asked is "Should a group have full communion with us?" one would assume that there are no voting representatives [from the group] at the table for the decision. It reminds me a bit of James and the Jewish-Christian leaders voting for Gentile inclusion at the Council of Jerusalem. To move from a closed to a more accepting and inclusive society takes the work of the insiders predominantly. That being said, I wonder if it is hard in your system to get a fair hearing for the LGBT community when both history and conservative theology are on the side of those in structural power.

The suggestion by Jeff that it may be those having "structural power" in the institution who can easily inhibit the possibility of the "LGBT community" getting a "fair hearing" is provocative and begs for more conversation (more about that later when we consider the role of leaders in the discernment process).

Jeff's concluding reflection is that "we [SPC] could have done a better job at engaging people in the LGBT community in our conversation as a group" by listening to "their story."

> But the big learning for me was what Julie suggested for both her experience at Eastern as well as her question for Jessica and me: we could have done a better job at engaging people in the LGBT community in our conversation as a group. The reality was that while each of us individually had our own experiences . . . and while together we set about engaging them through articles and books, we never actually sat down with a member of the LGBT community in our group and heard their story. Why didn't we do this? I'm not quite sure, but I wish we had, because while reading stories and discussing theological propositions are helpful, there is nothing that can substitute for face-to-face relationships and conversation.

Jeff follows this reflection with a poignant story of how one "face-to-face relationship and conversation" with a married gay couple "changed" him.

> I know this [that there is no substitute for face to face relationships and conversation] to be true because for me, my epiphany came when I had the chance to meet with a married gay couple who had started to attend our church. They had come to SPC because they were followers of Jesus and felt like this was a place where they sensed Jesus was present and active (the kind of compliment every pastor loves to hear!).

> But let me tell you a secret—I was nervous to meet with them, mostly because I had never actually met with a married gay couple and heard their story before. As we sat down at the local Starbucks, one of the men told me of his lifelong self-hatred because of his sexual orientation and his belief that God's hatred for him matched his own. This was a man who had given up a decade of his life serving Christ by playing in a music ministry that traveled the globe—yet all the while living in despair and without much hope. And yet now, through many years of study, prayer, and discernment, he had come to a place of peace that God loved him as he was, warts and all, and that even if this was not God's original intention for mankind, it was God's way of wholeness for him in the midst of his brokenness. Here was a man who was sincerely committed to the Scriptures and desired to live them out; who saw his fidelity to his husband as an extension of that devotion.
>
> I must say, that conversation changed me. Let me be clear—it didn't convince me of the biblical/hermeneutical lens that my friend was using to arrive at his conclusion, but it changed me, nonetheless.

Julie also notes here concern about the lack of LGBT representation in the discernment processes at all three institutions, pointing out that the "fatal flaw" (my words, not hers) in not listening to the members of the LGBT community is that "we 'do not know what we do not know' because of the limitations of our experiences and perspectives" (a confession that Jeff shares in one of his postings).

> Perhaps my concern is also the insight I've learned from going through the process at Eastern, and now reading their stories. Neither Jeff nor Jessica mentions that any of the key members involved are LGBT. One of the reasons we all have to build our knowledge in this area is that we are not LGBT. I remember as an undergraduate student in the mid-1980s that I sat on a faculty committee whose job was to develop the first sexual harassment policy for the university. As luck would have it, one of the members was sexually harassing me. When I asked the chair of the committee about it, he said that it was not considered sexual harassment since this faculty member was in sociology, while I was a nineteen-year old student in communications. Ha! This seems ridiculous now. We know so much more about the dynamics and consequences of sexual harassment and its connections with all manifestations of power. The point of my tangent is that the one in power (male and the chair of the committee)

> could not begin to understand the situation from my (female and student) perspective. Without voices at our tables who represent difference in sexual orientation and gender identification, we are not able to grasp the whole story because we "do not know what we do not know" because of the limitations of our experiences and perspectives.

Jessica notes that the exclusion of LGBT voices in the discernment process at Zion was at least partially motivated by a desire to minimize the "opportunities for people to say hurtful things to others." But, in light of this eCircle conversation, she now recognizes the importance of including LGBT voices if Zion is to "move forward."

> I think the encouragement from Julia to remember the voices of the LGBTQ communities within our congregational discernment are important for us as we move forward. I think initially, because of the heightened emotion surrounding the conversations, we as a leadership team were trying to "control" the opportunities for people to say hurtful things to others.

A SPLENDID BY-PRODUCT OF DISCERNMENT: CLARIFYING WHO WE ARE AS A COMMUNITY

A careful reading of the stories told by Julie, Jeff, and Jessica about their respective discernment processes reveal that the processes helped each institution to more carefully define who they were as communities. For example, Julie even asserts that "defining who we are as a community" was something hoped for from the very beginning.

> At various points, each group [at Eastern] felt that their perspective did not matter. It seemed that some believed that it was useless to share their opinions. For some, they feared that no minds would be changed. Was "changing minds" the point of the dialogue? If the rhetoric of the process turned into war rhetoric, with one side winning, the other side losing. If the process turned into counting the number of "soldiers" on each team, then the point of the dialogue was lost. Entering into conversation, with genuine care, has the possibility to change an individual. The dialogue was not about "winning souls," it was about defining who we are as a community.

Julie later elaborates in terms of her understanding of what it means to be an "academic" community.

> Throughout the process, motivation to engage varied from person to person. Our data confirms that those who engaged in the process learned from it, and some even changed their position. Those who did not engage, did not learn, nor did they change their position. While "changing positions" was not the goal, *becoming informed and thinking critically in an academic environment matched the culture of the university*. I don't think the answer was to require attendance, but I wish there was a way to get more people involved in the process. (Italics mine.)

Julie's proposal is that "becoming informed and thinking critically is central to the mission an academic community." I concur with Julie's proposal since I believe that the most fundamental mission of any Christian institution of higher learning is to seek after "Truth" about all aspects of God's Creation, and "becoming informed and thinking critically" is certainly "central" to that quest.

Julie then illustrates her proposal by sharing a poignant account of how her own undergraduate education at Eastern, apparently informed by the university's commitment to helping students to become informed and to think critically, "saved" her by giving her the "foundation . . . needed to continue to wrestle with my faith, rather than abandoning it."

> I am an LGBT alumna of Eastern. When I was at Eastern, I knew several students who were LGBT and I can name a hundred ways in which knowing them enriched my experience. I did not come out while at Eastern and I was unsure at the time of what I believed about Christianity and homosexuality, but there can be no mistake that going to Eastern saved me. What I mean is this: at some point, if I had not received the rich Christian education, steeped in the classics of the faith, that Eastern provided, I would have reached a point where I had to choose between faith and the church on one hand and the realization that who I was fell outside of traditionally-accepted norms for Christians on the other. The education I received enabled me to see that Christianity is no simple thing and God has used all kinds, warts and all. It gave me the foundation I needed to continue to wrestle with my faith, rather than abandoning it.

While not ignoring the differences between Christian institutions of higher education and Christian churches (which would call for another conversation), I will now boldly suggest a common purpose that all these institutions should aspire to, based on the accounts above of how Eastern, SPC, and Zion all hoped to "change hearts" toward commitment to and love for each other, which includes openness to changing your perspective on someone who disagrees with you, and their agreement that the path toward changing your perspective on someone who disagrees with you is to build a "personal relationship of trust" with that person by "listening well."

> *A community of Christian faith enables followers of Jesus to fellowship with one another in unity by providing a safe space to build relationships of mutual trust characterized by listening and talking to one another with respect and love regarding their disagreements toward the goal of seeking a better understanding of the nature of truth.*

I close this section with some reflections, based on my own experience with Christian institutions of higher education, on one obstacle that too often prevents such educational institutions from exemplifying the "ideal" that I propose above: the obstacle of "fear."

Recall Julie's account of how "fear" was an impediment to the discernment process at Eastern: fear about how others in the community would perceive them if they expressed a "progressive" (or "conservative") position; fear of faculty and administrators that they may lose their jobs; fear of students that "their grades would suffer" if they expressed views that disagreed with their professors.

The fears noted above were all based on the "internal dynamics" that can be operative at Christian institutions of higher education, all of which need to be addressed if an institution aspires to the above ideal. But I now add another dimension to the "fear" that prevents a number of Christian institutions of higher education from "talking about differences" relative to LGBT people and issues, fears that comes from the "outside, such as *fear that the institution's constituents (financial supporters and parents of potential students) will withdraw support if the institution sanctions open discussion about these controversial issues.*

The stark contradiction that I believe is operative at Christian institutions of higher education where "fear" precludes open, honest, respectful conversations about LGBT people and issues is that it inhibits the quest for truth that is included in my "ideal" for all Christian institutions of higher education (and churches).

To seek to measure up to the "ideal" type of Christian community proposed above will require a rare type of leadership, a topic that Julie, Jeff, and Jessica address.

THE CHALLENGES OF LEADERSHIP

The conversation between Julie, Jeff, and Jessica suggests four characteristics that institutional leaders need to exemplify if a discernment process regarding LGBT issues (or any other controversial issue) is to be fruitful in measuring up to the "community ideal" that I propose above.

CREATING A SAFE SPACE FOR EXPRESSIONS OF DISAGREEMENT

Jeff commends Jessica for creating a discernment process where not everyone has to agree with the views of the leader, thereby providing space for members of the community to "make their own discoveries."

> I also appreciated the fact that you didn't mandate a certain ideology or position, or expect people to see things as you do. As a leader, that is often very hard to do. Instead, you provided room at the table for everyone to be where they were at and make their own discoveries. That inductive type of teaching and learning is the best kind, in my opinion.

Jeff also commends Eastern both for the way in which "the president and the administration" exhibited "openness" to allowing the concerns of students and faculty to be heard, which is a sign of having created a safe space for conversation.

> One of the things I most appreciate about the conversation you all are having is the maturity of the president and the administration to allow the hurt and concerns of students and faculty to come to the forefront and the willingness of the president to both apologize and to lean into the conversation. That to me is a sign of a great leader.

This points to another important characteristic of being a "great leader."

MODELING GENUINE LISTENING AND ENGAGEMENT

Julie returns Jeff's compliment by expressing appreciation for how Jeff (and Jessica) modeled "compassionate dialogue," which exemplified "genuine listening and "engagement."

> What was it about these churches that allowed them to engage without splitting? I think one critical aspect was senior leadership. Both Jeff (senior pastor) and Jessica (pastor) modeled

> compassionate dialogue. Both modeled genuine listening and engagement. At Eastern, the task force was appointed by the university president. Certainly, his leadership provided the opportunity (and perhaps the safety) to engage in the dialogue. The appointment of trusted leaders to the task force was also critical to our success. One in particular modeled compassionate dialogue. The idea of "trickle-down leadership" seems to be a good fit when evaluating our processes. These leaders were able to create dialogue, whereas other leaders have simply dictated the policy of the church, with no engagement of the community.

Julie's reflections above also point to another important characteristic of effective leadership; what she calls "trickle-down leadership" that, in my own words, empowers other gifted members of the community to share in leadership responsibilities.

EMPOWERING OTHERS TO SHARE IN LEADERSHIP

Julie points to the experience of Eastern as an example of "trickle-down leadership at its best," characterized by the willingness of the president to empower a HSTF (Human Sexuality Task Force) that represented a "diversity of opinion" and included a gifted cochair who was empowered and given the space to effectively lead the discernment process.

> ... one of the chief reasons the dialogue process was such a success was due to the leadership of the HSTF. Faculty were selected to serve on this Task Force because they represented diversity of opinion, and because they were held in high regard in the community. Two students (one representing a conservative opinion, the other a progressive) also served as *equal* members of the Task Force. Faculty and Administration members of the Task Force specifically asked for their input at every turn.
>
> The leadership provided by the HSTF to the community was greatly influenced by one of the co-chairs, a retired faculty member, well-respected by all. Her emphasis on an inclusive process and modeling it during every meeting (typical meetings lasted more than two hours) set the tone for the HSTF, and the community. Trickle-down leadership at its best.

Along these same lines, Jessica notes that such sharing of leadership at Zion was simply an expression of the "community-centered leadership" that characterizes the Mennonite Christian tradition, which is related to the aforementioned resistance at Zion against rushing to a decision.

> This emphasis on not making a decision or not debating or discerning was frustrating to most people. They didn't understand the point of meeting if we weren't going to make a decision. Anxiety continued to grow, but we pastors strongly emphasized the need for all people to be in attendance if they wanted to be heard, which again, is a key piece of what we understand to be Anabaptist Mennonite community-centered leadership.

OPENNESS TO THE POSSIBILITY THAT ONE'S OWN VIEWS MAY BE "WRONG"

This is one of the most elusive characteristics of effective leadership because as human beings we are often quick to say "this is what I believe" (which we should be willing to say with clarity and deep conviction) but the qualification "I may be wrong" is a rarity (for all of us, not just leaders of Christian institutions).[6]

It appears that at SPC, Jeff had the freedom to entertain the possibility that his views on LGBT issues may be "wrong," as revealed in his fascinating reflections on the question "Which way would I rather be wrong?"

> That question started ringing in my ears and it continues to this day. I realize this may appear to be an unorthodox way to do theology, but hear me out.
>
> If we assume that none of us has the corner on the market on the total and complete understanding of the Scriptures (which we must assume with the wide variety of emphases and interpretations of the book throughout the Christian world); and if we also assume that this particular issue of homosexuality is not a salvation issue but really an issue of discipleship (which I realize is not a universal belief but was a conclusion I had already come to in my own life), then I had to ask myself a deeper question: *What if my viewpoint is wrong? If my stance is wrong, what does it cost me and, more importantly, what does it cost those who are on the other side?*
>
> As I thought this through, I came to some sober conclusions. If I was right and my gay married friends were wrong, then they would not be living in the fullness of God's design (as

---

6. For my reflections on why it is so hard for humans to say "I may be wrong," see Heie, "Modeling."

I fail to do in many parts of my life as well, I am sure). As their pastor, then, I should admonish them to break up or at least remain celibate for the rest of their lives if they wanted to most faithfully follow Jesus Christ. This is a plausible conclusion and is widely accepted by many in the Christian world. It is the classic God's will versus humanity's will, the desire to live consistent with the text and tradition of Scripture versus adopting a new or popular cultural interpretation. Holding to this line may have been the right answer.

But then I started to get nervous . . . *What if I'm wrong?* What if, as a growing group of disciples in the Christian world believe, the few Scriptures concerning homosexuality aren't really aimed at this current understanding of same gender marriage that is possible today? What if, like gender issues and slavery (to name a few) our current context forces us to reinterpret our understanding of God's Word on this issue? If that was the case, then I (as their pastor) would be robbing these followers of Jesus a chance to be in a covenanted relationship that they believed imaged the relationship of God and his church. I would be hamstringing these disciples of Jesus with a burden they shouldn't have to bear (possibly like Paul's admonition to the Galatian believers regarding the Gentiles and circumcision). Worst of all, if these disciples experienced this prohibition as my new friend had experienced it for decades—a rejection by the living God—then what if they went into eternity believing in that rejection? The words of Jesus, "Let the little children come to me and do not hinder them," rung in my ears. What if I was keeping these children from God because I was so committed to my belief in what amounted to a non-essential doctrine that doesn't affect one's salvation?

It made me nervous.

With that in mind, I started to consider the very real question of which way I would rather be wrong. When I stand before God's judgment seat someday, would I rather have God say, "You were way too open and accepting on this issue" or would I rather have him say, "Through your actions, some of my children, in their despair, never knew my love"?

In the end, I decided for myself that I'd rather err on the side of grace on this issue and be okay with an open posture of acceptance. I realize many of my beloved colleagues and friends find themselves on the other side. For them, this issue is much clearer . . . black and white. For me, however, through this process and through this conversation done in community, I am much less certain than I ever was before—mystery abounds—and ultimately I believe we made the hard right decision (even though I still have my questions). Jessica echoed my thoughts exactly at the end of her essay: "I think the fullest of what we are called to do as a community of Christ is to pour ourselves out on the behalf of others, to regard ourselves and our positions as less than our own. If each person could live in such a manner we would be able to exemplify an alternative to the polarized world we live in. This is the mission we are called to."

It is extremely important to reemphasize that the context for the SPC discernment process was that Jeff, as pastor, had the freedom to entertain the possibility that he was wrong, which made it possible for him to shape a process that created a safe space for disagreement about LGBT issues that modeled genuine listening and engagement. But not all leaders of Christian institutions have that freedom, an issue with which I close this section.

I will limit my reflections to Christian institutions of higher education (like Eastern University and the four Christian colleges where I served), although it appears to me that the dynamics I am about to describe may be applicable, in some form, to the relationships between the leaders of churches and the denominations to which they belong.

Some Christian institutions of higher education have a clearly articulated, unambiguous, "institutional position" that prohibits same-sex relationships, including same-sex marriage. Their institutional position is that limiting marriage to a covenant relationship between a man and a woman is not a "secondary" issue that is a "disputable matter" for Christians, but is, rather, central to their understanding of what it means for the institution to be faithful to the Christian faith.

The president of such an institution has not been granted the freedom to initiate a "comprehensive discernment process" where the possibility of changing the policy on same-sex relationships is open for discussion.

In contrast, It appears to me, from Julie's report on the discernment process at Eastern University that their president was given the freedom (by the university's Board of Trustees, I assume) to initiate a discernment process regarding LGBT issues where there were no preconditions as to what the results could or could not be, thereby making it possible for the president to publicly acknowledge that his own views may be wrong, and to initiate a process that created a safe space for disagreement about LGBT issues that modeled genuine listening and engagement.

A LONG SLOW ROAD

It has already been suggested that a careful discernment process regarding LGBT issues takes a lot of time and can't be rushed because "building relationships of mutual trust" is time consuming. Julie, Jeff, and Jessica share additional reflections on why this is a "long slow road."

Jeff comments:

> Engaging in LGBT issues as a church requires a long, slow road. Don't rush it! While some in the family are wanting to fling open the doors, there are others who are afraid of what that will look like. It takes time, conversation, patience, love, more patience, and time (did I already say that?).

Jeff further notes:

> One thing we found was that while the topic was at its anxious peaks (for example, right after our denomination made its decisions on ordination and same-gender marriage), if we waited a little bit, the anxiety would dissipate and we could have more rational, thoughtful discussions.

In reflecting on Eastern's discernment process, Jeff "wonder[s] if [the Eastern] community is rushing the decision a little bit," even suggesting that a bit of procrastination may be best.

> I also wonder if your community is rushing the decision a little bit. Steven Sample in his leadership book *The Contrarian's Guide to Leadership*[7] says, "*Never make a decision today that can reasonably be put off to tomorrow.*"
>
> In other words, sometimes we rush decisions out of anxiety or just because we want to close a loop, rather than being willing to wait and let the conversation run its course and we discover the right answer. I wonder if after this relatively short season of conversation at Eastern, the issue has been discussed adequately. These are not really questions I can answer, but just ponderings as I hear your story.

Based on her experience at Zion, Jessica echoes Jeff's suggestion that this discernment process takes time, noting that the purpose of their "first conversation" was to "slow the congregation down and help them peel back the layers of their assumptions concerning 'morality,' the Bible, and how they use Scripture."

---

7. Sample, *The Contrarian's Guide.*

Jessica also says that "the importance of taking time to process decisions well" was one of the important learnings she took away from this conversation with Julia and Jeff; then expressing regret that "Zion's initial process was that it was set up against a time barrier and that it was conducted within the height of conflict."

Of course, the existence of external pressures to "reach a decision" can militate against taking too much time. To the extent that it may be possible, such external pressures should be resisted. Another approach is to be more proactive than reactive; initiating a careful discernment process before external pressures demand a quick decision.

HOW DO WE READ THE BIBLE?

As the reader of this book has already discovered, in addition to the in-depth reflections on "Biblical Understandings" shared by biblical scholars Jim Brownson and Mark Strauss in chapter 2, the crucial question as to the most adequate interpretations of the biblical passages pertaining to homosexuality has been addressed by a number of my other "conversation partners" during my nine-month eCircle. Jessica and Jeff add some reflections.

First, Jessica points out that her Anabaptist Mennonite tradition comes to the task of interpreting any Scripture with "Jesus [as] . . . the central lens through which we read the Bible."

> . . . after sorting out the variety of truth sources for decision-making we approached how we read, interpret, and apply the Bible. As Anabaptist Mennonites we would say that Jesus is the radical center of our faith and therefore the central lens through which we read the Bible. "If the Scripture doesn't agree, Jesus is the referee."

Jessica adds that "Our denomination, in the spirit of Anabaptism, continues to try to toe the line of being a congregationally based denomination in which the community is entrusted with its own interpretation of Scripture."

However, Jessica also notes that this "assumed standard" for reading the Bible within the Mennonite Church was not known to many of her church members, and, therefore, it was important, at Zion, to go back to foundational discussion of how different Christians who share a belief in "scriptural authority" arrive at "very different interpretations."

> Reading Scripture through Jesus is the assumed standard for MC USA and its sister institutions, but often we have found that there are people within the Mennonite Church who still practice

> a "flat-Bible" reading of Scripture. Discussing the differences of how Scripture can be read was key (and eye opening to some) in our being able to say how it is possible that two people can hold a high view of scriptural authority and come out at very different interpretations.

Jeff expresses appreciation for the way in which Zion used their discernment process as an opportunity to teach their members about foundational truths regarding "Scriptural authority and interpretation."

> One of the things I really appreciated about the process you [Jessica] . . . took your congregation through was the way you located the conversation in the broader Mennonite context. It seems to me that any time we can say, "This conversation is natural because our ancestors have done this before us," it lowers people's anxiety and puts the congregation in a hopeful, positive frame of mind. That positioning unlocks the past (our theological tradition) in order to unlock the future (our congregation's path going forward). I thought you . . . located the heart of the issue—scriptural authority and hermeneutics—and used this opportunity to teach your people some important, foundational lessons that we often assume our people understand but don't. One of the things I learned in this process is how important it is for us as pastors to take the opportunities life and culture affords to teach simple truths. I personally came to enjoy this conversation at our church, even if it was often tense and had big stakes. I think that happened because there was a refreshing joy in talking about simple truths with faithful people. Not only that, but I know I learned a lot in the process as well. It seemed to me from hearing your story that you took away the same joyful learnings.

CHRISTIAN WITNESS TO A FRACTURED WORLD

I believe it is fair to say that a defining characteristic of contemporary American culture is that it is highly polarized, where those who disagree about important issues are quick to "choose sides," hoping to be "winners"; rather than engaging respectfully in an attempt to find common ground.

Given that present reality, Jessica issues a clarion call, with which Jeff enthusiastically agrees, that the "community of Christ" needs to "exemplify an alternative to the polarized world we live in."

Jeff accurately points out how *not* to exemplify such an alternative to polarization, by continuing the "schism and splitting up" that has been a common result of disagreements among Christians regarding LGBT issues, adding that such polarization was not "a good witness to a fractured world."

> Because while I myself landed on the more traditional side of this conversation, I had both colleagues as well as parishioners who I considered faithful to Jesus Christ, lovers and students of the Scriptures, Christian friends I would trust with my life and considered my family; and yet, saw things differently than me. As the pastor of this particular flock, I wanted us to be faithful to Jesus Christ and faithful to God's Word, of course. But part of that faithfulness had to be being faithful to each other in the midst of it. And in a world filled with quick divorces and unfaithful relationships, I couldn't believe that schism and splitting up from each other or even our denomination (which as a pastor I made ordination vows to and as a church we were birthed into life and supported by to this very day) was a good witness to a fractured world.

Jessica points out that Christians can be a better witness to a fractured world if we show that we are "different in the way we engage conflict and disagreement with fellow believers."

> What I have learned the most from these two institutions [Eastern and SPC] is the value of an open-ended process which involves all along the spectrum of opinions and experiences, as well as a full engagement with Scripture and tradition.
>
> I think the church universal has an opportunity to show the rest of the world that followers of Jesus are different in the way we engage conflict and disagreement with fellow believers, let alone with the rest of the world. We need to be able to show people a different way of being broken in this world, because ultimately we are all broken people. Can we together do it well, with the amazing grace, and the surpassing love of Jesus Christ our Lord?

Jessica points out that this "way of being community" could even be so "intriguing to the watching world that they want to ask questions and hopefully be inspired to join along."

> I believe it is this way of being community that is a sign of God's new covenant in Christ. If we, the church, are to be the sign of the new covenant, God's new people pointing toward the kingdom of God, we have to be able to exemplify a new way of behaving. We have to be so intriguing to the watching world

that they want to ask questions and hopefully be inspired to join along.

Jessica also makes the radical proposal that our "posture" of "love [that] I am willing to show" can have a greater impact on our "unchurched neighbor" than our particular "ethical or moral views."

> I think as disciples of Jesus Christ, we need to remember that our posture communicates so much more to the watching world than does the values we espouse or the strong opinions we hold.
>
> It does not matter at all to my unchurched neighbor the rightness or the wrongness of my ethical or moral views, but rather the love I am willing to show whoever I deem to be the foremost sinner.

In reflecting on what she has learned from this eCircle conversation, Julie adds the powerful suggestion that the Christian faith may be "more attractive to outsiders" if Christians demonstrated that they were on a journey to "figure things out" rather than claiming that they already have it "all figured out."

> Finally, have I changed my view of either institution [SPC or Zion]? No. I did not know them well enough before hand to form a view in need of change. But, my view of local communities of faith has changed in that I think each institution must be as proud of its process as it is of its positions. I am left wondering if Christianity might be more attractive to outsiders if we seemed more clearly like we were "figuring it out" rather than seeming to have "figured it out."

Jeff echoes Julie's sentiment in his expression of confidence that "If we [at SPC] come at every conversation with love and respect," SPC can continue to navigate their "long way to go" in a way that will be "more attractive to outsiders"; a way that models being on a journey rather than having arrived at final answers.

> Do we still have a long way to go at SPC? Of course. We haven't even brushed the surface of other gender issues that continue to be explored. But one thing I am confident of—If we come at every conversation with love and respect, we can accomplish what Julie so eloquently said at the end of her essay, "I am left wondering if Christianity might be more attractive to outsiders if we seemed more clearly like we were figuring it out rather than seeming to have figured it out."

Case Study Conversations about LGBT People and Issues

I close this section and this chapter with a personal reflection on how what Julie, Jeff, and Jessica have said about the witness that Christians need to present to a fractured world, the modeling of a way to deal with disagreements with love and respect, fits beautifully with Jesus prayer for "Christian Unity" recorded in John 17:20-21 (a prayer that, as far as I can tell, has yet to be answered).

> I ask not only on behalf of these [the twelve original disciples of Jesus], but also on behalf of those who will believe in me through their word, that they all may be one. As you, Father, are in me and I am in you, may they also be in us, *so that the world may believe that you have sent me*. (italics mine)

Despite the many volumes that have been written about witnessing to the Christian faith (doing Christian apologetics), an oft-neglected dimension of the witness to the world to which Jesus calls those who profess to be his followers is to demonstrate Christian unity (possibly neglected because it is so scarce). Of course, what I mean by Christian unity, as this entire book seeks to model, is not "uniformity" of beliefs about controversial issues, like LGBT issues, but, rather, the modeling of love and respect for one another in the midst of our disagreements. If we can really model such love and respect for those with whom we disagree, it is conceivable that more people in our fractured world who do not share our Christian faith will give Christianity serious consideration.

10

Conclusion

A Possible Way Forward

The myriad complex details of the give-and-take between the sets of traditional and nontraditional conversation partners reported in chapters 1–9 can be overwhelming. In this concluding chapter, I present a framework by means of which I have tried to make coherent sense of it all, with the goal of proposing a possible way forward.

RESOLUTION OF DISAGREEMENTS WILL NOT HAPPEN SOON

Recall the view of Matthew Anderson and Isaac Sharp that the present LGBT controversies will not soon fade away, their consensus prediction (made with some hesitation) being that "we [in Christendom] will have increasingly smaller and older Christian institutions that have clarified that they will continue to uphold the 'traditional' teachings on sexuality and will continue the debate as a minority position in a broader culture that disagrees."

Based on his four decades providing pastoral care in the nitty-gritty of church life, Weldon Nisly also shared the view that the significant disagreements about LGBT issues will not be resolved soon.

I believe that a careful reading of chapters 1–9 also supports the view that these controversies will not soon fade away. These chapters reveal that Christians having great competence in the fields related to the various Leading Questions can present cogent arguments for opposing positions.

The issues are so complex and some of the disagreements so stark that the resolution of these disagreements is not on the immediate horizon. So, what should we do, if anything, in the meantime?

DOING NOTHING UNTIL WE HAVE IT ALL FIGURED OUT IS NOT AN OPTION

I am haunted by the following tragic words submitted to my eCircle by a gay reader, well into his sixties, during our first conversation.

> All that heartache could not, in the end, be worth it. I should have been one of those guys who hung himself in the rafters of the empty garage with the abandoned house next door, or perhaps who found a wild moment to jump from the college bell tower or high rise science buildings. Instead, I just doggedly went on and on and on.

He is not alone. Some of our gay conversation partners have also reported the brutal treatment they have received from other Christians. And I have heard similar stories in private conversations.

What a number of our gay brothers and sisters in Christ find to be extremely painful is that they have often been marginalized or completely silenced within our Christian communities. They yearn to tell their stories of how they aspire to be faithful followers of Jesus, but too few "straight" Christians are willing to listen.

This status quo cannot continue. Members of Christian churches and other Christian organizations need to find a better way to engage gay Christians now; not waiting until we have sorted through our disagreements. I will eventually be proposing some concrete steps for a way forward. But what is the goal?

WINNING IS NOT THE GOAL

We live in a culture that seems preoccupied with winning; whether in games, elections, or debates. But, echoing the reflections of Julia Stronks, focusing on an attempt to win others over to your point of view about LGBT issues is not a viable way forward.

You should surely be willing to express your point of view with clarity and deep conviction. But, given the current major disagreements about LGBT issues that will not be resolved in the near future, a way forward will be elusive if we focus on winning the argument.

LIVING WELL TOGETHER SHOULD BE OUR PRIMARY GOAL

As Julia Stronks has also suggested, the "primary issue," for both the Christian community and the larger culture, is "how we will live together despite our differences."

My view is that it will be possible for Christians to live well together, given their significant disagreements about numerous controversial issues, like LGBT issues, if they can share commitment to the following three foundational Christian values: the centrality of the quest for *truth*; the need to extend Christian *love* to all our brothers and sisters in Christ; and the importance of modeling *Christian unity* as a witness in a fractured and polarized world.

THREE CHRISTIAN VALUES AS FOUNDATIONS FOR A WAY FORWARD

SEEKING TRUTH

Recall Tim Otto's desire to find "safe spaces" for discussing LGBT issues, which he did not equate with "comfortable spaces."

> ... I don't think "safe" means "comfortable." Safe means something like, "A place where we are all allowed to speak *the truth as we see it*, and we can all try to hear it, because we know ourselves to be—above all—beloved by God. Safe means a place where truth is spoken and welcomed. (italics mine)

But the "truth as I see it" may be all wrong; it may be untrue. So, I need to distinguish between the "truth" about the issue at hand (which refers to "God's understanding") and my "belief" about that truth, which could be wrong (untrue).

In other words, I believe that only God knows the full truth about many controversial issues. Because I am a finite and fallible human being, I do not have a "God's-eye" view of that truth. I only have my belief about that truth, which reflects aspects of my particular social location such as my biography, the tradition of thought in which I am embedded, my gender, my sexual orientation, and my social and economic status. In biblical terms, I only "see through a glass darkly" (1 Cor 13:12).

But, as the pages of this book reveal, there is significant disagreement about whether traditional or nontraditional beliefs regarding LGBT issues capture the truth about these issues.

On the one hand, many of those taking a traditional view of same-sex relationships believe that one's view about same-sex relationships is not a "disputable" matter for Christians. Rather, the belief that marriage is intended by God to be "between one man and one woman" is so central to the Christian story as they understand it that to deny that belief is tantamount to rejecting the Christian faith. In holding that view, they believe that their belief about marriage is identical to the truth.

In parallel fashion, many of those taking a nontraditional view about same-sex relationships, like their traditional counterparts, also assert that their beliefs about same-sex marriage are indisputably true. But that truth is that God blesses same-sex monogamous, lifelong "marriage" covenants.

I respectfully propose that those in either of these camps are wrong when they take the positions that their beliefs about same-sex marriage are indisputable.

In brief, I believe that a belief about an issue is disputable for Christians if there are a significant number of deeply committed Christians, all holding to the authority and inspiration of Scripture, who embrace divergent positions on that issue.[1] And the evidence I present for my asserting that beliefs about same-sex relationships are "disputable" are the numerous narratives posted during my eCircle. My conversation partners embraced divergent beliefs on the various LGBT issues that were discussed at the same time that their postings revealed that in the midst of their disagreements they unambiguously held to the full authority and inspiration of Scripture.

If those on both sides of LGBT issues see their respective beliefs as indisputable, then I see little hope for a way forward. The conversation is essentially over. But, if I am correct that beliefs about same-sex relationships are disputable, then the ongoing task for both traditionalists and nontraditionalists is for them to continue engaging in respectful conversations about their many disagreements in the hope that together they may converge on a better approximation to truth.

Some readers may wonder whether my unyielding commitment to the search for truth can ever be in conflict with the authority of the church. For example, a Christian in the Catholic tradition may wonder what authority, if any, I give to the pronouncements of the Catholic magisterium. The same question can be asked of the pronouncements of the leaders of any church denomination or tradition. Such pronouncements must be treated with the

---

1. The catalogue of issues that Christians have judged to be disputable is extensive, tracing back to the early Christian church. For example, as reported in Acts 15, Jewish Christians disputed whether Gentile Christians needed to be "circumcised according to the custom of Moses" (v. 1). As reported in Romans 14 and 15, the appropriateness of Christians eating meats that had been offered to idols was a disputable matter.

utmost respect and seriousness. But, dare I say it: even the pope or any other church leader(s) can hold to beliefs that are wrong (untrue). My ultimate authority is the authority of truth.

But, of course, my beliefs about what is true may be wrong. Therefore, I need to evidence a significant measure of "humility."

A Call to Humility: I hold to my Beliefs with Deep Conviction, But "I May Be Wrong": I must now tread carefully, since I am not suggesting that those Christians who agree with me that same-sex issues are disputable are humble while those who believe otherwise are proud or arrogant.

An underlying problem, once again, is that many Christians, including a number of my conversation partners, do not share my view that LGBT issues are disputable issues. Rather, they believe that to say "I may be wrong" about marriage being reserved for a man and a woman is tantamount to rejecting the Christian faith and is not a sign of pride or arrogance. What can I say to those who hold that belief?

I want to encourage such persons to think along with me as to the most fundamental meaning of what it means to be a Christian. Does holding a nontraditional view on LGBT issues *really* disqualify one from being a Christian? The conversations that have been reported in this book emphatically answer "no." Both the traditional and nontraditional conversation partners evidence deep commitment to the Christian faith.

As to my own perspective, I believe that persons on both sides of the same-sex marriage dispute can be deeply committed Christians, based on my rather minimalist statement as to the essence of commitment to the Christian faith, as follows:

> I believe that someone is a Christian if he/she personally trusts in the death and resurrection of Jesus Christ as decisive for salvation and the redemption of the entire created order, and if he/she aspires to be a "follower of Jesus" by means of obedience to the two great "love commandments" taught by Jesus: love for God and love for neighbor.

Recall Isaac Sharp's suggestion that that "the very possibility of ongoing dialogue between the coalescing 'non-affirming' and 'affirming' sides of US Christianity is predicated on *the ability to view one another as mistaken, but still Christian*" (italics mine). So, even if the nontraditionalists (or traditionalists) are mistaken, they are still Christians.

Why is it so hard for Christians on both sides of LGBT issues (and other controversial issues) to say "I may be wrong"? I dare to suggest that our hesitancy to say "I may be wrong" reflects an inadequate measure of humility, properly understood.

For me, humility does not mean that I am wishy-washy about my beliefs. I hold my beliefs with deep conviction, and am happy to articulate my deeply held beliefs in public discourse. But I aspire to exemplify that rare combination of deep commitment to what I believe to be true with openness to the possibility that I may be wrong and can, therefore, learn from engaging in respectful conversation with someone who disagrees with me. The late renowned Christian scholar Ian Barbour has suggested that exemplifying this rare combination is a sign of "religious maturity."

> It is by no means easy to hold beliefs for which you would be willing to die, and yet to remain open to new insights; but it is precisely such a combination of commitment and inquiry that constitutes religious maturity.[2]

This combination of "commitment" and "openness" is a rarity in our world. Too many people gravitate toward one extreme or the other. At one pole, commitment, without openness, too easily leads to fanaticism, even terrorism (as C. S. Lewis has observed, to which recent world events tragically testify: "Those who are readiest to die for a cause may easily become those who are readiest to kill for it"[3]). At the other pole, openness to the beliefs of others without commitment to your own beliefs too easily leads to sheer relativism (you have your "truth," I have my "truth"). It is a challenge to live within the tension between these two poles. But that is a challenge that all Christians need to embrace.

In summary, whatever your beliefs about LGBT issues, you should express your beliefs and your reasons for holding those beliefs with clarity and deep conviction. But if you believe that your beliefs about LGBT issues are indisputable, then I see little chance of a way forward in engaging other Christians who disagree with you. There is a way forward only if you are willing to say that at least some of these issues are disputable for Christians and some of your current beliefs may be wrong, which will open then door to ongoing conversation with those who disagree with you in a quest for greater understanding of the truth.[4]

But, a commitment to seek a better understanding of the truth about LGBT issues is only one of three foundations for a way forward. A second foundation is a commitment to love all your brothers and sisters in Christ, including those who disagree with you.

---

2. Barbour, *Myths*, 138.
3. Lewis, *Reflections*, 28.
4. Barbour, *Myths*, 138.

LOVE: A FAMILY VALUE

In reflecting on the work of the initial study group that struggled with LGBT issues at Sammamish Presbyterian Church, Jeff Lincicome notes ways in which members of the group became "family," noting that family" is frequently used in scripture as a metaphor "describing the church."

> For almost three years, this group met at least once a month, eating dinner together, getting to know each other, praying for each other, reading Scripture together, digesting articles, books, and YouTube talks from all sides of the issue together. And while we most certainly became the resident experts on the subject of homosexuality and the church, what we realized through this process was that what we REALLY became was not just experts, but family. In fact, family became an important metaphor for our group (which next to the "body of Christ" is the second most used metaphor in the Scriptures regarding the church—we aren't called "brothers and sisters" for nothing!). And while our study and conversation was eye opening, what we came to see most of all was a new set of family values—that just as we would never think of throwing someone out of our nuclear family for a difference of opinion, we would never turn away from each other as a church family as well, just because we saw things differently on these issues. *And so we met and fell more and more in love with each other as we studied and prayed on this difficult issue.* (italics mine)

Granting the existence of a significant number of dysfunctional families, the ideal pointed to by Jeff is clear: As "brothers and sisters in Christ," some of whom are straight and some of whom are LGBT, we can disagree strongly about controversial issues, but we are still family committed to loving one another in the midst of our disagreements and our differing sexual orientations.

This ideal is clearly taught by Jesus: "By this everyone will know that you are my disciples, if you have love for one another" (John 13:35). While Christians will not deny this clear teaching, there are disagreements as to how to express that love toward other Christians. A focus of this book is to emphasize a way for loving others that is too often neglected by Christians.

In brief, I believe that it is a deep expression of love for another person who disagrees with you about any issue when you provide that person with a safe and welcoming space to express their disagreements and you then engage that person in respectful conversation about your agreements and disagreements, seeking first to find common ground and then seeking to illuminate remaining disagreements, in a manner that will conducive to ongoing conversation. This firm belief has driven many of my activities over the course of my Christian pilgrimage.

The Christian family value of love also calls for loving all of our LGBT brothers and sisters in Christ. All human beings need to be able to give and receive love. Whatever your beliefs about LGBT issues, you need to help LGBT individuals to give and receive love (more about that later).

There is a third foundation for a way forward. In addition to a commitment to seek a better understanding of the truth relative to LGBT issues and a commitment to love those who disagree with you, including all your LGBT brothers and sisters in Christ, you also need to commit to fostering Christian unity.

CHRISTIAN UNITY AS A WITNESS IN A FRACTURED WORLD

Recall Jessica Schrock Ringenberg's assertion that the community of Christ needs to "exemplify an alternative to the polarized world we live in." This may be possible if we learn from a prayer that Jesus once uttered, which has yet to be answered.

> I ask not only on behalf of these [the original disciples of Jesus], but also on behalf of those who will believe in me through their word, *that they may all be one*. As you, Father, are in me and I am in you, may they also be in us, *so that the world may believe that you have sent me*. (John 17:20–21, emphasis mine)

The disunity among those who profess to be followers of Jesus is and always has been a scandal. All too often, when we disagree about LGBT issues, and other issues great and small, we gravitate toward those who agree with us, excluding from our fellowship, or even calling into question the genuineness of the Christian commitment of those whose partial glimpse of the truth differs from ours.

The unity for which Jesus prayed is not uniformity of belief or ecclesiastical practice. Rather it involves "sticking together" around a common commitment to being followers of Jesus in the midst of our disagreements regarding many issues.

The most meddlesome thing about the prayer of Jesus quoted above is the suggestion that the ultimate apologetic for the credibility of the Christian faith is unity among Christians. In that light, it is indeed strange that the vast literature on Christian apologetics says too little about the "witness" to the Christian faith that would occur if Christians exemplified unity. When those who do not follow Jesus witness the disunity among Christians, it is no wonder that they find our attempts to witness less than convincing.

I believe it is fair to say that despite their many significant disagreements, the vast majority, if not all, of the conversations partners for my eCircle shared a commitment to the foundational Christian values outlined above: the centrality of the quest for *truth*; the need to extend Christian *love* to all our brothers and sisters in Christ, straight or LGBT; and the importance of modeling *Christian unity* as a witness in a fractured and polarized world.

If the majority of Christians could agree on embracing these foundational Christian values, then I can envision, through the eyes of faith, a number of concrete actions that could provide a way forward, a pathway that calls for ongoing respectful conversations.

A POSSIBLE WAY FORWARD

It is my hope and prayer that Christians who hold divergent traditional or nontraditional views regarding LGBT issues, as well as straight and LGBT sisters and brothers in Christ, will take those concrete steps outlined below that pertain to them.

CELEBRATE COMMON GROUND

Almost a decade ago when I was involved in my first conversation about human sexuality issues in a meeting at my home church, lack of any common ground militated against any meaningful results. We spent the bulk of our time talking past one another. The sticking point that prevented the conversation from getting off the ground was the assumption on the part of many attendees that since there was absolute clarity about what the Bible says about same-sex relationships, anyone who allows for the possibility of same-sex marriage obviously has a low view of the authority of Scripture and can, therefore, be dismissed as an inferior Christian. End of conversation!

I hope every reader of this book has been disabused of that falsehood. My conversation partners have demonstrated in an admirable fashion that there are deeply committed Christians who hold to the full authority of Scripture while taking opposing views regarding same-sex marriage. That demonstration is no small accomplishment and is to be celebrated. And that is only one area of common ground that emerged during my eCircle, all of which should be celebrated.

CONFESS THE HARM DONE AND REPENT

I celebrate the fact, revealed in some of the stories recounted in chapters 1-9, that there are Christians, traditionalists as well as nontraditionalists relative to LGBT issues, who are extending love to their LGBT and sisters in Christ, including a commitment to listen to and walk with their LGBT friends in their pain.

But as other stories in chapters 1-9 reveal, some Christians, and their churches, have brutalized LGBT brothers and sisters in Christ. I think again of the sixty-something reader whose church experience was so painful that he wonders why he didn't hang himself in the rafters of an empty garage or jump from the college bell tower.

I think also of the report of one of our gay conversation partners, Tim Otto, as to how his painful experience in a conservative church led him to grow up "loathing himself" and carrying out "self-destructive behaviors aimed at medicating [his] . . . self-hate."

Only God is in a position to render ultimate judgment about our behavior as professing Christians. But I respectfully suggest that those professing Christians who have caused harm to their LGBT brothers and sisters in Christ need to confess their sin and repent. There will be no way forward for them and the LGBT individuals they interact with until that is first done.

LISTEN TO THE STORIES OF YOUR LGBT BROTHERS AND SISTERS IN CHRIST AND LISTEN TO THOSE WHO DISAGREE WITH YOU ABOUT LGBT ISSUES

As already noted, the case studies for Eastern University, Sammamish Presbyterian Church (SPC), and Zion Mennonite Church testify to the positive changes in perspective about those who disagree with one another that can take place when persons having differing views get to know each another on a personal level. Recall the report that those who left SPC over the LGBT controversy were primarily those who had not developed personal relationships with those with whom they disagreed. Apparently, there was a good amount of listening going on, up to a point.

As the conversation partners for these case studies point out, that extensive listening did not adequately include listening to the voices of LGBT Christians. Therefore, there was much more conversation "about" LGBT Christians than "with" LGBT Christians. That needs to change if there is to be a positive way forward.

We need to listen to the stories of our LGBT brothers and sisters in Christ, so that we can begin to understand their pain. We need to listen to and understand the ways in which they seek to faithfully live out their commitments to be followers of Jesus. Only after such careful listening as to how they believe God is working in their lives will be able to discern how we can support and encourage them by cooperating with what God is doing in their lives. As will soon be suggested, this will require that we create safe spaces for respectfully listening to and talking to one another.

BE OPEN TO TAKING A FRESH LOOK AT SCRIPTURE BASED ON THE STORIES HEARD FROM LGBT CHRISTIANS

There is ample empirical evidence, as noted in previous chapters, that when we get to know LGBT Christians, as friends and relatives, our beliefs about same-sex relationships often change to be more sympathetic. In particular, it gives us pause when we hear stories from LGBT Christians, or get glimpses of how they live, and discover that they also aspire to be faithful followers of Jesus if they have married a member of the same sex, or wish to do so. They also want to live together in a covenantal monogamous relationship characterized by the giving and receiving of love.

That is not to suggest that "experience trumps Scripture"; leading us to simply overlook the passages in Scripture that appear to clearly prohibit same-sex sexual intimacy. But, as a few of our conversation partners have suggested, such experience should lead us to take a "fresh look" at Scripture; further considering the adequacy of the prevalent interpretations of these specific biblical passages and the overarching biblical message.

The following areas of agreement among conversation partners who situate themselves on different sides of LGBT issues could inform this process of taking a "fresh look" at Scripture.

- The bible is "contextually given."
- The moral logic of the Bible requires that we dig beneath the surface of "biblical rules," seeking to discern the "purposes" ("reasons") for those rules.
- The "purposes" of some "biblical rules" seem to be related to "human flourishing," as in the teaching in Mark 2:27 that "The Sabbath was made for humankind, and "not humankind for then Sabbath."

CREATE "SAFE SPACES" FOR CONVERSATION THAT COUNTERACT "FEAR"

Recall Julie Morgan's report about the rampant fear that was an impediment to the discernment process at Eastern University: fear about how others in the community would perceive you if you expressed a "progressive" (or "conservative") position; fear of faculty and administrators that they may lose their jobs; fear of students that "their grades would suffer" if they expressed views that disagreed with their professors.

In addition to these fears that are driven by the internal dynamics of an institution, there are a host of fears driven by external factors that prevent Christian institutions from talking about disagreements relative to LGBT people and issues, such as fear that "people will leave" or fear that those who support the institution will withdraw their support.

Too many conversations about LGBT issues have been driven by, or inhibited by fear. There is no way forward unless we can create venues for conversation that that are not governed by fear.

PRACTICE COURAGEOUS LEADERSHIP

In light of the internal and external pressures that often create fear about discussing controversial LGBT issues at Christian institutions, a significant measure of courage is required of the leader(s) of such institutions to create safe spaces for these conversations.

The three case studies presented in chapter 9 revealed three indispensable prerequisites for such courageous leadership. The leader must:

- Present his/her beliefs about the issue at hand with deep conviction and clarity while being open to the possibility that his/her beliefs may be wrong, thereby opening up the possibility for mutual learning by means of conversation.
- Model genuine listening and respectful engagement with those who disagree with his/her beliefs.
- Empower others to share in leadership.[5]

---

5. Recall that the case study for Eastern University reported in chapter 9 referred to this willingness to empower others to share in leadership as "trickle down leadership." It was characterized by the willingness of the college president to empower a Human Sexuality Task Force that represented a diversity of opinion and included a gifted cochair who was empowered and given the space to effectively lead the discernment process. This characteristic of courageous leadership is captured most eloquently by Parker Palmer: "Jesus exercises the only kind of leadership that can evoke authentic

Since the first prerequisite noted above is at the heart of this entire book, I will elaborate somewhat with the help of renowned Christian historian George Marsden. After many years of persistent advocacy on behalf of the legitimacy of Christian scholarship in a pluralistic academy, Marsden notes that one of the important lessons he "has learned over the years is the importance of the personal dimension if we [Christian scholars] are to have a positive influence within university culture." This lesson has led Marsden to endorse the idea "that for Christians to successfully engage culture, they must do so by personally getting to know and take seriously people from other outlooks," his punch line (and mine) being that *"the personal dynamics of acting as a loving Christian are as important as what one says."*[6]

Yes! Yes! A thousand times yes! How one expresses one's beliefs in public is as important at the content of one's beliefs—even more important, since few people will listen if you present your beliefs bombastically from an assumed perch of superiority; others may listen, and even be persuaded, if you present your beliefs with clarity and conviction, but with a generous conversational style that creates a safe space for others to disagree with you; a style that models empathetic listening and respectful engagement (as per the second prerequisite noted above).

I can anticipate an objection to my three prerequisites for dealing with difficult issues, like LGBT issues, that they are a sign of weakness. From this perspective, a strong leader should never admit to the possibility of being wrong. That will only lead to losing control of the narrative. I think this perspective has weakness and strength all backwards.

To embrace the three prerequisites noted above is a sign of great strength, not weakness. The "command and control" model of leadership is bankrupt. A need to be in control often reflects insecurity. And this mode of leadership prevents the leader from reaping benefits from the best thinking

---

community—a leadership that risks failure (and even crucifixion) by making space for other people to act. When a leader takes up all the space and preempts all the action, he or she may make something happen, but the something is not community. Nor is it abundance, because the leader is only one person, and one person's resources invariably run out. But, when a leader is willing to trust the abundance that people have and can generate together, willing to take the risk of inviting people to share from that abundance, then and only then may true community emerge" (Palmer, *The Active Life*, 138). This "sharing of leadership" does not mean that a courageous leader abdicates her designated responsibilities for decision-making. But it does mean that she realizes that if she carries out her responsibilities as a "lone ranger," the result will only reflect her gifts. When she shares leadership with others, the results will reflect the combined gifts of everyone and genuine community will be fostered.

6. Marsden, "Being an Intentional Christian Scholar."

and giftedness of others or fostering the kind of genuine community that can only be created by a more collegial approach to leadership.

In stark contrast, a sign of true strength when you have the "power" to control outcomes is a willingness to hold to one's power lightly, albeit without abdicating the designated responsibilities of one's institutional position. Consider the ways in which those who led the discernment processes reported in chapter 9 gave evidence of a willingness to hold to power lightly, given the existence of some stark power differentials.

Recall, first, that the most significant power differential problem at all three institutions was that many LGBT individuals felt marginalized and powerless within these institutions. Other problems were the fear that a student at a Christian college may have about speaking out relative to LGBT issues due to the powered differentials between students and teachers; or the fear that a faculty member at such a college may have about possibly losing his/her job if he/she embraces a minority position.

In light of such power differentials, each leader could have appealed to the authority of his/her position and "commanded" a certain outcome regarding LGBT issues (or convinced another "high power," like a Church Consistory, to make a definitive decision). But that is not how college President Robert Duffett and pastors Jeff Lincicome and Jessica Schrock Ringenberg (and the other pastors at Zion Mennonite Church) proceeded. Rather, they held lightly[7] to the power of their positions, creating safe spaces for all members of their communities to be respectfully heard during a careful discernment process. And they did so without abdicating their responsibilities to foster the flourishing of their respective communities.

HELP EVERYONE TO GIVE AND RECEIVE LOVE

I believe it is fair to say that all of our conversation partners believe that all human beings have a need to belong, which includes a need to give and receive love.

Since the need to give and receive love is a universal human need, all Christians and all churches, whatever their views about LGBT issues, need to foster ways for both "straight" and LGBT brothers and sisters in Christ to "give and receive love."

As Eve Tushnet, a gay conversation partner who believes that LGBT Christians are called to a life of celibacy, has suggested, neglected forms of

---

7. Although it may be a stretch, I wonder if it may be possible to think of the redemptive work of Jesus as the ultimate exemplification of a willingness to hold to power lightly.

giving and receiving love that are alternatives to the marriage bond include friendship, service, and celibate partnerships. All churches, including those that take the position that marriage is reserved for one-man and one-woman, should actively provide for such neglected forms of giving and receiving love for all Christians who worship with them.

CONTINUE CONVERSATIONS ABOUT DISAGREEMENTS IN CHURCHES AND CHRISTIAN INSTITUTIONS OF HIGHER EDUCATION

For "independent" churches not affiliated with a particular Christian denomination, my overarching recommendation for a way forward is simple (to say, if not to do): Engage your members in a careful local discernment process that focuses on developing personal relationships of mutual understanding and trust, similar to the processes carried out at Sammamish Presbyterian Church, and Zion Mennonite Church, being careful to adapt these processes to your local contexts.

I also highly recommend that churches dealing with LGBT issues explore the resources for discernment provided by The Colossian Forum (TCF).[8] The overarching mission of TCF is to facilitate "dialogue on divisive issues within the church."[9] Toward that end, they have already hosted conversations about LGBT issues at a number of churches and have developed curricular materials regarding LGBT issues for use in churches.

I also encourage Christian institutions of higher education to continue the conversations reported in this book as an important contribution to a way forward. Since most of my career has been devoted to teaching and administering at four Christian liberal arts colleges that are members of the Council for Christian Colleges and Universities (CCCU), an organization that I have loved and served for many years, I especially encourage member institutions of the CCCU to focus ongoing conversations on four thorny questions for which no consensus emerged among my conversation partners, the first two of which deal with interconnected public policy issues.

> To what extent, if any should "biblical understanding" inform a Christian's advocacy for particular public policies relative to same-sex relationships within our pluralistic culture?

---

8. In the interest of full disclosure, I note that I currently serve as a Senior Fellow at The Colossian Forum.

9. www.colossianforum.org.

Conclusion

> How can one balance the need to protect the dignity and rights of LGBT individuals and the "religious freedom" of organizations that take a traditional view on same-sex issues?

Relative to the first question, recall that one perspective was a "principled pluralist" position that in our pluralistic society, government should not impose on all citizens public policies relative to marriage that reflects the moral views of one particular group, Christian or otherwise. The competing view was a "natural law" position: there are certain "natural laws" about human sexuality that are not dependent on the diversity of beliefs of citizens that should determine what our public polices should be. What are the pros and cons of these two positions and is there is a way out of this apparent impasse?

The second question above is particularly relevant these days as states and the federal government struggle to formulate "anti-discrimination" laws. The balance hoped for appears to be elusive, which will probably lead to judicial litigation for many years to come. Is there a viable balance?

I highly recommend that these two difficult public policy questions be addressed by faculty members, and their students, in political science departments at CCCU institutions, in conversation with faculty from other academic disciplines who can speak to public policy issues (e.g., historians who can provide an historical perspective on differing views regarding the relationship between public policies and the US Constitution).

A second set of interrelated questions that especially beg for ongoing conversation is as follows:

> What are the most adequate interpretations of biblical passages related to same-sex relationships?

> What are the scientific findings that are relevant to same-sex issues?

Note that these two challenging questions deal separately with issues of biblical interpretation and scientific findings, as addressed in chapters 2 and 3 respectively. But recall the shared view of both David Myers and Chris Grace that "we both respect, and seek to integrate, science and Scripture."

The key word here is *integrate*, which Christian institutions of higher education point to as one of their most fundamental distinctives, usually captured in the phrase "integration of faith and learning." Such integration of faith and learning for a Christian includes, at a minimum, an attempt to uncover "integral connections" between knowledge claims in the academic disciplines and one's biblical and theological understanding.[10]

---

10. Limited space here does not permit me to elaborate further on what I believe the phrase integration of faith and learning means, about which Christian educators

Therefore, in light of this fundamental distinctive of Christian higher education, all Christian institutions of higher education are well poised to have ongoing conversations that attempt to uncover integral connections between biblical interpretation and scientific findings relative to LGBT issues. I strongly encourage that ongoing conversation at all CCCU institutions.

CCCU institutions and all other Christian institutions of higher education could make an invaluable contribution to a way forward if they would orchestrate ongoing respectful conversations regarding the unresolved disagreements presented in this book, with particular attention to the four questions noted above.

What is the likelihood that such ongoing conversations about LGBT issues will take place at CCCU institutions? I am not in a position to give a definitive answer to that question. But I have a few educated guesses based on my experience and some anecdotal evidence.

Some CCCU schools will not sanction campus conversations about LGBT issues because they have embraced a traditional view on such matters that they believe to be indisputably true. To even talk about these issues is to call into question the tenets of the Christian faith. I respect their desire to know the truth and their commitment to their understanding of that truth, hoping that they will also respect those Christians who disagree with them.

But, I also know that the reason some CCCU schools will not sanction campus conversations about LGBT issues has little to do with questions of truth. Rather, there is significant fear that supporters and constituents of their schools will withdraw their support, and possibly not send students, if campus conversations regarding such matters are officially sanctioned.

I hope that the leaders of CCCU schools falling into this second category will at least consider my claim that the truth relative to LGBT issues is disputable. I would especially encourage them to build relationships of mutual understanding and trust with some other Christians who disagree with them about LGBT issues as well as with some LGBT individuals. I urge them to give listening and talking a chance before bringing closure as to whether to officially sanction the type of campus conversations that I recommend above.

---

often disagree. Suffice it to say for my purpose here that at least one component seeks to uncover "integral connections" between knowledge claims in the academic disciplines and one's biblical and theological understanding (or alternative "worldview" understanding for those committed to other "faiths," religious or secular). For a few of my own writings on this integrative theme, see Heie and Wolfe. eds., *The Reality*; Heie and Wolfe, *Slogans*; and Heie, "Developing a Christian Perspective." See also Hasker, "Faith-Learning Integration."

NAVIGATE DENOMINATIONAL CONFLICT

As I have already suggested, there is significant potential for divisiveness when a church that is struggling with LGBT issues is affiliated with a particular Christian denomination. Therefore, I will address such difficult situations in some detail.

As a way forward for those churches affiliated with a particular Christian denomination, I appeal to the principle of subsidiarity that originated in the Roman Catholic Church. This principle asserts that "social and political issues should be dealt with at the most immediate (or local level) that is consistent with their resolution."[11] In other words, "a central authority should perform only those tasks which cannot be performed effectively at a more immediate or local level."[12]

I believe that the two case studies on churches presented in chapter 9 are excellent exemplifications of "respectful conversations about LGBT issues" at the local level called for by the principle of subsidiarity. In both cases, there were extended conversations among church members that enabled those who disagreed with one another to get to know one another well enough to build relationships of mutual understanding and trust. As acknowledged by those reporting on the three case studies, a shared weakness was that the views of LGBT individuals were not adequately represented. But the conversations that did take place were characterized by careful listening to the contrary beliefs of others and to talking about disagreements. These are splendid examples of difficult issues being addressed at the local level, where relationships of mutual understanding and trust can be develop, rather than at a "higher" level, where it is much more difficult to develop such personal relationships.

In the case of churches that are affiliated with denominations, there are often two "higher" levels of authority. The next highest level of authority is often regional (e.g., a regional conference like the Ohio Conference of the Mennonite Church USA reported in one of the case studies, or in the case of the Reformed Church in which I worship, a regional "classis"). Above that regional level, one frequently finds a national or international body (e.g., the Mennonite Church USA or the Reformed Church in America).

The question, then, is whether the type of conversations that took place at the local level in our two church case studies could have been effectively carried out at one of these "higher" levels of authority.

---

11. Wikipedia.
12. Ibid.

I simply do not know the answer to that question, given the importance of understanding context pointed to by our case study leaders, which precludes simple transferable answers, and given the fact that I have never been personally involved in such higher level conversations. (In retrospect, I now wish that I had included a case study dealing with LGBT issues at one of these higher levels.) But I have had a few informal conversations with persons who have been involved in such higher-level conversations about LGBT issues, and the following reflections flow from this admittedly anecdotal evidence.

One apparent difficulty with such higher-level conversations is that it is a challenge, possibly not insurmountable, for participants in such conversations to have the extended time needed to develop the personal relationships of mutual understanding and trust that enhance the possibility of finding some common ground and a way forward.

But another deeper difficulty, in my estimation, is that whatever the results of such higher level conversations may be, those results were not forged with adequate input and conversations from the local bodies that are expected to live with those results; they are simply handed down from above without adequate attention being paid to the beliefs of the local organization.

So, in light of these perceived difficulties, what is an adequate way forward that does justice to these various levels of authority?

First, I need to make it abundantly clear that I am not calling into question the legitimacy and authority of Christian denominational bodies or their intermediate bodies like regional conferences. In particular, although I believe that the fracturing of the followers of Jesus into countless denominations is lamentable (since it works against fostering unity within the body of Christ), I also believe that each of the major Christian traditions has an important contribution to make to a full-orbed understanding and practice of the Christian faith, provided that no tradition believes it has a "corner on God's truth." For example, those who worship in the Reformed tradition, or the Anabaptist tradition, the Wesleyan tradition, the Catholic tradition. or the Eastern Orthodox tradition, and the colleges and universities associated with these traditions, should continue to mine the theological depths of their respective traditions, with my hope being that they will then engage with those working out of other traditions to learn from each other's theological emphases.

Beyond keeping alive various important theological emphases, at a pragmatic level these higher bodies of authority also make possible ministries of redemption that cannot be adequately carried out by individual churches or institutions of higher education, such as extensive missionary

Conclusion

and humanitarian efforts that denominations carry out from resources pooled from individual churches.

But the question remains as to how to best navigate the connections between the decision-making responsibilities of these various levels of authority relative to LGBT issues. It is my view that the response depends on whether LGBT issues are viewed as disputable or indisputable.

On the one hand, let us assume that a particular Christian denomination that has some type of governance jurisdiction over regional conferences, or one of those regional conferences that has some type of governance jurisdiction over local church congregations, has taken a traditional position on LGBT issues that it views as indisputable. How should a local congregation respond?

I recommend that such a local congregation should initiate a discernment process that begins by considering the question as to whether LGBT issues are disputable matters. If the congregation decides that the traditional position embraced by the higher authoritative body is indisputably true, then there is no need for further deliberation.

But if the local congregation decides that LGBT issues are disputable matters, then that local congregation should continue its discernment process, using careful local processes similar to those followed by the Sammamish Presbyterian Church and the Zion Mennonite Church.

If the result of that further discernment process is that the local congregation embraces a traditional position, then there is no need for further deliberation.

But, if the end result of the discernment process is that the local congregation embraces a nontraditional position that is in conflict with the traditional position taken by the relevant higher authoritative body, which is deemed to be indisputable, then it appears to me that the local congregation has three options.

I believe the first option that should be explored is for the local congregation, in collaboration with other denominational congregations that take a nontraditional position, to try to persuade the "higher body" that LGBT issues are disputable issues about which equally committed Christians can disagree without fracturing the unity of the larger church body. That this should be the first option is in accord with my earlier suggestion that winning the LGBT debate is not the goal. Rather the goal is to find a way for Christians within the "higher body" to live well together, guided by a shared commitment to the foundational Christian values of continually seeking after God's Truth about these matters, extending Christian love to all brothers and sisters in Christ and modeling Christian unity.

If such persuasion is unsuccessful, then it appears to me that two options remain. The next option is to ask the higher authoritative body to grant an "exception" to its traditional position (and I will soon suggest one possible mechanism for the granting of such exceptions).

But if an exception is not granted, then the local congregation must be true to the result of its local discernment process and must, with deep regret but in good conscience, separate itself from the higher authoritative body.

Exceptions for "Affinity Groups": Rather than dealing in abstractions relative to the challenge of navigating the hazardous waters where a local church takes a nontraditional (or traditional) view relative to LGBT issues when a "higher authority" (a conference of church congregations or a Christian denominational body) takes an opposite traditional (or nontraditional) view, I will deal with two actual cases with which I have some familiarity, albeit no firsthand involvement.

The first case focuses on current deliberations within the Reformed Church in America (RCA), the denominational body to which the church where I worship in Orange City (Iowa) belongs, and the second case focuses on Shalom Mennonite Church (SMC) in Harrisonburg (Virginia), the church where my son Jeff and his family worship. Although there are very significant differences between the RCA and the Mennonite Church USA (the denomination to which SMC belongs), there is some parallelism in a method that is emerging (or could emerge) for navigating these troubled waters.

Starting with the RCA, an "RCA Special Council" met in Chicago in April of 2016 to address "questions of human sexuality as it relates to ordination and marriage."[13] One of the recommendations that this Special Council decided to bring to General Synod 2016 (in the summer of 2016) was:

> That Synod establish at least one affinity classis that includes people and congregations regardless of their perspective on human sexuality to ensure and allow relationship and mission together.[14]

In its commentary on this "Recommended Action of General Synod," this Special Council suggests that synodical approval of this recommendation

---

13. RCA Special Council, report from the "Group of Five."

14. Ibid. In RCA polity, each RCA congregation belongs to a "regional classis." Although the RCA Synod has taken the "traditional" position on marriage that "marriage is between a man and a woman," it is now left to each regional classis to decide on "accountability" (or not) relative to that synodical position.

"might provide a way for those with differing interpretations of Scripture to remain in the RCA."[15]

While not using any words like "affinity group," the idea of allowing for such groups has evolved de facto[16] within the Mennonite Church USA, as illustrated by the experience of Shalom Mennonite Church.

SMC has taken a welcoming and affirming position relative to LGBT Christians, which allows for LGBT persons to assume positions of leadership within the church as well as the ordination of LGBT persons and the performance of same-sex marriages at the church.

The position that SMC takes relative to same-sex marriage differs from the position of the Mennonite Church USA that marriage is "between a man and a woman." At the time that SMC took this position, it was a member of the Virginia Mennonite Conference, one or the twenty or so conferences by which Mennonite Church USA is organized.[17] However, it became apparent that the position taken by SMC on same-sex marriage was a better fit with the views of the members of the Central District Conference than with the views of the members of the Virginia Conference, and SMC was granted permission by the Virginia Conference to join the Central District Conference. This bears similarities to the idea of the RCA possibly allowing for RCA churches to become members of an "affinity classis" consisting of RCA churches (not necessarily regional) that share their views on human sexuality.

How does a Christian denomination decide whether it wishes to sanction such affinity groups that share views on human sexuality that are contrary to the stated denominational position? It appears to me that there would be little incentive for a denomination to sanction such affinity groups if the denomination held that the traditional view of marriage is indisputable. But it is conceivable that there could be an opening for such sanctioning if the denomination took a strong position on the importance of Christian unity and decided that it wanted to create a polity that does not

---

15. Ibid. What happened in the June 2016 meeting of the RCA synod is that a motion that would have allowed for same-sex marriage was defeated (apparently the attempt at persuasion that I proposed as the first option to be taken was unsuccessful). Also defeated was a motion to create at least one affinity classis (as I proposed in my second option). The synod did approve a motion to amend the RCA constitution to add an "Order of Christian Marriage" liturgy, which describes marriage as "a joyful covenanting between a man and a woman" (which must be approved by two-thirds of the RCA's forty-four classes and ratified by the 2017 General Synod).

16. Private conversation with Ted Grimsrud, May 1, 2016.

17. The "Conference" is roughly equivalent to the "Classis" of RCA polity, although it is not necessarily regional, due to the complexities of the merger in 2002 of the General Conference Mennonite Church and the Mennonite Church.

exclude churches that are deeply committed to the "essential" theological and ecclesiological tenets of the particular denomination.

Of course, as the content of this book amply illustrates, the issue of which beliefs are "essential" to the Christian faith is itself disputable. So, the denomination would have to first decide whether it wishes to embrace churches that are strong proponents of most of the denomination's theological and ecclesiological tenets.

Given my position that LGBT issues are disputable and my suggestion that it is best for LGBT issues to be addressed at the local congregational level, I endorse the idea of denominations allowing for the formation of such affinity groups relative to human sexuality as one important component of a way forward.

A Recommendation for the CCCU: It is my love and best wishes for the CCCU that prompts me to present a recommendation for CCCU consideration.

The context for my recommendations is my understanding, from the outside looking in, of some recent developments at the CCCU regarding LGBT issues, as follows.

Two CCCU institutions, Eastern Mennonite University and Goshen College, recently withdrew from the CCCU after they adopted policies that allowed for the hiring of LGBT faculty. I understand that these two institutions voluntarily withdrew from the CCCU when it became apparent that a significant number of other CCCU institutions would withdraw from the CCCU if EMU and Goshen were allowed to continue as members.

This situation has led the CCCU to reconsider its membership requirements. The present requirement for CCCU membership includes the stipulation that the institution be "Christ-centered and rooted in the historic Christian faith."[18] As this book reveals, there is lack of agreement among Christians as to whether a nontraditional view on human sexuality is adequately "rooted in the historic Christian faith." It is my understanding that the CCCU is currently struggling with the question of whether they should revise their current membership requirements to explicitly include reference to a traditional view on human sexuality.

As the CCCU and its member institutions address these thorny issues, I recommend that the CCCU consider the possibility of establishing a category of CCCU member institutions that are analogous to the affinity groups noted above—a group of Christian colleges and universities that have embraced nontraditional views on human sexuality as a result of their local discernment processes that are clearly Christ-centered and can

---

18. http:www.cccu.org/members_and_affiliates.

still make an important contribution to the overarching cause of Christian higher education.

BUILD RELATIONSHIPS OF MUTUAL UNDERSTANDING AND TRUST WITH THOSE WITH WHOM YOU DISAGREE

It should be obvious by now that a number of the action-steps suggested above as comprising a way forward, such as talking to our LGBT brothers and sisters in Christ and orchestrating conversations at Christian colleges, will require that Christians become better at talking respectful to one another about their disagreements. *A precondition that opens the door for the possibility of such respectful conversations is the building of relationships of mutual understanding and trust with those with whom you disagree.*

I cannot overstate the critical importance of this action step: *Without taking this step, there is no way forward.* I believe there is ample evidence from my reports in chapters 1–9 that most, if not all, of the various sets of conversation partners developed strong relationships of mutual trust and understanding despite some major disagreements. There is also strong evidence from the three case studies reported on in chapter 9 that building such personal relationships is a necessary first step in adequately addressing contentious LGBT issues in a Christian school or church.

Why is this important first step of building strong relationships of mutual understanding and trust with those with whom we disagree so often neglected? Psychologists and sociologists may have a better response than me. My brief take is that we don't naturally gravitate toward those who disagree with us. We generally feel most comfortable with people who are like us; people who think as we do. Therefore, it is all too seldom that we take the time to develop a personal relationship with someone with whom we have strong disagreements.

Public Exhibit A is what you witness in the political realm. The politicians or political pundits who bash each other on TV or talk radio probably do not know each other very well on a personal level. And it is all too easy to demonize a person you hardly know, or to simply dismiss him as stupid, biased, a liar, or evil.

One aspect of what can emerge when you develop a personal relationship with someone who disagrees with you is that you gain a better understanding of the reasons for her taking a position that you believe is wrong. You are able to uncover the experiences and other aspects of her social location that inform her beliefs on the issue about which you disagree. She will also be able to uncover the reasons you have for your position.

An important way for Christians to develop such a personal relationship is to worship together. During times of worship you are able to see that the person who strongly disagrees with you about a controversial issue still worships the same God that you worship and is a deeply committed Christian.

Developing such a personal relationship may not change either of your positions. But your perspectives about each other may change radically (both of you may have what a few of our conversation partners called a "change in heart").

Such a change in perspective about the person who disagrees with you can open the door for ongoing conversations about your disagreements. You may find that a level of mutual understanding and trust has evolved that makes you more open to listening to her beliefs with an empathetic ear.

As I have already suggested, I believe that a careful reading of the conversations reported in this book will reveal that the conversation partners for the various topics came to know each other well enough, even without face-to-face encounters, to understand the reasons behind their differing positions and to appreciate and respect the deep Christian commitment of those with whom they disagreed. That it is no small accomplishment.

Excursus: The Educational Value of Exposure to Otherness: What follows may initially seem like an unnecessary digression that draws excessively on my own personal experiences.[19] But if you bear with me, you will soon understand why I believe that "building relationships of mutual understanding and mutual trust with those with whom you disagree" (about LGBT issues or any other contentious issues) is the indispensable starting point for Christians to sort through their disagreements and for realizing a significant measure of "Christian unity" in the midst of those disagreements.

As a teenager in my Lutheran home church in Brooklyn, I assumed that we Lutherans had captured the truth about doctrinal issues. I was never exposed to other beliefs about the content of Christian truth and that was fine by me at the time.

But later in my Christian pilgrimage, I was exposed to other beliefs about truth held by Christians immersed in the Reformed and Anabaptist traditions. I got to know these Christians on a personal level though developing relationships of mutual understanding and trust. Out of these relationships emerged a realization in my part that these non-Lutherans were also deeply committed Christians who held to the full inspiration and authority of Scripture, as I did, but were interpreting some of those Scriptures

---

19. For a significant elaboration of what I share in this excursus, see Heie, *Learning to Listen*.

in ways that were not congruent with the interpretations of Lutherans. This mutual understanding and trust laid the foundation for us to be able to respectfully talk about our agreements and disagreements and to learn from one another.[20]

That was only the tip of the iceberg in my exposure to "otherness." I eventually found that my exposure to other persons whose particularities as to race, gender, socioeconomic status, and, yes, sexual orientation, gave me a deep appreciation for the marvelous diversity among Christians who are equally committed to being followers of Jesus, aspiring to live faithfully in the light of their respective understandings of the Scriptures to which they all attributed full inspiration and authority.[21]

My latest profound experience of this diversity of Christian belief has been reported in this book. My twenty-one conversation partners have strong disagreements about LGBT issues, including differing beliefs about the most adequate interpretations of relevant scriptures. Yet those on both sides of these issues have borne witness to their shared Christian commitment and to their shared belief in the full inspiration and authority of scripture.

This emerging realization of this amazing diversity of belief among equally committed Christians has led me to my minimalist view of what it means to be a "Christian," a view that does not embrace all the tenets of any one Christian tradition but focuses on the shared commitment to be followers of Jesus.[22]

---

20. In a nutshell, what I learned from these conversations led me to question the "two-kingdoms" view that is prevalent among Lutherans and to embrace a Reformed view relative to God's redemptive purposes (God wishes to redeem all of creation), while committing myself to an Anabaptist view that the means for my being an agent for God's redemptive purposes must embrace peacemaking. This summary begs for elaboration, which I cannot provide here (again, see Heie, *Learning to Listen*.)

21. Mark Noll points with approval to this marvelous diversity among Christians when he states that he leans strongly toward "efforts at encouraging . . . respect for the extraordinary diversity within the body of Christ" (private correspondence on June 10, 2016). Elsewhere, Noll suggests that "God accepts this diversity as a good thing": "The best explanation for why Christian traditions differ among themselves is that God is responsible for the diversity of human cultures, God accepts that diversity as a good thing, and God allows that Christian faith to be adapted to the shape of diverse human cultures." (Noll, "British," 220.)

22. Recall my earlier statement that "I believe that someone is a Christian if he/she personally trusts in the death and resurrection of Jesus Christ as decisive for salvation and the redemption of the entire created order, and if he/she aspires to be a "follower of Jesus" by means of obedience to the two great "love commandments" taught by Jesus: love for God and love for neighbor."

So, what is my point? I close with two thoughts for your consideration. The first general point is to highlight the "educational value of exposure to otherness." If Christians spend all of their time within insular Christian communities, they too easily fall prey to the temptation to "othering"; setting up "us versus them" categories that exclude deeply committed Christians because they do not share all of our beliefs. My experience suggests that the best way to avoid succumbing to this temptation is to create venues wherein Christians are adequately exposed to "otherness." If I am right about that, it has profound implications for programming at both Christian institutions of education and Christian churches.

My second point takes me back to the centrality of building relationships of mutual understanding and trust with those with whom you disagree. Throughout my career, from my early teaching days in the 1960s through the project that led to this book, the way forward in sorting though disagreements has always been for me to first build strong relationships of mutual understanding and trust with those with whom I had disagreements. And building such relationships is also the indispensable starting point for realizing a significant measure of Christian unity in the midst of disagreements, a quest to which Jesus calls all who aspire to be his followers.

WHAT WILL THE FUTURE HOLD?

I enter all conversations with the conviction that one cannot predict beforehand the results of a respectful conversation. Therefore, my hope for the future for navigating contentious LGBT issues focuses on the *process* that I propose in my way forward, with particular emphasis on my calls for ongoing respectful conversations.

While I cannot foresee the results of implementing that conversational process, it is my hope and prayer that Christians commit themselves to this process, and that, in doing so, they will bear witness to the Christian values of love and Christian unity. I can also envision, through the eyes of faith, that the results eventually emerging from these ongoing conversations will yield greater clarity as to the truth, as God knows it, relative to same-sex issues.

But a thorny prior issue must first be addressed: Are beliefs about LGBT issues disputable for Christians?

If a reader believes that his/her beliefs about LGBT issues (whether traditional or nontraditional) are indisputable, then there is no motivation for conversation. Fruitful conversation will be possible among those who disagree only if they believe, as I do, that Christian beliefs about LGBT issues are disputable, by which I mean that there are deeply committed Christians, all holding to the inspiration and authority of Scripture, who hold to divergent positions on these issues.

The evidence I have already cited for my assertion that beliefs about LGBT issues are disputable are the numerous narratives posted during my eCircle, in which my conversation partners respectfully discussed their divergent positions in postings that revealed their unambiguous adherence to the full inspiration and authority of Scripture.

If you share my conviction that beliefs about LGBT issues are disputable for Christians, conversation will be possible, hopefully guided by the two primary components of a conversational process to which I believe Christians should make a commitment.

- By means of respectful conversations, Christians need to build relationships of mutual understanding and trust with those with whom they disagree about LGBT issues.
- Christians need to listen to the stories of their LGBT brothers and sisters in Christ, empathizing with the pain that many of them have experienced and seeking to understand the ways in which they seek to faithfully live out their commitments to be followers of Jesus.

If Christians will start with these two primary commitments, there is no telling beforehand where the ongoing conversations may lead.

However, the question still looms as to how these two primary components of a conversational process can be worked out in a community of believers such as a local congregation. Since I believe that LGBT issue are disputable matters, I favor the "third way" approach for Christian communities that I posed to my conversation partners in chapter 9 as accepting LGBT persons in our churches, without taking a community-wide position that chooses between the binary of welcoming, but not affirming, or welcoming and affirming. In contrast to expecting everyone in a church to share a belief in one of these binary choices, this third way would create a safe space for Christians who hold to either of these to views to fellowship together as brothers and sisters in Christ.

But I now find the word *accepting* to be ambiguous. It can too easily be interpreted in the weak sense of "mere tolerance"; where I only "put up with" an LGBT person in my church. The word *acceptance* only works for me if it used in the strong sense of "lovingly engaging" my LGBT brother or sister in Christ. To avoid the ambiguity, I now prefer the word *embrace*; I must "embrace" the LGBT persons in my church.

But what does it mean to embrace another? It means that *"The other is received as one who is beloved,"*[23] a person who is loved by God whom I then should also love.

Yes! I believe I am called to embrace my LGBT brother and sisters in Christ as beloved, building loving relationships of mutual trust and understanding, which starts by listening to their stories.

Churches that wish to pursue such a third way face considerable challenges. For example, one may ask why an LGBT person or a parent of an LGBT person would choose to worship in a third-way church, where a significant number of members are "non-affirming," when they could attend a church that is "affirming." Aren't they opening themselves up for the possibility of the brutish treatment that LGBT persons and their relatives/allies have too often experienced in Christian churches? Another concern is that the two primary components of the conversational process that I propose above may sound good as an aspirational ideal; but, how well will they be practiced in a third-way church?

I am not sure I have a compelling response to such concerns. But four thoughts come to mind. First, if an LGBT person or relative/ally of an LGBT person believes, as I do, that these two aspirational ideals are *deep expressions of love for another person*, then one may be willing to take the risk of embarking on this third way, as a venture of faith, hoping and praying that living out this third way will be a compelling witness to Christian unity.

Secondly, respectfully engaging others in a third-way church who disagree with you about LGBT issues, rather than limiting yourself to engaging only those Christians who agree with you, may be good "schooling" for engaging others in our pluralistic culture. As Ken Wilson puts it:

> We live in a pluralistic age. Our children will need to learn how to hold their convictions despite the fact that others, including people they love and admire, do not share them.[24]

Thirdly, the strong temptation toward exclusion, in either direction, of those church members who hold to "traditional" views on LGBT issues, or those who hold to nontraditional views, can be overcome by remembering that since we share the aspiration to be followers of Jesus, we are all brothers and sisters in Christ. As biological brothers and sisters ideally "hang in there together" in the midst of disagreements, so members of the body of Christ are called to embrace one another in the midst of their disagreements.[25]

23. Dunn, *Word Biblical Commentary*, 798, quoted by Wilson, *Letter*, 128, drawing on Volf, *Exclusion*, 140-47.

24. Wilson, *Letter*, 122.

25. The need for Christians to avoid excluding those who disagree with them about

Finally, as pointed out by Ken Wilson, "A third way provides space and time for a community to eventually resolve some disputes peacefully."[26] He elaborates as follows:

> Allowing the tension of a disputable matter provides time for the practical evidence, *for the fruit of the two positions to become manifest*.... Disputable matters may remain in dispute indefinitely, or with time, a common discernment may form in the community, and the dispute disappears, as is the case historically with other issues (Sabbath observance, women in leadership, slavery, etc.) The third way provides room for the Spirit to work in the community—to practice acceptance during the disagreement and to eventually settle some matters.[27]

Wilson's reference to "the fruit of the two positions to become manifest" brings to mind some recent experiences that have deeply informed my own views about LGBT persons and issues. It is only recently that I have developed relationships of mutual understanding and trust with some LGBT persons inside and outside of my church congregation. When I have listened to their stories, hearing about the ways in which they aspire to be faithful followers of Jesus, and have seen the fruit of the spirit evident in their lives ("love, joy, peace, patience, kindness, generosity, faithfulness, gentleness, and self-control"[28]), I know that I must embrace them. As I have already said, I am not saying that my recent experience trumps scripture. But it does lead me to be willing to look once again at Scripture with fresh eyes.

I encourage my readers who are embroiled in contentious LGBT issues, in their churches or other settings, to commit themselves to the two primary components of a conversational process that I propose above (plus the other aspects of my proposed way forward). But I give you fair warning: You cannot just assume that those you wish to draw into that process will talk to one another respectfully. You must make that expectation clear before you start talking, as suggested below.

LGBT issues is eloquently stated by the renowned Christian ethicist Richard Hays (who holds to traditional positions regarding LGBT issues): "... for the foreseeable future we must find ways to live within the church in a situation of serious moral disagreement while still respecting one another as brothers and sisters in Christ. If the church is going to start practicing the discipline of exclusion from the community, there are other issues far more important than homosexuality where we should begin to draw a line in the dirt: violence and materialism, for example." Hays, *Moral Vision*, 400.

26. Wilson, *Letter*, 115

27. Ibid., 116.

28. Gal 5:33.

GUIDELINES FOR RESPECTFUL CONVERSATION

When extending invitations to my conversation partners for this project, I clearly stated my expectation that all who accepted my invitation had to agree up-front to abide by a set of "Conversation Guidelines."[29] I close this book by presenting these guidelines, with a suggestion that if any reader wishes to orchestrate a respectful conversation about LGBT issues (or any other contentious issue) within his or her sphere of influence, it would be wise to make such an expectation clear to all who are invited to participate in the conversation.

EXPECTATIONS FOR ECIRCLE CONTRIBUTORS

Contributors to an eCircle will be expected to provide a welcoming space for respectful conversation by aspiring to the following ideals.

- I will try to listen well, providing each person with a welcoming space to express her perspective on the issue at hand.
- I will seek to empathetically understand the reasons another person has for her perspective.
- I will express my perspective, and my reasons for holding that perspective, with commitment and conviction, but with a non-coercive style that invites conversation with a person who disagrees with me.
- In my conversation with a person who disagrees with me, I will explore whether we can find some common ground that can further the conversation. But, if we cannot find common ground, I will conclude that "we can only agree to disagree"; yet I will do so in a way that demonstrates respect for the other and concern for her well-being and does not foreclose the possibility of future conversations.
- In aspiring to these ideals for conversation, I will also aspire to be characterized by humility, courage, patience, and love.

---

29. My website also made it clear that I would be screening all comments posted by readers, approving only those submissions that satisfied published criteria (for a statement of these criteria go to the "Conversation Guidelines" page under the "About" section of my website www.respectfulconversation.net).

Recommended Readings

The following is a composite list of recommendations for further reading from the conversation partners, to which I have added five entries.

Achtemeier, Mark. *The Bible's Yes to Same-Sex Marriage: An Evangelical's Change of Heart.* Louisville: Westminster John Knox, 2014.

Anderson, Ryan T. *Truth Overruled: The Future of Marriage and Religious Freedom.* Washington, DC: Regnery, 2015.

Beck, Richard. *Unclean: Meditations on Purity, Hospitality, and Mortality.* Eugene, OR: Cascade, 2011.

Beckwith, Francis. "Interracial Marriage and Same-Sex Marriage," Public Discourse. Witherspoon Institute, May 2010. http://www.thepublicdiscourse.com/2010/05/1324/.

Bray, Alan. *The Friend.* Chicago: The University of Chicago Press, 2003.

Bradshaw, Timothy, ed. *The Way Forward? Christian Voices on Homosexuality and the Church.* Grand Rapids: Eerdmans, 2004.

Brownson, James. *Bible, Gender, Sexuality: Reframing the Church's Debate on Same-Sex Relationships.* Grand Rapids: Eerdmans, 2013.

Chu, Jeff. *Does Jesus Really Love Me?: A Gay Christian's Pilgrimage in Search of God in America.* New York: Harper Perennial, 2014.

Coontz, Stephanie. *Marriage, a History: From Obedience to Intimacy, or How Love Conquered Marriage.* New York: Viking, 2005.

Danforth, John. *The Relevance of Religion: How Faithful People Can Change Politics.* New York: Random House, 2015.

DeFranza, Megan K. *Sex Difference in Christian Theology: Male, Female, and Intersex in the Image of God.* Grand Rapids: Eerdmans, 2015.

De Young, Kevin. *What Does the Bible Teach about Homosexuality?* Wheaton, IL: Crossway, 2015.

Ellison, Marvin M., and Kelly Brown Douglas, eds. *Sexuality and the Sacred: Sources for Theological Reflection.* Louisville: Westminster John Knox, 2010.

Evangelicals Concerned web resources, including Ralph Blair's 2015 historical review: "Looking Back: Evangelicals and Homosexuality." www.ecinc.org.

Farley, Margaret A. *Just Love: a Framework for Christian Sexual Ethics*. New York: Continuum, 2006.

Gagnon, Robert A. J. *The Bible and Homosexual Practice: Texts and Hermeneutics*. Nashville: Abingdon, 2001.

Greer, Peter, and Chris Horst. *Mission Drift: The Unspoken Crisis Facing Leaders, Charities and Churches*. Bloomington, MN: Bethany, 2014.

Grenz, Stanley. *Welcoming but Not Affirming: An Evangelical Response to Homosexuality*. Louisville: Westminster John Knox, 1998.

Grimsrud, Ted, and Mark Thiessen Nation. *Reasoning Together: A Conversation on Homosexuality*. Scottdale, PA: Herald, 2008.

Gushee, David P. *Changing Our Mind*. Canton, MI: Read the Spirit, 2015.

Hays, Richard. *The Moral Vision of the New Testament: Community, Cross, New Creation, A Contemporary Introduction to New Testament Ethics*. New York: HarperCollins, 1996.

Hill, Wesley. *Spiritual Friendship: Finding Love in the Church as a Celibate Gay Christian*. Grand Rapids: Brazos, 2015.

———. *Washed and Waiting: Reflections on Christian Faithfulness and Homosexuality*. Grand Rapids: Zondervan, 2010.

Hirsch, Deborah. *Redeeming Sex: Naked Conversations about Sexuality and Spirituality*. Downers Grove, IL: InterVarsity, 2015.

Jordan, Mark D. *The Ethics of Sex*. Oxford: Blackwell, 2002.

Kemeny, P. C., ed. *Church, State and Public Justice: Five Views*. Downers Grove, IL: IVP Academic, 2007.

King, Michael A., ed. *Stumbling Toward a Genuine Conversation on Homosexuality*. Telford, PA: Cascadia, 2007.

Lee, Justin. *Torn: Rescuing the Gospel from then Gays vs. Christians Debate*. New York: Jericho, 2012.

Lee, Patrick, and Robert P. George, *Conjugal Union: What Marriage Is and Why It Matters*. New York: Cambridge University Press, 2014.

LeVay, Simon. *Gay, Straight, and the Reason Why: The Science of Sexual Orientation*. Oxford: Oxford University Press, 2011.

Lyons, Gabe, and David Kinnaman. *Good Faith: Being a Christian When Society Thinks You Are Irrelevant and Extreme*. Grand Rapids: Baker, 2016.

MacLeod, Adam J. "Rights, Privileges, and the Future of Marriage Law." *Regent University Law Review* 28.71 (2015) 71–110.

Marin, Andrew. *Love is an Orientation: Elevating the Conversation with the Gay Community*. Downers Grove, IL: InterVarsity, 2009.

Martin, Dale B. *Sex and the Single Savior: Gender and Sexuality in Biblical Interpretation*. Louisville: Westminster John Knox, 2006.

Monsma, Stephen. *Healing for a Broken World: Christian Perspectives on Public Policy*. Wheaton, IL: Crossway, 2008.

Monsma, Stephen, and Stanley Carlson-Thies. *Free to Serve: Protecting the Religious Freedom of Faith Based Organizations*. Grand Rapids: Baker, 2015.

Myers, David, and Letha Scanzoni. *What God Has Joined Together: The Christian Case for Gay Marriage*. New York: Harper One, 2006.

Otto, Tim. *Oriented to Faith: Transforming the Debate Over Gay Relationships*. Eugene, OR: Cascade, 2014.

Paris, Jenell. *The Good News about Conflict: Transforming Religious Struggle over Sexuality*. Eugene, OR: Cascade, 2016.
Schmidt, Thomas E. *Straight and Narrow? Compassion & Clarity in the Homosexuality Debate*. Downers Grove, IL: InterVarsity, 1995.
Sprinkle, Preston. *People to Be Loved: Why Homosexuality is Not Just an Issue*. Grand Rapids: Zondervan, 2015.
Stoner, James R., Jr. "Does the Law and the Constitution of the Family Have to Change?" *Perspectives on Political Science* 45.2 (2016) 80–86.
Tushnet, Eve. *Gay and Catholic: Accepting My Sexuality, Finding Community, Living My Faith*. Notre Dame, IN: Ave Maria, 2014.
Vines, Matthew. *God and the Gay Christian: The Biblical Case in Support of Same-Sex Relationships*. New York: Convergent, 2015.
Wilson, Ken. *A Letter to My Congregation*. Canton, MI: Read the Spirit, 2014.
Wolfe, Christopher, ed. *That Eminent Tribunal: Judicial Supremacy and the Constitution*. Princeton, NJ: Princeton University Press, 2004.
Yarhouse, Mark A. *Understanding Sexual Identity: A Resource for Youth Ministry*. Grand Rapids: Zondervan, 2013.

Bibliography

Barbour, Ian G. *Myths, Models, and Paradigms: A Comparative Study of Science and Religion*. New York: Harper & Row, 1974.

Bradshaw, Timothy, ed. *The Way Forward? Christian Voices on Homosexuality and the Church*. Grand Rapids: Eerdmans, 2003.

Brooks, David. "The Next Culture War." *The New York Times*, June 30, 2015. https://www.nytimes.com/2015/06/30/opinion/david-brooks-the-next-culture-war.html.

Dunn, James D. G. *Word Biblical Commentary, Volume 38A, Romans 1-8*. Nashville: Thomas Nelson, 1988.

Enns, Peter. *The Bible Tells Me So: Why Defending Scripture Has Made Us Unable to Read It*. New York: HarperCollins, 2014.

Farley, Margaret A. *Just Love: A Framework for Christian Sexual Ethics*. New York: Continuum, 2006.

George, Robert, et al. *What is Marriage? Man and Woman: A Defense*. New York: Encounter, 2012.

Hasker, William. "Faith-Learning Integration: An Overview." *Christian Scholar's Review* 21 (1992) 234-48.

Hays, Richard. *The Moral Vision of the New Testament: A Contemporary Introduction to New Testament Ethics*. New York: HarperCollins, 1996.

Heie, Harold. "Coming Alongside Others: Redemptive Engagement." In *Mutual Treasure: Seeking Better Ways for Christians and Culture to Converse*, edited by Harold Heie and Michael A. King, 176-97. Telford, PA: Cascadia, 2009.

———. "Dialogic Discourse: Christian Scholars Engaging the Larger Academy." *Christian Scholar's Review* 37 (2008) 347-56.

———. "Developing a Christian Perspective on the Nature of Mathematics." In *Teaching as an Act of Faith: Theory and Practice in Church-Related Higher Education*, edited by Arlin A. Migliazzo, 95-116. New York: Fordham University Press, 2002.

———. *A Future for American Evangelicalism: Commitment, Openness, and Conversation*. Eugene OR: Wipf & Stock, 2015.

———. *Learning to Listen, Ready to Talk: A Pilgrimage Toward Peacemaking*. New York: iUniverse, 2007.

———. "Letting Truth and Civility Meet." *Patheos*, October 14, 2015. http://www.patheos.com/topics/moving-past-hatred/letting-truth-and-civility-meet-harold-heie-101315.

———. "Modeling Humility and Love in Public Discourse." http://www.respectfulconversation.net/musings/2016/5/17/.

———. "Politics in the Trenches: Local Advocacy for Immigration Reform in Iowa." *Capital Commentary*, November 16, 2015. http://www.cpjustice.org/public/capital_commentary/article1313?utm_source=CPJ&utm.

———. "Values in Public Education: Dialogue Within Diversity." *Christian Scholar's Review* 22.2 (December 19, 1992) 131–43.

Heie, Harold, and David L. Wolfe. *Slogans or Distinctives: Reforming Christian Higher Education*. Lanham, MD: University Press of America, 1993.

Heie, Harold, and David L. Wolfe, eds. *The Reality of Christian Learning: Strategies for Faith-Discipline Integration*. Grand Rapids: Eerdmans, 1987; Eugene, OR: Wipf and Stock, 2004.

Hill, Wesley. *Spiritual Friendship: Finding Love in the Church as a Celibate Gay Christian*. Grand Rapids: Brazos, 2015.

———. *Washed and Waiting: Reflections on Christian Faithfulness and Homosexuality*. Grand Rapids: Zondervan, 2010.

Holben, L. R. *What Christians Think About Homosexuality: Six Representative Views*. North Richland Hills, TX: Bibal, 1999.

Holcomb, Justin S. "Why You Shouldn't Call That False Teaching a Heresy." *Christianity Today*, October 6, 2015, 38.

Johnson, Luke Timothy. *The Revelatory Body: Theology as Inductive Art*. Grand Rapids: Eerdmans, 2015.

Jones, Stanton L., and Mark A. Yarhouse. *Ex-Gays? A Longitudinal Study of Religiously Mediated Changes in Sexual Orientation*. Downers Grove, IL: InterVarsity, 2007.

King, Michael A. "Conversations on Homosexuality as a Quest to Love Enemy Prejudices." In *Mutual Treasure: Seeking Better Ways for Christians and Culture To Converse*, edited by Harold Heie and Michael A. King, 144–60. Telford, PA: Cascadia, 2009.

Lewis, C. S. *Mere Christianity*. San Francisco: HarperOne, 2009.

———. *Reflections on the Psalms*. New York: Harcourt, Brace & World, 1958.

Lovelace, Richard. *Dynamics of Spiritual Life: An Evangelical Theology of Renewal*. Downers Grove, IL: InterVarsity, 1979.

Macleod, Adam. "Rights, Privileges, and the Future of Marriage." *The Selected Works of Adam Macleod*. Available at http://works.bepress.com/adam_macleod/21.

Marsden, George. "Being an Intentional Christian Scholar Today," unpublished manuscript, presented at a Whitworth University conference on *Christians Engaging Culture: Models for Public Policy Practitioners, Politicians, and Scholars*, October 25, 2005, quoted by Harold Heie in his essay "Dialogic Discourse: Christians Engaging the Larger Academy," *Christian Scholar's Review* 37 (2008) 354.

Mohler, R. Albert, Jr. "Confessional Evangelicalism." In *Four Views on the Spectrum of Evangelicalism*, edited by David Naselli and Collin Hansen, 68–96. Grand Rapids: Zondervan, 2011.

Noll, Mark. "British Methodological Pointers for Writing a History of Theology in America." In *Seeing Things Their Way: Intellectual History and the Return of*

Religion, edited by Alister Chapman et al., 202–25. Notre Dame, IN: University of Notre Dame Press, 2009.

———. *The Civil War as a Theological Crisis*. Raleigh, NC: The University of North Carolina Press, 2006.

Olson, Roger E. *Reformed and Always Reforming: The Postconservative Approach to Evangelical Theology*. Acadia Studies in Bible and Theology. Grand Rapids: Baker, 2007.

Palmer, Parker. *The Active Life: A Spirituality of Work, Creativity, and Caring*. San Francisco: Harper & Row, 1990.

Putnam, Robert D., and David E. Campbell. *Amazing Grace: How Religion Divides and Unites Us*. New York: Simon & Schuster, 2010.

RCA Special Council. Report from the "Group of Five." Chicago, April 15–18, 2016.

Sample, Steven B. *The Contrarian's Guide to Leadership*. San Francisco: Jossey-Bass, 2002.

Schneider, Sandra M. *The Revelatory Text: Interpreting the New Testament as Sacred Scripture*. Collegeville, MN: Liturgical, 1999.

Schrock-Shenk, Carolyn. "Foreword." In *Stumbling Toward a Genuine Conversation on Homosexuality*, edited by Michael A. King, 13–18. Telford, PA: Cascadia, 2007.

Smith, Christian. *The Bible Made Impossible: Why Biblicism is Not a Truly Evangelical Reading of Scripture*. Grand Rapids: Brazos, 2012.

Swartley, Willard. *Homosexuality: Biblical Interpretation and Moral Discernment*. Scottdale, PA: Herald, 2003.

Volf, Miroslav. *Exclusion and Embrace: A Theological Exploration of Identity, Otherness and Reconciliation*. Nashville: Abingdon, 1996.

Wilson, Ken. *A Letter to my Congregation: An evangelical pastor's path to embracing people who are gay, lesbian and transgender into the company of Jesus*. Canton, MI: Read the Spirit, 2014.

Authors

Harold Heie is a Senior Fellow at The Colossian Forum. He previously served as Founding Director of the Center for Christian Studies (now the Center for Faith and Inquiry) at Gordon College and as Vice President for Academic Affairs at Messiah College and Northwestern College in Iowa, after teaching mathematics at Gordon College and The King's College. His web site, www.respectfulconversation.net, is devoted to encouraging and modeling respectful conversations concerning contentious issues about which Christians have strong disagreements. The eCircle on "Christian Faithfulness and Human Sexuality" that is the basis for this book is the third of three major eCircles he has hosted on his web site, the first two of which resulted in books: *Evangelicals on Public Policy Issues: Sustaining a Respectful Political Conversation*; and *A Future for American Evangelicalism: Commitment, Openness, and Conversation.*

George Marsden has taught history at Calvin College, Duke University Divinity School, and the University of Notre Dame where he is now professor emeritus. His highly acclaimed books include *Fundamentalism and American Culture, The Soul of the American University, The Outrageous Idea of Christian Scholarship, Jonathan Edwards: A Life, The Twilight of the American Enlightenment,* and *C. S. Lewis's* Mere Christianity, *A Biography.*

Conversation Partners

Matthew Lee Anderson is the Founder of the Mere Orthodoxy blog. He is studying for a DPhil in Christian Ethics at Oxford University, from which he holds an MPhil. His written work includes publications for the *Washington Post*, CNN, *Christianity Today*, *Books & Culture*, and *The City*.

Chelsea Langston Bombino is the Director of Equipping and Membership at the Institutional Religious Freedom Alliance, where she focuses on building IRFA's membership base and providing educational opportunities for faith-based organizations in the areas of organizational religious freedom policy, best practices, and public witness. She holds a JD from the University of Michigan. She previously worked for the National Association of Consumer Advocates (NACA) in Washington, DC and as a fellow for the Irish Center for Human Rights in Galway, Ireland.

Kathryn Brightbill is a board member at Safety Net, working to make Christian colleges and universities safe for LGBT students. She is also a board member and legislative policy analyst at the Coalition for Responsible Home Education. She holds a JD from the University of Florida Levin College of Law. She previously served on the English faculty at the Diplomatic Academy of Vietnam in Hanoi, Vietnam.

James Brownson is the James and Jean Cook Professor of New Testament at Western Theological Seminary in Holland, Michigan, where he has served for over twenty years. He holds a PhD from Princeton Theological Seminary in New Testament (Gospel of John). As a New Testament professor, he tries to keep his focus on issues of significance in the life of the church and to help the church center its life more deeply on the gospel.

Chris Grace is a Professor of Psychology at Biola University, and serves as the founding Director of the Biola University Center for Marriage and Relationships. His PhD is in Social Psychology from Colorado State University. He speaks at colleges, churches, and retreat centers nationwide on the topic of relationships and marriages. He is a member of the Association for Psychological Science, and on the editorial review board for *The Journal of Psychology and Theology*, as well as *Marriage and Family: A Christian Journal*.

Justin Lee is the founder and former executive director of The Gay Christian Network, an interdenominational nonprofit organization engaging Christians from differing theological perspectives to work together for a more loving, grace-filled church. His first book, *Torn: Rescuing the Gospel from the Gays-vs.-Christians Debate*, has been widely cited on both sides for its influence in promoting more nuanced Christian conversations about LGBT issues. Justin speaks frequently around the world and writes about matters of faith and culture on his blog, *Crumbs from the Communion Table*.

Kathryn A. Lee is chair and professor of political science at Whitworth University. She earned her PhD in political science at The Johns Hopkins University and her JD at Temple University. Her areas of focus include women in politics and American political institutions. Before joining the faculty at Whitworth, Kathryn taught seventeen years at Eastern University. She was a founding member of Christians in Political Science. She worked for two summers for the Department of Justice.

Jeff Lincicome is the Senior Pastor of Sammamish Presbyterian Church in Sammamish, Washington. He holds a DMin from George Fox Evangelical Seminary and an MDiv from Princeton Theological Seminary. As a member of the Presbyterian Church (USA), Jeff has recently walked his moderate evangelical church through the challenging discussions of marriage working towards unity without uniformity on issues concerning the LGBT community.

David Myers is a Hope College social psychologist who communicates psychological science to college students and the general public. His scientific writings have appeared in three dozen academic periodicals, four dozen magazines, and seventeen books, including textbooks for introductory and social psychology. He is a trustee of his alma mater, Whitworth University, and of the John Templeton Foundation.

Adam J. MacLeod is Associate Professor at Faulkner University, Jones School of Law; Thomas Edison Fellow in the Center for Protection of Intellectual Property at George Mason University; and a former visiting fellow in the James Madison Program in American Ideals and Institutions at Princeton University. He is the author of *Property and Practical Reason* (2015) and dozens of articles, essays, and reviews, and coeditor of *Foundations of Law* (2017). He has served as special Deputy Attorney General of Alabama and speaks widely about the foundations of private law. He received his JD from the University of Notre Dame Law School.

Julie W. Morgan is cochair and professor of Communication Studies at Eastern University. She earned her EdD at Nova Southeastern University. Her areas of research include conflict and dialogue and the intersection of faith and culture. She is currently doing research on applying the theology of Stanley Hauerwas to navigating conflict within faith communities and serves on the Christianity and Communication Studies Network advisory board.

Weldon Nisly retired in late 2013, after almost two decades as pastor at Seattle Mennonite Church and four decades of Mennonite pastoral and peace ministry. He has an active retirement ministry of Contemplative Just Peacebuilding, including part time with Christian Peacemaker Teams in Iraq and Palestine. He received an MA in Peace Studies from Anabaptist Mennonite Biblical Seminary and has served on peace teams in Nicaragua, Russia, and Iraq. He is a Benedictine Oblate with Saint Mary's Abbey in Collegeville, Minnesota. He is a co-founder of the Mennonite Catholic Bridgefolk movement.

Tim Otto is a pastor at the Church of the Sojourners, a live-together Christian community in the Mission District of San Francisco. He has a Masters of Theological Studies from Duke Divinity School. He worked for fourteen years as a Registered Nurse on the first AIDS ward in the United States. He maintains the website www.orientedtofaith.com, which strives to "wage peace in the church's conflict over LGBT sexuality." He may be followed at https://twitter.com/Tim_Otto.

Mikael L. Pelz received his PhD in political science from the University of Missouri-Columbia. He is an Assistant Professor in Political Science at Calvin College. His research is in the areas of public policy, political behavior, and religiosity. He has recently published studies on state education policy and the link between religiosity and public opinion among so-called millennial evangelicals. He is also a regular contributor on *Capital Commentary*, an online publication of the Center for Public Justice. He is currently a member of the Society for the Scientific Study of Religion and the Midwest Political Science Association.

Jessica Schrock Ringenberg is on the Pastoral Team at Zion Mennonite Church in Archbold, Ohio, with her primary responsibilities in the area of Worship and Formation, with particular emphasis on how Scripture informs our preaching and teaching. She is a regular blogger for The Mennonite online, a publication for the Mennonite Church USA. She has served on the Constituency Leadership Council, the advisory group to the Mennonite Church USA. She received her MDiv from Anabaptist Mennonite Biblical Seminary.

Isaac Sharp is a doctoral student in Ethics at Union Theological Seminary in New York. He previously received a Master of Divinity degree from Mercer University with a concentration in Christian Social Ethics. He is the coeditor, with David P. Gushee, of *Christian Social Ethics: A Reader* from Westminster John Knox Press's Library of Theological Ethics series.

Chris Schutte is the Rector of Christ Church Anglican in Phoenix, where he has served for almost ten years. He holds an MDiv degree from Gordon-Conwell Theological Seminary and is currently pursuing doctoral studies in theology through the University of Aberdeen in Scotland.

Mark L. Strauss is University Professor of New Testament at Bethel Seminary San Diego, where he has served since 1993. He holds a PhD from Aberdeen University. He is the author of numerous books and articles on hermeneutics, New Testament, and Bible translation. He also serves as Vice Chair of the Committee for Bible Translation for the *New International Version* and as an associate editor for the *NIV Study Bible*. He is a member of the Society of Biblical Literature, the Institute for Biblical Research and the Evangelical Theological Society.

Julia K. Stronks is the Edward B. Lindaman Chair and a professor of political science at Whitworth University. She holds a PhD from The University of Maryland and a JD from the University of Iowa College of Law. She has written numerous books, articles, and opinion pieces on the relationship between faith and public policy, including a focus on a faith-based approach to living in a pluralistic world.

Eve Tushnet is a writer in Washington, DC. She has written extensively on topics related to human sexuality and other topics, ranging from US men's figure skating to pro-life pregnancy counseling. She blogs at Patheos and does speaking engagements on topics such as gay Christian life, friendship as a form of kinship, and vocational discernment.

Micah Watson is the William Spoelhof Teacher-Scholar-In-Residence Chair and Associate Professor of Political Science at Calvin College. He formerly directed the Center for Politics and Religion at Union University, and was a 2010–11 William E. Simon Fellow in Religion and Public Life at Princeton University. He earned his PhD in politics at Princeton University, and an MA in Church-State Studies at Baylor University.

www.ingramcontent.com/pod-product-compliance
Lightning Source LLC
Chambersburg PA
CBHW021649230426
43668CB00008B/569